COMPUTER
USAGE

FUNDAMENTALS

McGRAW-HILL/COMPUTER USAGE SERIES

ERIC A. WEISS
SERIES EDITOR

WEISS: COMPUTER USAGE/FUNDAMENTALS
COMPUTER USAGE/360 ASSEMBLY PROGRAMMING
COMPUTER USAGE/360 FORTRAN PROGRAMMING
COMPUTER USAGE/APPLICATIONS
COMPUTER USAGE/360 COBOL PROGRAMMING

COMPUTER USAGE FUNDAMENTALS

COMPUTER USAGE COMPANY, INC.

ERIC A. WEISS, EDITOR
SUN OIL COMPANY

McGRAW-HILL BOOK COMPANY
NEW YORK   ST. LOUIS   SAN FRANCISCO
LONDON   SYDNEY   TORONTO
MEXICO   PANAMA

**COMPUTER
USAGE
FUNDAMENTALS**

Library of Congress Catalog Card Number 71-76142

12382

1 2 3 4 5 6 7 8 9 0   H D M M   7 6 5 4 3 2 1 0 6 9

Man has always strived to free himself of drudgery. The results of this search have become the cornerstones upon which our civilizations have been built. The wheel, boat, steam engine, electricity, automobile, atomic energy, and numerous other innovations freed man both physically and intellectually to pursue more creative endeavors. **1488966**

Probably no other invention in man's history has more potential to break the chains of drudgery than the computer. And likewise, no other creation of man brings such power to enhance his intellect and creativity. Because, in actuality, that is what the computer is—an extension of man's intelligence.

For this reason alone, as well as the fact that computers will play such a vital role in everyone's future, it is important that every educated individual understand the fundamentals of computing, regardless of his career.

The purpose of this book is to create such an understanding.

The material which provided the basis for this book and others in the Computer Usage series is the result of two years' intensive research and documentation by an acknowledged pioneer and leader in computing systems, Computer Usage Company, Inc.

The men and women who compiled this information are experts in their field. It is to their credit as computer professionals, and to the credit of the industry as a whole, that such a concise foundation of the basic concepts of such a dynamic discipline and constantly changing technology is presented in this book.

C. C. HURD
CHAIRMAN OF THE BOARD
COMPUTER USAGE COMPANY, INC.

In this, the first volume in the Computer Usage series, the reader is introduced to the fundamentals of computing through a study of background and basic concepts. The book can be either the prelude to the more advanced Computer Usage texts on 360 Assembly Language, Fortran, and Cobol or the text for a terminal course in computer appreciation and understanding for those who need only an overview of the field.

The student will find that the special language and jargon of the computer world are explained in detail and summarized in the Prose Glossary. The history, the industry, job opportunities, computer hardware, and computer programming are all covered in simple, straightforward language in the text. The subjects of greatest significance, such as programming and coding, are dealt with in some depth, but the overall plan is to provide extensive rather than intensive coverage. The intensive material for those who wish to pursue the subject further is presented in the other texts in the series.

Wherever possible the book refers to modern computers in general, but where specific examples are needed, the computer chosen is the IBM System/360. Chapter 4, "The Computer Manufacturing Industry," explains why.

Each chapter except the last two ends with a few questions. These are usually intended to summarize the chapter or to provoke the student into thinking about the broader aspects and implications of the subject. In the later chapters, the questions are sometimes used to tie the subject to what has gone before. Sometimes the questions try to make the student examine the subject with a slightly different approach from the text's. In a few cases the text presentation is reinforced with some drills or exercises. In no case are questions included which can be satisfied·by the mechanical regurgitation of the text or the Glossary.

A flowchart of the book appears at the beginning of each chapter. This chart presents a graphic display of the important fields of computing and illustrates how the chapters of the book cover them.

The Introduction is as important as any chapter, since it explains much of the book and is intended to give some motivation. The Prose Glossary should be read immediately after Chapter 1 so the student will have this reference material available when he first needs it. The remainder of the chapters should be read in sequence, because concepts that appear in later ones have been introduced, foreshadowed, and sometimes defined in the earlier ones. If there is too much material for the time available, the last chapters in the book can be safely omitted.

Some students will find Chapter 6, "What Is Coding?" difficult. They should take this as a signal that they may have difficulty in becoming computer professionals. The same comment does *not* apply to Chapter 10, "How Computers Operate." Students who find Chapter 10 difficult may very well become successful programmers but will probably never qualify as top-flight computer hardware designers. Students who find Chapter 15, "Techniques for Computing Scientific Problems," difficult but are attracted by Chapter 14, "Business Data Processing," and Chapter 8, "The Work and Tools of the Systems Analyst," can see that their computer career will be better in the commercial than in the scientific field. And vice versa.

It is considerations such as this—that the student wants to find out what areas of computer science appeal to him and are within his abilities—which justify a broad survey text of this nature.

ERIC A. WEISS

CONTENTS

Glossaries of technical terms are very often of little use to the novice since their alphabetic order does not reflect any other logical structure. Attempted here is a glossary arranged in a more or less logical fashion, with an index (pages xvii–xix) to help the nonserial user find a particular term. If the definition does not shed sufficient light, the context may.

1   **A computer** is a machine for performing complex processes on information
2   without manual intervention. **Analog computers** perform this function by
3   directly measuring continuous physical quantities such as electrical voltages.
4   The best-known analog computer is a slide rule. **Digital computers** represent
5   numerical quantities by discrete electrical states which can be manipulated
6   logically and hence arithmetically. Digital computers are sometimes referred
7   to as **electronic data processing machines, EDP,** or **processors.** In order to
8   distinguish the actual physical equipment from the programs which extend
9   its usefulness, the former is called **hardware.**

10   **The central processing unit (CPU)** or **main frame** is the portion of the
11   computer which performs the calculations and decisions; the **memory** or
12   **storage** is the part in which the data and programs are stored. The **core**
13   **memory** is the main memory of most modern machines; it is normally the
14   only memory directly accessible to the CPU. Its name derives from its
15   composition: small ferrite rings called **cores.** The computer may have
16   additional memory devices; information is transferred between these and the
17   core memory. The most usual such memories are **magnetic drums** (spinning
18   cylinders with a magnetizable recording sufrace) and **magnetic discs** (flat
19   spinning discs with magnetizable surfaces).

20   The capability of memory devices is measured in capacity and speed of access.
21   The **storage capacity** of a memory is measured in **words** (also called **cells** or
22   **registers**) which are usually of fixed length, consisting of 12 to 48 bits. This
23   number is called the machine's **word length.** A **bit** (binary digit) is the
24   minimum unit of information storage and has only two possible values.
25   Capacity can also be measured in **bytes,** units of 6 or 8 bits, each capable of
26   representing one alphabetic or numeric symbol.

27   **Access speed** of a memory is the time it takes for the processor to obtain a
28   word from memory. Core memory is called **random access** when any word

29 can be obtained at any time without regard to its serial order. Drum, tape,
30 and disc memories are **serial access,** because the words pass one at a time as
31 they move past the station where they may be accessed. Speed is usually
32 spoken of in terms of **milliseconds** (msec) (thousandths of a second),
33 **microseconds** (μsec) (millionths of a second), or **nanoseconds** (nsec)
34 (billionths of a second). One nanosecond is the time required for light to
35 travel almost one foot.
36 The central processor and the memory constitute the computer per se; to get
37 data and programs into the machine and the results out are the role of the
38 **input/output equipment** or **I/O.**

39 **Input devices** convert information to a form in which it can be stored in the
40 computer's memory. The commonest form of input is the **punched card** or
41 **Hollerith card** (after its inventor). Input devices which accept cards are called
42 **card readers** and the function they perform is commonly called **reading,** as is
43 that of all input devices. Cards have 80 **columns** with 12 possible punch
44 positions; normally, each column is used to represent one character. A set
45 of cards is called a **deck.** Another form of input is **punched paper tape—**
46 continuous tape approximately 1 inch wide, with holes punched across its
47 width to represent characters or numeric quantities. **Magnetic ink character**
48 **readers** have come to be used for input, particularly in banking; they can
49 interpret characters printed with a special ink. More recently, **optical**
50 **scanners** have appeared, which can read clearly printed or typed material of
51 given type fonts.

52 **Output devices** usually include a **card punch** (which converts the characters
53 stored in memory to punched holes in a card), a **tape punch** (which
54 performs the same function for punched paper tape), and a **line printer**
55 (which prints numerals, letters, and other characters of conventional design
56 on continuous rolls of paper). When it passes information to these devices, the
57 computer is **writing.** Recent additions to the output family include the
58 **display device** which exhibits readable characters or graphic information on
59 the face of a **cathode ray tube** or **CRT.** These images must be read at once,
60 of course, since they are not permanent.

61 Information which can be taken away in permanent form (such as the output
62 of a line printer) is called **hard copy.** A **plotter** is an output device which, under
63 computer control, can draw continuous lines or curves on paper, thus
64 producing graphs, maps, etc., in hard copy. **Magnetic tape** is widely used
65 both as a form of memory and I/O. It can be stored conveniently away from
66 the machine and can be read or written by the computer if it is put on a
67 **tape drive** attached to the computer. It is the fastest type of I/O and the slowest
68 type of memory except when used for serial reading.

69   I/O devices connected directly to the computer memory and under control
70   of the CPU are spoken of as being **on-line.** They are placed **off-line** when
71   they are used to perform independent functions. For example, it is common
72   to exchange information between punched cards and magnetic tape off-line.
73   Some devices are always off-line. They are **peripheral equipment** and are
74   generally called collectively **electromechanical accounting machines** or **EAM.**
75   These are frequently used independently of the computer and in fact antedate
76   computers by many years. The most common are the **keypunch,** used to
77   punch cards, the **reproducer,** which makes copies of decks of cards, and the
78   **sorter,** which places cards in different bins as a function of which holes are
79   punched. In some recent systems, another on-line I/O device has been
80   added, the **console** or **terminal.** These are intended for the user to interact
81   directly with the machine, and usually consist of a typewriterlike keyboard,
82   and either a typewriterlike printing mechanism or another display device for
83   output.

84   Information is stored in the computer's memory in the form of the presence
85   or absence of a magnetic charge. A collection of such "yes or no" physical
86   states is usually thought of as a **binary number** (a number whose only
87   possible digits are 0 and 1). Depending on context, such numbers can have
88   many meanings; in this sense, the numbers are **coded.** They can be interpreted
89   as numeric quantities, **characters** (letters, digits, punctuation marks) or
90   **instructions** or **commands** which will direct the computer to perform its
91   basic functions (add, compare, read, etc.).

92   A set of instructions to perform a specified function or solve a complete
93   problem is called a **program.** The computer performs such instructions
94   sequentially. However, as the computer can modify the data in its memory,
95   it can also modify its program. This capability to modify its own directions is a
96   case of the engineering principle called **feedback,** the modification of future
97   performance on the basis of past performance. It is because of this distinctive
98   feature that modern digital computers are sometimes called **stored program**
99   **computers.** Parts of programs are sometimes called **routines** or **subroutines.**
100 Subroutines which perform generally useful functions are sometimes combined
101 into a subroutine **library,** usually on magnetic tape. Copies of relevant
102 subroutines will be added to a program automatically and hence need not be
103 developed by hand. Single instructions in a program are sometimes called
104 **steps.** When a sequence of program steps is operated repeatedly, the process
105 is called a **loop.** Certain instructions compare two quantities and select either
106 of two program paths on the basis of the result: these are called **branching**
107 instructions.

108 The data on which a program acts are usually structured into **tables.**

109   Individual values which control the operation of programs or subroutines are
110   **parameters.** An organized collection of information in the computer or on
111   tape is called a **file,** like the organized set of papers in a file cabinet. A **data**
112   **base** or **data bank** is a large and complex set of tables which describe some
113   aspect of the world outside of the computer (a library catalog, a student
114   record file, a budget).

115   A **programmer** is a person who converts a problem into a set of directions to a
116   computer to solve it. The function is sometimes broken down into several
117   parts, particularly if the problem is very complex. The task of stating the
118   problem in a clear and unambiguous form is performed by an **analyst** or
119   **system analyst.** The technique of specifying methods of solution for
120   mathematical problems is **mathematical analysis** or **numerical analysis.** A
121   specific procedure for solving a problem is an **algorithm.** The process of
122   writing the detailed step-by-step instructions for the computer to follow is
123   **coding** done by a **coder.**

124   After a program is written, it is tested by letting it perform its function in the
125   computer on test data to which the proper solution is known. This process is
126   **code checking** or **debugging.** The coder will also produce some descriptions
127   of this program and how it operates so that others may understand how it
128   works, in case at a future date it is necessary to modify it. This **documentation**
129   may include a **flowchart:** a graphic description or diagram of the various
130   paths and branches followed by the program.

131   The repertory of instructions available to the programmer for a specific
132   computer is that computer's **machine language.** Other **higher-order languages**
133   have been developed to help the programmer by simplifying the tedious
134   aspects of writing machine language; these are called **procedure oriented**
135   **languages** or **problem oriented languages** or POL. Commonly used POLs are
136   **Fortran, Algol,** and **Cobol;** the first two were devised mainly for scientific
137   computation and the latter for business data processing. A new type is
138   represented by **list processing languages;** because of greater flexibilities in
139   dealing with data, these languages are particularly useful in nonnumeric
140   computations such as are frequently involved in research. Their particular
141   virtues are most apparent in **heuristic processes:** methods where the precise
142   method of solution is not spelled out but is discovered as the program
143   progresses and as it evaluates its progress toward an acceptable solution.
144   (Because this use of the "language" is somewhat misleading, human
145   languages such as English are distinguished as **natural languages.**)

146   Programs which convert higher-order languages into machine language are
147   called **compilers;** programs which perform similar functions but at a much
148   simpler level are **assemblers.** The term **translator** is used sometimes for

149   compiler, but it is used less frequently because of the possible confusion with
150   programs which perform translation between natural languages. **Interpreters**
151   do not compile the entire program but translate and perform one statement of
152   the program at a time; effectively, they perform both functions—compiling
153   and running a program.

154   **Software** is the term used to refer to the totality of programs and procedures
155   available on a computer; sometimes it is used more specifically to mean those
156   programs of general usefulness (such as compilers) which are available to all
157   users. These are sometimes called **utility programs.** All machines today have
158   **operating systems** to aid the user (and the operator) in sequencing jobs,
159   accounting, and calling up other utility programs. Operating systems or
160   programs are also called **control programs, supervisors,** or **executives.**

161   **Applications** are the problems to which a computer is applied; the names for
162   most common applications are self-explanatory, but some are not. A
163   **simulation** is the representation of a real or hypothetical system by a computer
164   process; its function is to indicate system performance under various
165   conditions by program performance. **Information retrieval** is the name applied
166   to processes which recover or locate information in a collection of documents.
167   An **information management system** helps a user maintain a data base, modify
168   it, and get reports from it. It is usually defined as a **general purpose device;**
169   this means that it can accommodate a large range of applications. A
170   **management information system** supplied to the management of an
171   organization the data that it requires to make decisions and to exercise
172   control. A **report generator** is a program which allows the user to specify in
173   some simple way the content and format of reports which the computer is to
174   produce.

175   To **run** a program is to cause it to be performed on the computer. Running a
176   program to solve a problem or produce real results (as opposed to
177   debugging) is called a **production run.** Installations in which the user runs his
178   own job are called **open shops.** Installations which have a **computer**
179   **operator** who runs the programs for the user are **closed shops.** Computers are
180   usually operated in **batch processing mode;** the operator assembles a batch
181   of programs waiting to be run and puts them serially into the computer; output
182   from all the programs is returned in one batch. **Turnaround time** is the time
183   between the user's delivering his job to the center and his receipt of his
184   output. **Time sharing** is a method of operation by means of which several jobs
185   are interleaved, giving the appearance of simultaneous operation. In many
186   timeshared systems, users have individual terminals which are on-line. Such
187   terminals may be located far from the computer; this is **remote access.** This
188   allows users to interact with the computer on a time scale appropriate for

189   human beings—on the order of a few seconds between responses. This
190   capability is called operating in **real time.** Using the computer for frequent
191   interaction with the user in this way is called an **interactive** or **conversational**
192   mode of computing.

193   Like all electronic devices, computers sometimes break down. The prevention
194   and correction of such situations is **maintenance. Preventive maintenance** finds
195   failing components before they actually break down. **Reliability** is the measure of
196   the frequency of failure of the computer. During **downtime** the machine is being
197   maintained or repaired; during **uptime** it is available for normal productive use.

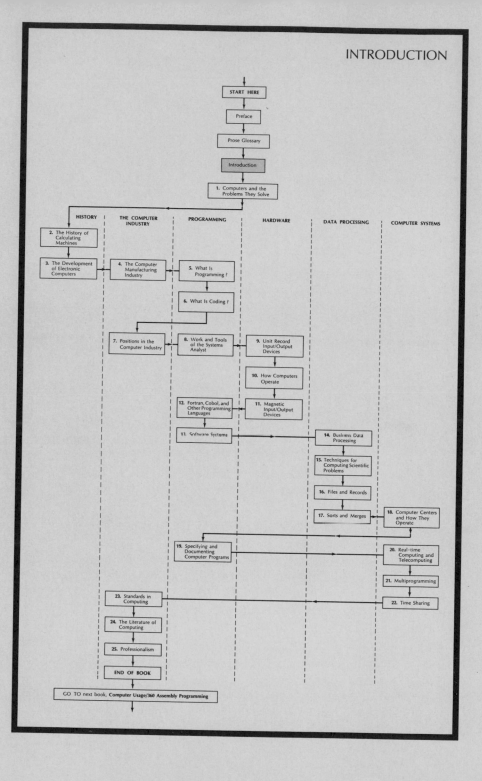

START HERE

Preface

Prose Glossary

Introduction

1. Computers and the Problems They Solve

| HISTORY | THE COMPUTER INDUSTRY | PROGRAMMING | HARDWARE | DATA PROCESSING | COMPUTER SYSTEMS |

2. The History of Calculating Machines

3. The Development of Electronic Computers

4. The Computer Manufacturing Industry

5. What Is Programming?

6. What Is Coding?

7. Positions in the Computer Industry

8. Work and Tools of the Systems Analyst

9. Unit Record Input/Output Devices

10. How Computers Operate

11. Magnetic Input/Output Devices

12. Fortran, Cobol, and Other Programming Languages

13. Software Systems

14. Business Data Processing

15. Techniques for Computing Scientific Problems

16. Files and Records

17. Sorts and Merges

18. Computer Centers and How They Operate

19. Specifying and Documenting Computer Programs

20. Real-time Computing and Telecomputing

21. Multiprogramming

22. Time Sharing

23. Standards in Computing

24. The Literature of Computing

25. Professionalism

END OF BOOK

GO TO next book, Computer Usage/360 Assembly Programming

WELCOME TO THE WORLD OF COMPUTERS

As you open this book, as you start your studies, you are taking a first step into one of the most fascinating, challenging, and rewarding professions the world has ever known. Just as the inventions of steam, gasoline, and electric power extended man's *muscles* so that he could literally move mountains, so the invention and development of the computer extends man's *mind* so that he can understand, manage, and extend modern technologies such as space travel, nuclear propulsion, and medical research.

Today, tens of thousands of computers are quietly and competently handling the everyday aspects of our daily lives—newspapers, food, transit, housing, clothing, education. Not a day passes without the installation of twenty to thirty new computers, and not a day passes without a dozen new computer applications being conceived. This very moment, computers are running twenty-four hours a day in Tokyo, Singapore, Frankfurt, Johannesburg, Manchester, Buenos Aires, Melbourne, and most American cities and towns.

Most of these computers are of one principal type: the general purpose electronic digital computer. The existence of tens of thousands of these computers has created an industry-wide demand for more and more people who can understand and use computers. These people have the prospect of steady employment and a high salary level.

What a vast challenge now lies before you! Learning to understand, master, and use computers, planning their work, instructing them in the execution of the simplest task—or the most complex—becomes your professional province. To be the first to develop a new use, to be first to use a new computer or a new programming language, to be the first to devise an improved system—these are but a few of the gratifying experiences awaiting you as an expert in computer use.

Wherever the action is, you'll find computer specialists: at Cape Kennedy, at the Stock Exchange, at the Olympics, in the control towers of jet airports. Systems analysts and programmers must also cope with the simplest everyday operations such as truck routing, food preparation, and gasoline distribution, but even these often turn out to be far more complex than you now visualize.

Computing is challenging. It is a big field, bewildering to the newcomer. It includes dozens of different types of jobs—sales, engineering, research, production, etc. It occupies hundreds of thousands of workers. It commands its own jargon: "read-only memory," "software," "syntax-driven," "megabits," "nanoseconds"—all of which you'll master before completing this course.

☐ THESE BOOKS

This is the first in a series of textbooks to teach the understanding and use of computers. This book is devoted to giving you knowledge of the basic concepts of computing, in order to lay the groundwork for study of the remaining books in the series. The later books will deal with applications of computers in business and industry and with the elementary details of programming for the IBM System/360. They will use symbolic machine assembly language as well as two higher-level languages, Fortran and Cobol.

The organization of the series of books is the result of careful planning by many computer and educational specialists. Its purpose is to acquaint you with the whole field of computer use while requiring a minimum of wasted motion on your part.

☐ WHAT YOU'LL LEARN

This series of books is aimed at giving you *knowledge* of the computer world, *knowledge* of how computer applications work, *skill* in programming a computer (IBM System/360), and *skill* in using a programming language (Fortran). When you have acquired these by faithfully studying the books, you will be professionally qualified to take a job using computers.

You acquire the *knowledge* from this book and from the treatment of computer applications in another book in the series. You acquire the *skills* by studying the books in the series that deal with assembly language, Fortran, and Cobol and by writing and testing the computer programs assigned in those books.

WHY SYSTEM/360 IS TAUGHT

Over 100 different types of computers have been developed. Each has many features in common, each has many differences. The experienced computer user will learn to handle any one of them in a short time, provided that he knows one computer well. Each type of computer has available well-written manuals.

It is the *first* computer learned that is important. After much thought, we have selected the IBM System/360 to teach. Note that it is an example of a computer and presented as such.

IBM System/360 is one of the most widely used machines, and it handles all aspects of computing.

WHY FORTRAN AND COBOL ARE TAUGHT

Later in this book you'll read about programming languages, and you'll study them in other books in the series. These are special English-like languages used to facilitate programming and to ease transition from one type of computer to another. Once you learn two programming languages, it is relatively easy to learn others.

Fortran and Cobol are the most widely used programming languages. Nearly all computers can accept programs written in Cobol and Fortran. Fortran is scientifically oriented; Cobol is business-oriented. Together they cover most areas of computer applications.

Many students will study these books, to qualify themselves to enter the field as professional computer programmers. Others will want to broaden their horizons so as to encompass the wide computer field—to move to better positions, to understand their own work more thoroughly, to learn more about the power of the computer.

But whatever your reason for studying, you must acquire both the *knowledge* and the *skills*. Each supports the other.

☐ ABOUT THIS BOOK

This book should be studied straight through from the Introduction to the last chapter. The chapters cover six different aspects of computers and computing, and as you go from chapter to chapter you will find that you are being led back and forth through six different fields while you develop the ability to understand more advanced and complicated subjects.

The six aspects of computers and computing are:

History
The computer industry
Programming
Hardware
Data processing
Computer systems

The chart on the next page shows these six areas and lists the chapters that deal with each of them. As you study the chapters in order, you will be led along the path shown by the arrows through this flowchart of the book.

☐ VOCABULARY

In studying this book you will run into many new words and many common words used in new and special ways. Care has been taken to explain each new word when it is introduced. To help you with these words, a Prose Glossary appears just before this Introduction. The Prose Glossary gives brief explanations of all the new computer words that you will meet in the book. The Glossary has its own index, which you can use to look up any word that bothers you. For more complete and extensive explanations than the Glossary can give, look up any unfamiliar word in the index in the back of the book.

Now, on to your new career!

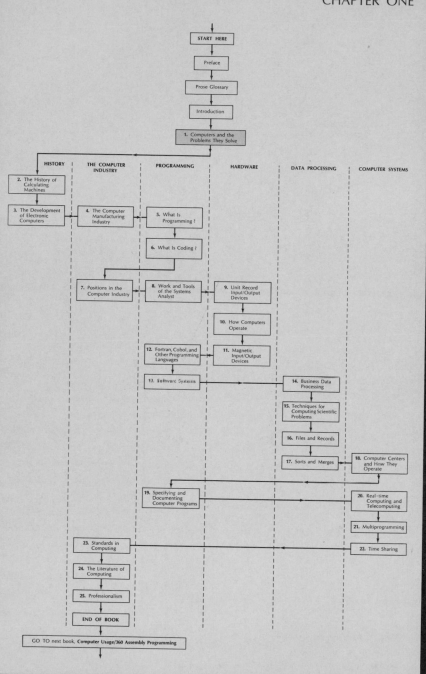

CHAPTER ONE

You may be studying this book because you wish to prepare to be a computer programmer. Or your objective may be to learn more about computers, to keep up with this increasingly important area of technology.

In either case, you will learn how a computer works and how to make use of it. You will be given a broad knowledge of the basic concepts of computers and computing. You will study the history and present state of the industry and get an understanding of the nature of computer jobs. You will learn what is involved in systems analysis (planning what a computer is to do) and in programming (telling a computer what it is to do). You will learn what the parts of a computer are and how they operate. You will be introduced to the programming languages Fortran and Cobol. You will study the elements of both business and scientific data processing and learn about the variety of different ways that computers are used.

☐ THE IMPORTANCE OF COMPUTERS

New applications for computers are constantly under development. Computers are used to streamline savings bank operations, keep track of parts inventories, generate trade names, set printing type automatically, design highways, prepare market research information, diagnose diseases, and track space vehicles. You will study all these applications (and many more) in another book in this series, *Computer Usage/Applications.*

Computers are important in giving support to people in occupations with heavy demand, such as doctors and teachers, and in performing tasks for which man's abilities have become (or are becoming) inadequate, as in air traffic control. In fact, many problem areas cannot even be attacked without the use of a computer. One such example is nuclear research, where incredible amounts of data must be manipulated.

☐ COMPUTERS IN USE

In 1950, there were 15 computers in the United States. By 1968, there were more than 50,000. Predictions are that there will be 200,000 by 1975, and 350,000 by 1980.

The value of the computing equipment in use will rise to more than 25 billion dollars by 1970 and perhaps 75 billion dollars by 1980. Although the majority of computers sold are in the small to medium range, by the end of 1967 there were about 2,000 large-scale machines in use, with an average sale price of $2,000,000 each.

Originally, most computers were made for the government. Nongovernmental

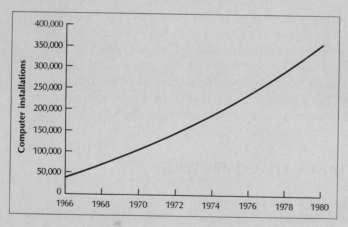

NUMBER OF COMPUTER INSTALLATIONS IN UNITED STATES. (ADAPTED BY PERMISSION FROM MODERN DATA SYSTEMS.)

use of computers increased from 21 percent of all computer installations in 1950 to 84 percent in 1965, as more and more businesses turned to computers for help.

☐ TYPES OF COMPUTERS

Some computers are very limited. *Special purpose computers* (which constitute only a fraction of all computers) are designed for just one application and are wired internally to go through the identical sequence of operations every time.

One example is that of the early airline reservations computers. They could do only three things: find out if the requested number of seats was available on a certain flight; subtract that number from the stored total of seats if a sale was made; and, in the case of cancellations, add the number of seats back into the stored inventory.

Such special purpose computers cannot be made to do something new by changing the instructions under which they operate. You can only make them do something new by taking a soldering iron and changing their wiring. The instructions which are given to a computer are called its *program,* so these special purpose computers are said to be *not programmable,* or if this lack is to be made a virtue, they are said not to need programming.

On the other hand, a *general purpose computer* can be made to do any of a variety of jobs simply by changing the instructions which are given to it. Its wiring remains the same. Only the program is changed. Such computers need programming but are extremely flexible, since a mere change in program changes what they are to do. You will learn more about programming in the chapters that follow. This book will deal only with general purpose computers—those which can be programmed.

Until recently, general purpose computers, which can take on a great variety of jobs, were divided into two main types, business and scientific. A *business computer* was designed to perform a comparatively small amount of computing with large amounts of data. *A scientific computer* performed lengthy mathematical calculations using a relatively small amount of data.

For several reasons (including the problems of providing programming support for two different types of computers), the distinction between business and scientific computers is rapidly disappearing. To illustrate, the

IBM System/360 was designed to perform any type of computation, from keeping records of parts inventory to plotting the path of an astronaut's flight.

In studying this book, you will be concerned only with *digital computers,* which compute using numbers directly. There is another family of machines called *analog computers.* That type solves problems by translating numbers into physical conditions (such as flow, length, angular position, or voltage), manipulating the physical equivalents to obtain a solution also in the form of a physical condition, and finally retranslating that condition into its numerical equivalent.

A slide rule is one type of analog computer. It translates numbers into lengths. The result of the calculation is always obtained by translating a position on a scale (representing length) to a number.

□ WHAT COMPUTERS LOOK LIKE

The *first generation* of digital computers was built with vacuum tubes. Some of these early computers were so large that they filled several rooms. The *second generation* of computers used transistors. Some of these were no

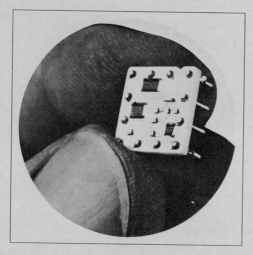

AN IBM SYSTEM/360 CIRCUIT.

THREE GENERATIONS OF COMPUTER CIRCUITS.

larger than an office desk. The *third generation*, whose best-known representative is the IBM System/360, is built of tiny microelectronic circuits, called solid logic technology by IBM. Some of these computers are smaller than a file drawer. Today's computers are more than 1,000 times faster than the first (1951) commercial models.

Strangely enough, an analog computer more closely resembles the common conception of a digital computer. It often has hundreds of wires dangling from large plugboards, dozens of knobs, several meters, and perhaps a graphic output device similar to a television picture tube.

Actually, most of a digital computer is in closed cabinets whose insides are seldom seen except by the maintenance technician. Most of the noise and

AN ANALOG COMPUTER.

movement at a computer installation is caused by the high-speed line printer, spewing out sheet after sheet of results. The rest is contributed by the card readers, card punches, magnetic tape units, and disc storage units. After you've been working with a computer a while, its appearance will probably make little impression on you. You'll be interested only in what it can *do*, rather than in how it *looks*.

☐ GENERAL PURPOSE DIGITAL COMPUTERS

Although general purpose digital computers differ widely in size, form, and method of operation, they all have common features that can be represented quite simply.

First, they must all have some device by which the information that the computer is to deal with is gotten into the computer. This is called the *input device.* It could be a punched card reader, a typewriter keyboard, an optical scanner, a magnetic tape unit, and many other things. We can represent such a device as a box labeled "INPUT."

INPUT

Second, computers must have some device by which the results produced are gotten out of the computer and delivered to the outside world. This could be a card punch, an automatic typewriter, a printer, a magnetic tape unit, a visual display device, and many other things. We can represent such a device as a box labeled "OUTPUT."

OUTPUT

Third, each computer must have a device where the operations are performed on the information brought in. This device will be made up of the electronic and electromagnetic circuits where the calculations are actually carried out. In many computers this is called the arithmetic unit. We can represent this part of any computer as a box labeled "ARITHMETIC UNIT."

ARITHMETIC UNIT

The computer must have the capability of remembering or storing information in electromagnetic form. This may be the information that it is about to operate on, or the partial results produced by the ARITHMETIC UNIT and not yet passed out through the OUTPUT, or the detailed instructions as to how this information is to be manipulated. The device with this capability is the memory or main storage and consists of tiny metallic doughnuts strung on wires that can be magnetized in one direction or another to represent and retain information. We can represent this part of the computer as a box labeled "STORAGE."

STORAGE

Finally, there must be a set of electronic circuits which automatically manage all parts of the computer, causing it to follow the detailed instructions stored in it so that information is taken in, manipulated according to the stored program, and stored temporarily in the memory, while the results are put out through the output device. This part of the computer is the control device, and we can represent it as a block labeled "SYSTEM CONTROL."

SYSTEM
CONTROL

If we connect these blocks with arrows that indicate the direction of flow of information and with dotted lines to indicate control, we get the computer diagram that will give a general representation of any computer.

Note that information flows from the INPUT to the ARITHMETIC UNIT and from there to the OUTPUT. Information flows both ways between the ARITHMETIC UNIT and STORAGE. The SYSTEM CONTROL controls the operation of all parts of the computer and gets information from STORAGE.

From the outside, computers seldom look like this diagram. Some computers are all in one box. Some computers consist of far more than five boxes. Some input devices share the same cabinet as the output device. In many computers the system control, arithmetic unit, and storage are not only in the same cabinet but have their electronic components so intermingled that

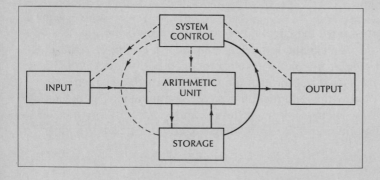

it is hard to say exactly where one ends and the other begins. Many computers have more than one storage device, several input and output devices, and more than one system control.

But in spite of this, the simple diagram represents the logical organization of any stored program, general purpose, digital computer and will aid you in reducing the most complex computer system to an understandable form.

☐ YOUR FIRST LOOK AT THE IBM SYSTEM/360

In this book it will often be necessary to explain a concept by giving a concrete example and by referring to a specific computer. The computer most frequently referred to will be the IBM System/360, a stored program, general purpose, digital computer manufactured by the International Business Machines Corporation. In this book you will learn some of the details of some of the important parts of System/360. Other books in this series will deal with more of the details; in particular, they will teach you how to program this computer.

Since the System/360 is a stored program, general purpose, digital computer, it has a block diagram like that on page 16. But there are certain specific features of the System/360 that we will want to emphasize later, so we draw its block diagram slightly differently, as shown on page 18.

Notice that the input devices and the output devices are not separated as they were before but are grouped together and called I/O devices. This is because some of the most important of these devices can be used as *either* input *or* output devices. That is, the computer can either *read in* information from a magnetic tape or magnetic disc or *write out* information on it.

Next notice that DATA CHANNELS appear between the I/O devices and the main part of the computer. These provide the data path and control for input/output devices as they communicate with the computer and transmit data to and from the main storage. Their function is an important consideration in System/360 programming, so they are specifically indicated.

REGISTERS in the System/360 are special electronic circuits that assist in performing the various computational operations on data in main storage. Consequently they may be thought of as carrying out the function of the box labeled "ARITHMETIC UNIT" in the general diagram.

The MAIN STORAGE block is purposely drawn larger than the other blocks

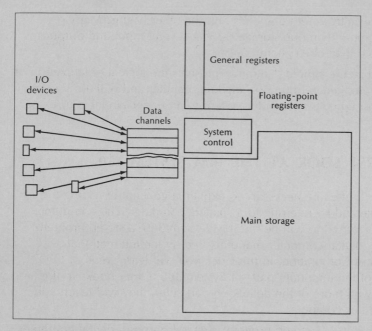

BLOCK DIAGRAM OF SYSTEM/360 COMPUTER.

to emphasize the vast amount of data that can be stored (often thousands of times as much information as the registers hold). The word MAIN has to be introduced here because, as you will find out later, the total storage capacity of a computer often consists of both main storage and supplementary or auxiliary storage.

Each of these blocks will be examined in greater detail in later chapters.

As you read this book you will learn that there are many common words which have specific computer meanings, such as *base, common, field, function, record, register,* and *word.* If you use them in other than their specific computer meaning, you will only cause confusion. Resolve to always use them properly.

HOW A PROGRAM IS EXECUTED BY SYSTEM 360
In the simplest case, the program is loaded into *main storage* from one of the *input devices.* The data to be operated on is also read from a device such as a punched card reader or a magnetic tape unit into the main

storage. When the program is ready to start work, the instructions that make up the program are automatically fetched from their places in main storage, one by one, and placed in the *system control section*.

According to the nature of the instruction, the various parts of System/360 perform the required operations. For instance, arithmetic operations may be performed in the *registers*. When the operations required by one instruction are completed, the next instruction to be executed is brought to system control. When it is time to write out results, either at the end of the

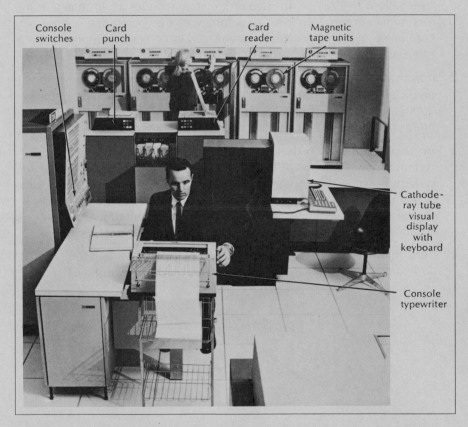

THE INPUT/OUTPUT EQUIPMENT AVAILABLE FOR SYSTEM/360 COVERS A WIDE VARIETY OF DEVICES, SOME OF WHICH ARE SHOWN. THESE INCLUDE PUNCHED CARD READERS AND CARD PUNCHES, TYPEWRITER-KEYBOARD DEVICES, PRINTERS, VISUAL DISPLAY DEVICES, AND MANY OTHERS.

program or, more usually, at a variety of points throughout the program, data is written out from main storage through a data channel to an output device such as a line printer or magnetic tape unit.

□ QUESTIONS

1   Assuming that each computer installation needs 10 full-time workers, calculate the number of people needed to man all United States computer installations in 1980. If this rate of growth continues as illustrated in the second figure in this chapter, how long will it be before the entire population of the United States is engaged in computer support? Why is this extrapolation ridiculous?

2   If the value of installed computing equipment continues to rise at the rate predicted for the period 1970 to 1980, what will the value be in the year 2000? In what year will this value equal the United States gross national product? Why is this extrapolation ridiculous?

3   An accountant and his desk calculator are an information processing system. Apply the terms of the five-block computer diagram to this system. What are the input, output, storage, control, and arithmetic units in this case? Apply the same terms to a typist and her typewriter; to a person using a telephone. What is the one significant difference between all these combination systems and a general purpose digital computer?

4   Read through the Prose Glossary in the front of the book, noting in particular the definitions of the new words introduced in this chapter.

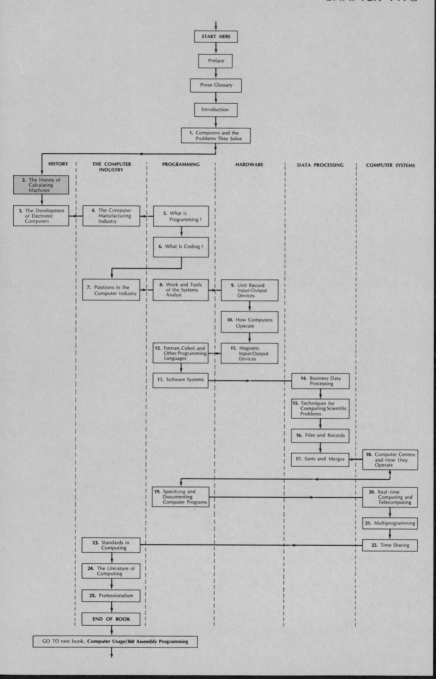

CHAPTER TWO

START HERE

Preface

Prose Glossary

Introduction

1. Computers and the Problems They Solve

| HISTORY | THE COMPUTER INDUSTRY | PROGRAMMING | HARDWARE | DATA PROCESSING | COMPUTER SYSTEMS |

2. The History of Calculating Machines

3. The Development of Electronic Computers

4. The Computer Manufacturing Industry

5. What Is Programming ?

6. What Is Coding ?

7. Positions in the Computer Industry

8. Work and Tools of the Systems Analyst

9. Unit Record Input/Output Devices

10. How Computers Operate

12. Fortran, Cobol, and Other Programming Languages

11. Magnetic Input/Output Devices

13. Software Systems

14. Business Data Processing

15. Techniques for Computing Scientific Problems

16. Files and Records

17. Sorts and Merges

18. Computer Centers and How They Operate

19. Specifying and Documenting Computer Programs

20. Real-time Computing and Telecomputing

21. Multiprogramming

23. Standards in Computing

22. Time Sharing

24. The Literature of Computing

25. Professionalism

END OF BOOK

GO TO next book, **Computer Usage/360 Assembly Programming**

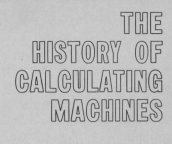

THE
HISTORY OF
CALCULATING
MACHINES

In this chapter you will study the early history of the computer. You are being taught computer history so that you will have a better basis for understanding how computers got where they are today. You will also be introduced to some concepts about their internal operation, which will serve as an introduction to Chapter 3.

☐ A YOUNG INDUSTRY

If you are over twenty, the entire field of electronic computers has developed since you were born. Electronic computers, like so many other devices of great importance today, have undergone all their growth since World War II. One reason for the computer's skyrocketing development is the rapidly increasing need for faster and faster ways of dealing with vast amounts of data generated by, and needed to guide, our complex technology.

☐ THE PROBLEM OF THE 1890 CENSUS

The problem of dealing with overwhelming numbers is not new. Back in 1888, the United States Census Office had a big problem too. The 1880 census had taken seven and a half years to complete, using standard hand methods to compile its reports on the nation's 50 million inhabitants. The 1890 census was only two years away. With an anticipated 62 million heads to be counted at that time, it was feared that the data might not be processed by the time of the 1900 census. If so, the figures would be obsolete before they could be analyzed.

Could the job be done by any available mechanical devices? If so, what equipment was available then? Not very much, as the following will show.

☐ ABACUS

For more than 3,000 years, the only device available to assist with arithmetic calculations was the *abacus*. This beads-on-rods calculator has been used in many countries, including ancient Egypt, India, and the Roman Empire, and is still in wide use in the Orient. Addition and subtraction are simple enough, but multiplication and division require complicated mental calculations, mostly to handle the carries from one column to the next, which the abacus obviously cannot do by itself.

☐ EARLY MECHANICAL CALCULATORS

Blaise Pascal, tired of adding long columns of figures in his father's tax office in Rouen, invented the first mechanical adding machine in 1642, when he was only nineteen. This shoe-box size *"arithmetic machine,"* which was operated with a stylus, took over the troublesome business of adding sols and deniers to francs (12 deniers = 1 sol; 20 sols = 1 franc). Its most important feature, however, was its ability to carry a *one* to the next

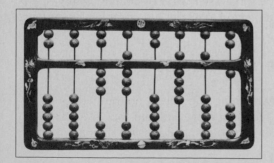

CHINESE ABACUS.

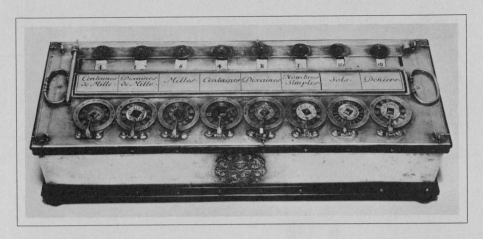

PASCAL'S ARITHMETIC MACHINE.

column. When a wheel moved from 9 to 0, the next wheel to the left advanced one digit. Pascal went on to become one of France's greatest philosophers and mathematicians.

Thirty years later, in 1672, Gottfried Leibnitz of Germany proposed a

THOMAS'S ARITHMOMETER.

machine to perform multiplication by repeated addition. One was built in 1694, but it was never dependable in operation.

C. X. Thomas of Colmar, in Alsace, improved the Leibnitz machine to the point where it was the first machine that could perform all four basic arithmetic operations well enough for commercial use. The *Arithmometer*, built in 1820, won for its inventor the ribbon of a Chevalier of the Legion of Honor from the grateful French government. However, only a few of the Thomas machines were built, and mechanical calculators were not to become important commercially for more than sixty years.

JACQUARD'S LOOM.

☐ JACQUARD'S CARDS

A watchmaker named Jacques de Vaucanson invented, in 1741, a delicate *automatic loom* for weaving figured silks. The designs in the silks were established by patterns of holes punched in a metal drum. The holes controlled the selection of threads by raising and lowering the treadles.

In 1804, Joseph Marie Jacquard adapted the same idea to a much larger scale for weaving multicolored tapestries, rugs, and other heavier materials. To increase the utility of his automatic loom, Jacquard used as controls punched sheets of stiff paper which could be changed fairly easily. A repetitive pattern could be woven using only a few cards, strung together to form a loop. But 24,000 cards were needed to produce a famous portrait of Jacquard himself. Within eight years, 11,000 Jacquard looms were operating in France.

☐ BABBAGE AND HIS ENGINES

Charles Babbage, in 1823, talked the British government into financing the construction of his *"difference engine."* He had spent the previous ten years designing and building portions of a small working model. The full-size device was to perform complex calculations and print out the results. However, it turned out that the precision parts required could not then be made. The government eventually withdrew its support in 1833 and the machine was never completed.

That same year, 1833, Babbage conceived his extremely ambitious *"analytical engine,"* and worked on it with his own money until he died in 1871. As designed, the machine had all the basic parts of a modern general purpose digital computer: memory (storage unit), control, arithmetic unit, and input/output. The memory was to hold 50,000 digits, and control was to be carried out by punched cards similar to those of Jacquard. The arithmetic unit was supposed to add or subtract in one second, and multiply 50 digits by 50 digits in about one minute.

This was the age of Watt's steam engine, when the criterion for the "close" fit of a piston within the cylinder wall was that a thin sixpence could just be slipped between the two. Built to such tolerances, Babbage's analytical engine, like his previous machine, could never be made to produce reliable answers.

With its large storage capacity and all its elaborate controls, the construction

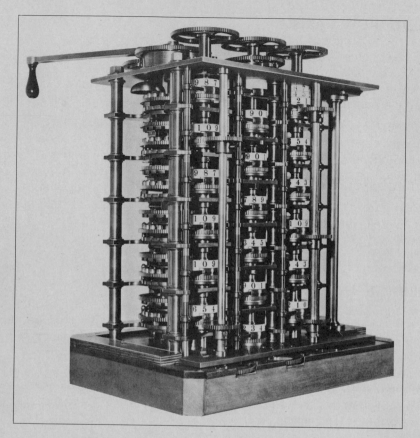

PART OF BABBAGE'S DIFFERENCE ENGINE.

of Babbage's computers would be a big project even by today's standards. If his objectives had been more modest, he might have succeeded in completing a working machine which, although not as powerful as desired, would have been powerful enough to be highly successful. Instead, his machines became only historical curiosities, with just a few parts ever completed.

☐ AMERICAN COMMERCIAL DEVICES (PRE-1890)

The Felt "*macaroni box*" was invented in 1885 in the United States. This experimental key-driven calculating machine was built from a wooden macaroni box, with meat skewers for keys, staples for key guides, and rubber bands for springs. In 1886 a metal model was built. This was the forerunner of the Comptometer, made by the Felt and Tarrant Manufacturing Company, now the Victor Comptometer Coporation.

William S. Burroughs, of the United States, built in 1889 a calculator called the *"listing accountant."* It was somewhat similar to the Felt machine, but used a carry mechanism similar to Pascal's. This was the first calculator of the Burroughs Adding Machine Company, now the Burroughs Corporation. It was probably the first adding machine designed for production in quantity.

☐ HERMAN HOLLERITH AND THE INVENTION OF PUNCHED CARD MACHINES

These devices, from the abacus to the Burroughs calculator, were all that had been developed in three thousand years of civilization. None of them could do the job required by the Census Office.

After Herman Hollerith received his Bachelor's degree from Columbia University in 1879, at the age of nineteen, he went to work for the Census Office of the U.S. Department of the Interior. He noted the tedious, slow system that required all data to be handwritten on cards, the cards sorted by hand into various categories, each classification counted, then the cards re-sorted and counted again and again.

Hollerith left the Census Office to become an instructor in mechanical engineering at M.I.T. Here, in 1882, he conducted his first experiments on what he called a *Census Machine*. Hollerith remembered having seen a

HOLLERITH'S CENSUS MACHINE.

train conductor hand-punching tickets that recorded a rough description of passengers, to prevent use by anyone else. Hollerith thought it should be possible to punch a card for each individual in the United States. The cards, similar to those of Jacquard, were made the same size as the large dollar bills in use at that time, for "standard size and ease of handling." Each card was divided into 240 areas, each square having a distinct meaning. One group of holes was for age, another for education, income, etc. One particular hole, for instance, meant that the individual was between the ages of 30 and 35. The holes were made with a train conductor's hand punch.

After being punched, the cards were inserted, one at a time, in the Census Machine, which had a pin for every possible hole in the card. The handle was then pulled down. Wherever there was a hole, a spring-loaded pin passed through to make contact with an individual cup of mercury, making an electrical circuit. This caused a counter connected to that cup to add a *one*. There were 40 counters altogether, with dials like clocks (printing was a refinement not yet used).

The electrical impulse that energized the counter also opened one of the lids in the accompanying sorting box. The operator then removed the card by hand from the reader, placed it in the open slot of the sorting box, and closed the lid with his hand. It was a crude but effective form of sorting.

The conductor's punch was replaced by a desk-top punch in time for the 1890 census. It had been estimated that a punch operator would be able to punch 500 cards a day, but an average of 700 was reached and some operators managed to punch 2,000 a day. The Hollerith machines completed the 1890 census of 62 million Americans in less than three years.

A storm broke when the figures were announced, as the count had been expected to go over 65 million. People claimed that these new machines had counted wrong. Prominent scientists rushed to Hollerith's defense and proclaimed that, if anything, the 1890 count was the most accurate yet recorded.

In 1894, Hollerith redesigned the card into its present form, with holes for 0 through 9 in 80 columns. In 1896, he formed the Tabulating Machine Company. Word of his success spread rapidly. Before 1900, he set up an installation for the New York Central to keep track of their railroad cars. Insurance companies used his machines for actuarial work; Marshall Field's store in Chicago used them for sales analysis. Hollerith even went to Russia to help the government with its census.

Hollerith continued to modify and improve his machines, which were used for the 1900 census. In 1910, even though Hollerith had developed a system of hopper-fed machines that eliminated feeding cards by hand, he was unable to reach an agreement with the Census Bureau for their use. When his Tabulating Machine Company became too large for individual control, Hollerith sold it. In 1917, the company, which by then had merged with two other companies, entered the Canadian market under the name of International Business Machines Co., Ltd. In 1924, the American company became International Business Machines Corporation.

☐ SCIENTIFIC USE OF PUNCHED CARD MACHINES

Scientists, overburdened with calculating chores requiring thousands and millions of computations, soon made use of the new *punched card equipment*. Although these machines were pitifully slow compared with the computers that became available fifteen to twenty years later, the scientists could not have waited even if they had known what the future would bring. The first scientific application of the Hollerith system, as it is often still called in Europe, was undertaken by the British National Almanac Office in 1927. Information from tables of positions of the moon was punched into half a million cards. These cards were then used to compute the position of the moon at noon and at midnight, for all dates from 1935 to 2000 A.D. One hundred million figures were produced, and the results printed out over a period of seven months. These tables were of great use to astronomers and, when printed in the *Nautical Almanac*, highly important to marine navigation.

☐ HARVARD MARK I
(AUTOMATIC SEQUENCE CONTROLLED CALCULATOR)

Scientific and statistical use of punched card machines began to grow. And as more uses developed, so did the demand for faster machines.

The demand for a faster machine was met by Professor Howard Aiken of Harvard University. Working with IBM engineers, he developed an electromechanical calculator called the Automatic Sequence Controlled Calculator, but most often referred to as the *Harvard Mark I calculator*. Begun in 1939, it was completed in August, 1944.

Mark I was 51 feet long and 8 feet high and weighed about 5 tons. It used the Jacquard type of wide, continuous punched paper tape and incorporated many of the principles advanced by Babbage. The relays, counters, cam contacts, typewriters, card feeds, and card punches used in Mark I were all standard parts of IBM tabulating machines.

Mark I could add and subtract in $3/10$ second. Multiplication took at most 6 seconds, with an average of 4 seconds. Division took at most 16 seconds,

THE HARVARD MARK I.

with an average of 11 seconds. Mark I could perform any specified sequence of five fundamental operations: addition, subtraction, multiplication, division, and reference to tables of previously computed results. The Hollerith accumulator was the calculating element in Mark I. It produced some very important mathematical tables that were soon put into wide use. Mark I was in operation for more than fifteen years. Results of its work are used in almost every computation laboratory.

☐ BELL LABORATORIES RELAY COMPUTERS

Many World War II projects cried out for faster and faster computations, especially in airplane and ordnance development. The atom-bomb project required calculations of a complexity never before encountered. The first computers to answer these military needs were *relay computers*. During the years 1944 to 1947, four types of relay computers were put into operation on scientific problems. They were the Harvard Mark I, Harvard Mark II, Bell Telephone Laboratories Relay Computers, and the IBM Pluggable Sequence Relay Calculator.

Development of relay computing devices began in 1938 at the Bell Telephone Laboratories. These devices were needed to handle computations of the complex numbers used in electronic engineering design; that is, numbers involving the square root of minus one, $\sqrt{-1}$. However, its users soon found that the "Complex Number Computer" could solve other types of problems.

The *Complex Computer,* as it soon came to be called, had features desirable in many modern installations. It could be used from three different, separate operator stations, and it could be operated remotely over a teletypewriter circuit.

With the advent of World War II, demands on the Complex Computer increased and many military projects were speeded through its use. Other models were built, the last of which was a modern computer in contrast with *Model I,* which became in retrospect little more than an elaborate desk calculator. *Model II* was built for the National Defense Research Council and, in 1943, began handling problems of fire control for guns. Model II had 31 instructions and used paper tape for input and output; its operating sequence was controlled by a punched paper tape loop. *Model IV* could also handle trigonometric functions, such as sine and tangent.

The success of these small machines led to the construction of two large systems (Model V) for American government agencies. *Model V* had a maximum of six computing units, with ten locations into which problems could be fed, allowing the computing units to function continuously. Problems were fed into idle problem locations. A computing unit, after finishing one problem, automatically started another. Each problem location had one tape reader for input data, up to five readers for program instructions, and up to six readers for tabular data. Permanently wired into the machine were tables of logarithms, antilogarithms, sines, cosines, and arctangents.

Model VI, the last of the family, was built for Bell Laboratories' own use. It had many improvements, including magnetic tape storage units. Models V and VI bridged the gap between the beginnings of the art and the modern age of electronic computers.

An important difference between the Harvard Mark II machine and the Bell Laboratories machines resulted from the different attitudes taken by their designers as to the inclusion of checking circuits. The Harvard Mark II followed the tradition of Mark I: the whole burden of checking, including checks on the operations performed by the machine, was placed on the programmer. The designers of the Bell Laboratories machines, however, did all they could to make them self-checking, and these machines would stop rather than make an error.

☐ THE TURING MACHINE

In the midst of all this discussion of machines, let's look at a very significant machine that was never built. In 1938, several years before the beginning of modern computer technology, British mathematician Alan M. Turing proposed a computing concept now known as the *Turing machine.* No Turing machine has ever been built, as its value is more theoretical than practical. However, it has been verified that the Turing machine is a useful and practical tool—not only for problem solving and for checking out possible approaches to problem solving, but also for teaching students the fundamentals of computing.

The description of a Turing machine is deceptively simple. There are three parts: a control unit, a read-write head, and a tape of infinite length, divided into squares, any of which can contain any symbol from a specific list of characters.

The reading head scans one square of the tape, upon command. It can read the symbol written there and, under directions from the control element, can write a new symbol (after erasing the old one) and also move the tape one square to the right or left.

The control unit is a device with a predetermined number of internal "states." (All machines contain a specific number of elements, and each element can have two or more conditions. The "state" of a machine is a summary of the conditions of all the elements at a particular instant. For instance, an automobile can be considered as having a variety of states, depending on how many elements are to be considered: motor on or off; lights on or off; heater on, half-on, or off; radio tuned to station X, Y, or Z; and so on. The state of the automobile at any instant is the *condition at that moment of all the elements involved.*)

At any particular time, the next operation that the Turing machine will perform depends on the current state of the control unit and the symbol being read by the reading head. This next operation will consist of three parts: first, printing a new symbol in the present square (which may, of course, be the same symbol as the one just read); second, the control unit goes into a new state (which may also be the same as the previous state); and third, movement of the tape under the reading head, one square to the right or left.

In operation, some of the tape squares are prepared with a starting set of symbols, the rest of the tape being left blank. The reading head is placed at a particular starting square and the machine proceeds to computing, starting with the first operation in its control unit.

Turing demonstrated that if a Turing machine can perform the above functions, it can carry out an amazingly wide range of calculations. Applying this principle to today's computers, if a computing machine can perform all Turing functions, it can compute a wide range of calculations.

The importance of the Turing machine is in the application to its fundamental theory. Using Turing-machine *theory,* logicians can predict

1488966

what could happen in the computation of any problem. One can thus know in advance if a problem can be solved by a computer or, if not, how far toward a solution the computer can go.

☐ THE NEXT STEP

The development of electromechanical computers was given a big push during World War II. Within a few years the theory had been worked out, and the basic principles of computing had been tested and proved.

The next step was a giant one—to vastly increase the speed and flexibility of computers by using electronic components such as vacuum tubes. The first automatic electronic computer was designe at the Moore School of Electrical Engineering—but that's another story, to be covered in Chapter 3.

☐ QUESTIONS

1 Was the rate of increase in Jacquard looms in France in the early nineteenth century greater or less than the rate of increase in computers cited in Chapter 1?

2 Babbage planned to be able to multiply 50 digits by 50 digits in a minute. How long would it take to do this with pencil and paper? Time yourself, with a random string of digits. Time a mechanical desk calculator multiplying the longest string of digits it can. How long did the input take? How long did the output take? How do your speeds compare with what Aiken's Mark I could do?

3 How often is the United States census taken? Why? What was the original purpose of the census? What are its present purposes?

4 Discuss the differences in the Harvard and Bell Laboratories design philosophies with regard to checking. What are the advantages and disadvantages of the two approaches? Is one significantly superior to the other? How would the choice of approaches be related to the level of computer technology available, that is, to how reliable the computer was thought to be? To the purpose of the calculations? To the cost of manpower?

5 Consider the discussion of "states" in the section on the Turing Machine. How many states does an electric wall switch have? How many states does the lamp it controls have? How many states does the automobile described in that section have? (Ignore the phrase "and so on.")

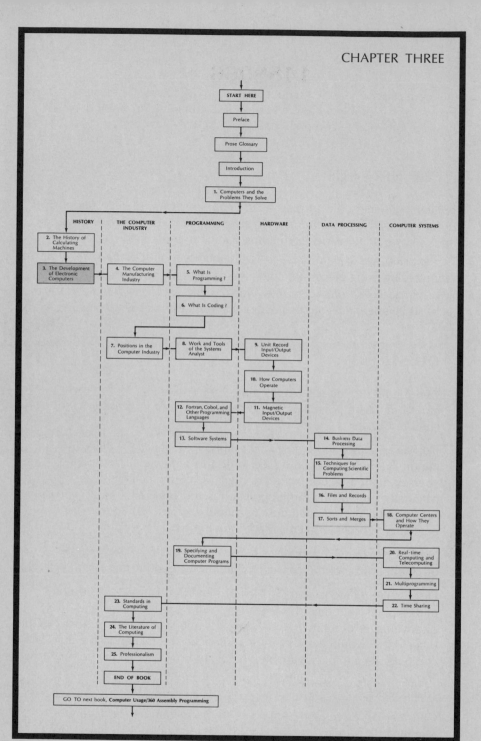

CHAPTER THREE

START HERE

Preface

Prose Glossary

Introduction

1. Computers and the Problems They Solve

HISTORY	THE COMPUTER INDUSTRY	PROGRAMMING	HARDWARE	DATA PROCESSING	COMPUTER SYSTEMS

2. The History of Calculating Machines

3. The Development of Electronic Computers

4. The Computer Manufacturing Industry

5. What Is Programming?

6. What Is Coding?

7. Positions in the Computer Industry

8. Work and Tools of the Systems Analyst

9. Unit Record Input/Output Devices

10. How Computers Operate

12. Fortran, Cobol, and Other Programming Languages

11. Magnetic Input/Output Devices

13. Software Systems

14. Business Data Processing

15. Techniques for Computing Scientific Problems

16. Files and Records

17. Sorts and Merges

18. Computer Centers and How They Operate

19. Specifying and Documenting Computer Programs

20. Real-time Computing and Telecomputing

21. Multiprogramming

23. Standards in Computing

22. Time Sharing

24. The Literature of Computing

25. Professionalism

END OF BOOK

GO TO next book, **Computer Usage/360 Assembly Programming**

THE DEVELOPMENT OF ELECTRONIC COMPUTERS

☐ ENIAC, THE FIRST ELECTRONIC COMPUTER

In 1941 a physicist, Dr. John W. Mauchly, joined the staff of the University of Pennsylvania's Moore School of Electrical Engineering in Philadelphia. He hoped to find some way of applying electronics to the task of handling the great mass of numerical information that scientists were gathering about the earth—about electricity in the atmosphere, magnetism in the earth, the weather, etc.

However, the problems of war soon pushed aside all other considerations. The Army needed firing tables to tell its artillerymen how to aim the new guns. The Moore School had been calculating these tables, but with methods that were proving too slow. Dr. Mauchly suggested that a machine using electronic tubes be built for the calculations. The Army agreed and provided funds. Mauchly began to design a computer, working with one of the electronics engineering students, J. Presper Eckert, Jr. Their machine was called ENIAC, from the first letters of the full name, Electronic Numerical Integrater And Calculator. When completed it made all relay calculators obsolete. Relay machines such as Mark I could perform no more than about 10 additions a second; ENIAC could do 5,000 additions a second.

Originally designed as a special purpose machine to calculate firing tables, ENIAC's plans were later modified to enable the machine to solve a very wide variety of problems, perhaps because the war was coming to an end. Completed in the summer of 1946, ENIAC was the first electronic automatic general purpose computer. All computing and storage of numbers were performed by electronic circuits; there were no moving parts except for the input and output mechanisms.

ENIAC was built primarily with standard radio tubes and parts. There were over 18,800 vacuum tubes linked by half a million hand-soldered connections. ENIAC was a slow-footed giant by comparison with today's standards—it weighed more than 30 tons and occupied a space 30 by 50 feet. But it had taken a giant step and started a revolution—a technological revolution based on the development of the computer.

According to Dr. Eckert, ENIAC could have been built 10 or 15 years earlier, because all the components were available then. But, as Dr. Mauchly has said, the demand wasn't there. In 1930, only about a third of the United States labor force was doing paper work, instead of the half engaged in this work today, even with the computer. In those days the demand was largely met, as far as the automation of office clerical jobs was concerned, by a growing array of punched card equipment. Dr. Eckert believes that today the single most serious problem facing the computing industry is the programming problem: the problem of writing out the detailed instructions for every task that the computer must do. Dr. Mauchly has said he wouldn't be surprised if "it was a worse problem five years from today than it is now."

One of the two major drawbacks of ENIAC was its limited storage capacity. Twelve vacuum tubes were required to store one decimal digit. With storage as expensive as this, only the capacity for 20 ten-digit numbers could be provided.

HOW ENIAC WAS "PROGRAMMED"
The other drawback of ENIAC was its extremely awkward setup procedure. When originally installed in 1947 at the Ballistic Research Laboratories, Aberdeen Proving Ground, Maryland, ENIAC required a lengthy procedure for being instructed how to do a problem. The machine had some 6,000 switches, most of them with several positions, which were used for programming and for the storage of various constants in function tables.

Each switch required hand setting. Although the ENIAC programming scheme was flexible, it was also quite complicated. Each of the 20 main-memory registers (circuits which temporarily stored numbers) also functioned as an accumulator that could add and subtract as well as store. Each accumulator or other number handling circuit, such as the multiplier, had associated with it a number of "program controls" of various types. Each program control was an electronic circuit containing nine or more tubes plus switches that determined such things as the number of consecutive cycles the program control was to operate, or whether a given accumulator was to add, subtract, or just receive. Plugwires were used to connect the accumulators and other units to trunk wires and to interconnect the various program controls for the sequencing of operations. This system gave ENIAC the ability to perform several arithmetic operations simultaneously, to alter the sequence of operations in accordance with the results of intermediate calculations, and to repeat sequences of operations, all at electronic speeds.

Many hours were required to alter the thousands of switches and the multitude of plugwires when changing from one program to another. This long and difficult job was subject to many errors. It required a long period of checking of all settings. The connections and settings generally took a full working day to set up and check. This constituted a serious limitation on the flexibility of the system. (Contrast this with modern computer programming, which no longer requires the programmer to set switches and insert plugwires, but allows him to write his computer instructions out with pencil and paper in an office, at home, or anywhere he can think and work undisturbed.)

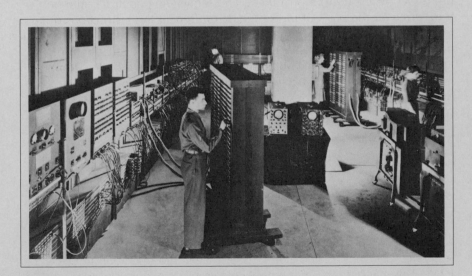

ENIAC.

Even though this limitation of ENIAC was not a serious obstacle to the calculation of ballistic and firing tables, it was eased in the late 1940s when a more flexible wired programming system was devised. ENIAC was modified to accommodate what was called the "von Neumann programming method." Dr. von Neumann recognized that the programming information contained in the switch settings and plugwire connections was digital information that could be coded in a digital form very similar to that of digital data. Assuming sufficient storage capacity, *the program as well as the data* could be stored in the computer. The large-capacity storage system could also hold function-table data, (trigonometric, logarithmic, etc.), thus allowing the switches previously used for this purpose to be eliminated.

ENIAC's wiring was made permanent, and the function tables were used to store *instructions* rather than values of functions. ENIAC then read the function tables in sequence and followed these instructions. The remainder of the machine was wired in one standard fashion, which seldom needed to be changed. However, the instructions did not then constitute an internally stored program, since they were manually set on the function-table switches.

ENIAC contained an important concept that is only now finding acceptance in digital systems: the simultaneous performance of several operations. ENIAC also made the first use of subroutines. When a certain series of instructions was completed, an internal test could be made to see whether or not it was necessary to repeat them, and sequencing control could be transferred on the basis of this test, either to repeat the instructions or go on to another set. Subroutines are important, because a program may use a large number of them. Any often-used subroutine is usually available from a library of subroutines. This library is most often supplied by the computer manufacturer; there are also libraries of special subroutines peculiar to a particular company or industry.

□ SSEC

IBM, which had at that time a sizable market in punched card equipment, contributed to the field by producing the Mark I computer jointly with Harvard University. After Mark I was given to Harvard, IBM continued its developmental work on computers. IBM's next computer, the Selective Sequence Electronic Calculator, or SSEC, went into operation in December, 1947. This machine was not entirely electronic, since it used relays as well as tubes. It was very large, having about 23,000 relays and about 13,000

SSEC.

tubes. The SSEC became one of the most prominent computers of its day. It was put on display in the windows of IBM World Headquarters in New York City.

☐ EDVAC

EDVAC (Electronic Discrete Variable Computer) was the second high-speed digital machine constructed at the Moore School of Electrical Engineering at the University of Pennsylvania. EDVAC occupied much less space than ENIAC (about 140 square feet, compared with 1,500 square feet). EDVAC contained only about 3,500 vacuum tubes—roughly one-sixth the number used in ENIAC. Other than the method for programming, the main difference lay in the use of mercury delay lines for internal storage of numbers. (The mercury delay line was an early method of main-memory storage, in which data was passed through a column of mercury at the speed of sound—so much slower than the electronic speed of the rest of the computer that the data was, in effect, stored temporarily. Mercury delay lines have been completely replaced by magnetic-core storage.) These delay lines in EDVAC gave it enough capacity to make it the first digital system, electronic or otherwise, to use the *stored program* principle.

Because EDVAC had progressed quite far by 1946, it is often referred to as the first electronic computer following ENIAC in the chain of development. However, EDVAC did not become operational until 1952, so that in terms of date of completion, it followed a number of other computers.

EDVAC.

EDVAC used acoustic delay lines, in the form of sealed tubes full of mercury, to give it a main memory with a total of 1,024 words. The instructions, each consisting of four addresses and an operation code, were stored in main memory along with the data to be used in the computation. Input/output equipment included paper tape, a typewriter, and punched cards. Addition required one thousandth of a second (one millisecond); multiplication and division required about three milliseconds.

EDVAC had an auxiliary storage with a capacity of about 20,000 numbers, but with a much longer access time (the time required to fetch information from storage) than the mercury delay line storage. The auxiliary storage consisted of reels of nickel-plated bronze wire on which the digits were recorded magnetically. This was an adaptation of the wire-recording technique developed in Germany and popular here right after World War II. Magnetic wire recording, both for computers and for sound, eventually gave way to magnetic tape systems.

☐ EDSAC AND SEAC

EDSAC, a computer built at Cambridge University in England, was the first stored program computer, complete with input and output facilities, to be placed in operation—in May, 1949.

The Standards Electronic Automatic Computer (SEAC) was built by the National Bureau of Standards. Design began in June, 1946, and the computer began operation in May, 1950. It was built under the sponsorship of the Air Force, mainly for mathematical investigations of techniques for solving problems in logistics (the military science of moving, supplying, and housing troops). SEAC was built as a stored program computer, with its design based on that of EDVAC. It was planned and constructed as a nucleus to which improvements could be added to increase its problem-solving capabilities. With about 750 tubes and 10,500 semiconductor diodes, the original installation consisted mainly of the computing and control circuits, a mercury delay line memory providing a storage of 512 words, a manual

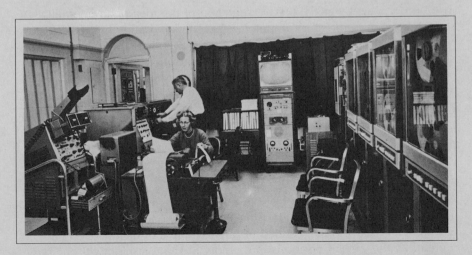

SEAC.

keyboard for direct input, and a teletypewriter for direct output. Additions made from time to time included additional memory, an electric typewriter which read and punched paper tape, and magnetic tape for input and output. SEAC proved to be a workhorse computer and was not retired from active duty until April, 1964. Portions of SEAC are now on display at the Smithsonian Institution in Washington.

☐ JOHN VON NEUMANN AND THE IAS COMPUTER

A most important early influence in computer technology was provided by Dr. John von Neumann, a mathematician at the Institute of Advanced Study (IAS) at Princeton, New Jersey. His suggested modification of ENIAC supplied a model for most digital computers. Not only did he develop the stored program concept; he introduced the idea of a flowchart.

The ideas generated upon reviewing the design of ENIAC were collected together in a report titled "Preliminary Discussion of the Logical Design of an Electronic Computing Instrument," by A. W. Burks, H. H. Goldstine, and Dr. von Neumann, prepared under a contract between the Army Ordnance Department and the Institute of Advanced Study. The material in this report, suggesting design principles for new computers, was widely disseminated by means of a summer session at the University of Pennsylvania in 1946, and influenced computer design for the next decade.

The historic paper was the first presentation of the idea of an internally stored program to direct a computer. It also covered other desirable features of a digital computer so thoroughly that for many years there were very few significant differences between the machine proposed by the three authors and the machines actually built.

At the time the IAS paper was written, the principle of automatic calculation had been well established (with Harvard's Mark I), as was the great advance gained by electronics (with ENIAC). The jump from that state of the art to the details of the IAS paper is difficult to measure, although it might be compared to writing a full description of a jet plane shortly after the Wright brothers had made a few flights.

Among the significant features of the IAS computer were (1) storing both data and instructions in memory; (2) using the same sequence of instructions with different sets of data, located in different parts of memory; (3) numbering the various positions in memory in serial fashion with memory

DR. JOHN VON NEUMANN AND THE IAS COMPUTER.

addresses; (4) conditional transfer, in which the computer switches to another set of instructions depending upon certain conditions at a particular moment; (5) parallel arithmetic; (6) decimal-to-binary and binary-to-decimal conversion within the computer; (7) synchronous computing, in which the timing of the entire computer is governed by a single clock-pulse source; (8) simultaneous operation of the computer and the input/output devices; and (9) replacement of punched paper tapes by magnetic recording tapes for external storage.

The design of the IAS computer was started in 1946, and the machine was completed six years later under the direction of Dr. von Neumann. Its development and construction were initially sponsored by the Army Ordnance Corps; later the project was also sponsored by the Office of Naval Research, the Air Force, and the Atomic Energy Commission.

The IAS computer was an electronic parallel machine. It was unusually small, 2 x 8 x 8 feet, not including the input/output equipment. It used an electrostatic memory composed of 40 cathode-ray tubes. A magnetic drum was added later. For input and output, punched cards and perforated paper tape were employed.

It made use of three principal registers. One was an "accumulator," a device capable of holding a number and adding another number to it. For instance, during addition the accumulator would hold the augend and then the sum (addend + augend = sum). A second register was called the "arithmetic register," designed to hold the multiplier and the product during multiplication, and the quotient during division. The third register was a "memory register" that contained the addend during addition, the multiplicand during multiplication, and the divisor during division. This concept is visible in current computers like the IBM System/360, which is treated in detail in another book in this series.

☐ WHIRLWIND

An assignment to build a real time aircraft simulator was given in 1945 to a group that eventually became the Digital Computer Laboratory of the

INSIDE WHIRLWIND.

Massachusetts Institute of Technology. Beginning in 1947, most of the effort was devoted to the design and construction of an electronic digital computer known as Whirlwind, sponsored by the Office of Naval Research and the Air Force. The machine was put into operation in March, 1951.

Whirlwind, following the IAS principle, was a parallel computer. It consisted of an arithmetic element, a control unit, a program counter, memory, input/output equipment, and extensive test and checking equipment.

The arithmetic element consisted of three registers. The first was an accumulator, which also held the product during multiplication. The second held the multiplicand during multiplication. The third register was a register holding the multiplier.

Whirlwind was a stored program computer, with the instructions stored in the internal memory. There were 32 instructions, including addition, subtraction, multiplication, division, shifting, branching, and conditional branching.

The memory of Whirlwind originally consisted of 16 specially designed electrostatic storage tubes, a form of computer memory no longer in use. Later a magnetic-core memory was substituted and magnetic tape units and magnetic drums were added. Many modern programming concepts were developed by the Whirlwind group.

☐ UNIVAC

In 1950, Remington Rand was the second-largest manufacturer of office equipment in the United States. RemRand, as it was then called, got into the computer business in 1950 by buying the Eckert-Mauchly Computer Corporation, which had been founded in 1947 by J. Presper Eckert and John W. Mauchly about a year after their ENIAC computer started operations. The Eckert-Mauchly company had already contracted to sell a computer to the Bureau of the Census. This computer was the UNIVAC I. At the same time, RemRand also acquired Engineering Research Associates, which had developed the ERA 1101 computer.

UNIVAC I (Universal Automatic Computer) was a direct descendant of the two other computers that had been built at the University of Pennsylvania, ENIAC and EDVAC. UNIVAC I contained about 5,000 vacuum tubes and was considerably smaller than ENIAC. A stored program computer, it could add in 2 microseconds and multiply in 10 microseconds. It had 45

UNIVAC I, CONSOLE AND TAPE UNITS.

instructions and was one of the first computers to make significant use of magnetic tape as an input/output medium.

UNIVAC I received a large amount of publicity when it was used in 1952 to predict the outcome of the presidential election on the basis of incomplete early returns. It predicted the correct winner—Eisenhower—with near-certain probability, so quickly that those in charge of the television program thought it had made a mistake, and the information was withheld from the public for a time.

UNIVAC I is important because it was the first commercially available computer. Remington Rand eventually built 48 UNIVAC I computers. The first one to be completed went into operation in March, 1951, for the Bureau of the Census, where punched card machines got their start under Hollerith, and was put to work editing data from the 1950 census. Machines had come full circle. The foundation for the "Computer Age" had been laid.

□ **QUESTIONS**

1   Make a table of all the computers named in this chapter showing the dates of first operation, parent organization, programming method, storage or memory method, memory size, number of instructions, and multiply and add speeds.

2   Compare the multiply and add speeds for the computers described here with those treated in the previous chapters.

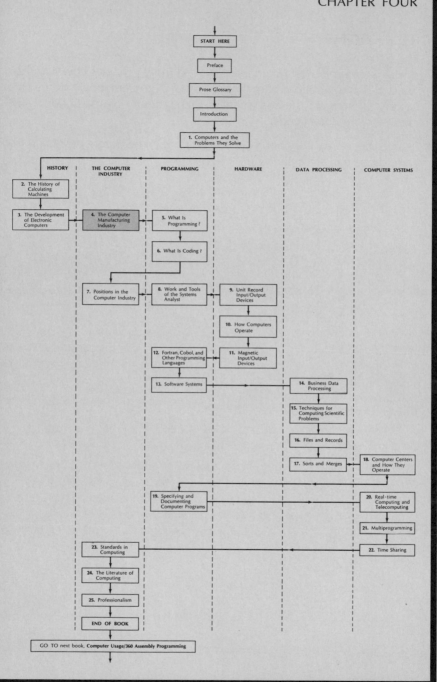

CHAPTER FOUR

START HERE

Preface

Prose Glossary

Introduction

1. Computers and the Problems They Solve

HISTORY | THE COMPUTER INDUSTRY | PROGRAMMING | HARDWARE | DATA PROCESSING | COMPUTER SYSTEMS

2. The History of Calculating Machines

3. The Development of Electronic Computers

4. The Computer Manufacturing Industry

5. What Is Programming?

6. What Is Coding?

7. Positions in the Computer Industry

8. Work and Tools of the Systems Analyst

9. Unit Record Input/Output Devices

10. How Computers Operate

11. Magnetic Input/Output Devices

12. Fortran, Cobol, and Other Programming Languages

13. Software Systems

14. Business Data Processing

15. Techniques for Computing Scientific Problems

16. Files and Records

17. Sorts and Merges

18. Computer Centers and How They Operate

19. Specifying and Documenting Computer Programs

20. Real-time Computing and Telecomputing

21. Multiprogramming

22. Time Sharing

23. Standards in Computing

24. The Literature of Computing

25. Professionalism

END OF BOOK

GO TO next book, **Computer Usage/360 Assembly Programming**

THE COMPUTER MANUFACTURING INDUSTRY

Never before has a single piece of equipment generated such a technically sophisticated, competitive, expansion-minded, and well-financed industrial venture. The computer manufacturing industry is growing at a faster rate than any other major industry. At the beginning of 1968 there were more than 50,000 computers, with a total value of 13.6 billion dollars, installed in the United States. The order backlog for all manufacturers was more than 25,000 machines. In other words, unfilled orders equalled half of all computers installed over the years—an enormous growth rate.

What has occurred in the industry to account for this growth? According to the experts, one of the major factors for the great surge is the many new applications for computers that have been developed. Computer users have become far more sophisticated and are constantly searching for new applications for the machines. Interestingly enough, this is affecting not just one but all manufacturers, so that no company is suffering in the midst of the boom.

It is necessary that you be fully aware of the extensiveness of the computer manufacturing industry and of the international nature of its market Although this lesson will familiarize you only with manufacturing and marketing here in the United States, it is important to remember that in Russia, China, Japan, and throughout Europe, companies or governments are constantly designing, building, and installing these machines, although the total foreign segment is much smaller than the United States market.

☐ CHARACTERISTICS OF THE COMPUTER MANUFACTURING INDUSTRY

The computer manufacturing industry, not unlike other industries, has a personality and characteristics uniquely its own. It is a business in which billions of dollars are constantly risked on research and development. It is an industry selling machines having fantastic scientific advances that are almost obsolete when they hit the market.

The computer industry is a unique union of *science* and *business*. It is a union so advanced and so high-powered that it makes many other technical manufacturing industries seem like child's play.

☐ FOUR PREREQUISITES FOR COMPUTER MANUFACTURERS

It is easy enough to deduce that in an industry having the characteristics already mentioned, there are bound to be certain prerequisites for any company wishing to enter the field. First a company must have *tremendous capital* to invest in research, engineering, marketing, production, etc. Secondly, a company must have creative *computer designers*. Third in the list is *technical know-how*, so that the company can begin building computers which will be marketable about three years in the future. This requires an ability to analyze and predict future trends, as well as demanding a willingness to invest sums to develop a product that may or may not sell well. Finally, a company must have its next computer always in the *planning* state so that the next model's production is assured.

☐ THE COMPANIES

There are about two dozen companies manufacturing computers. It is predicted by those knowledgeable in the industry that these will probably shrink to become a handful of giant corporations—all highly competitive.

Already there are acknowledged leaders in the industry, so that we need only concern ourselves with the nine largest companies. These come from

A TYPICAL COMPUTER MANUFACTURING OPERATION.

three primary groups:

1 Companies evolving from the manufacturers of business machines:
    International Business Machines (IBM)
    Sperry Rand Corporation's UNIVAC Division
    Burroughs Corporation
    National Cash Register Corporation (NCR)
2 Companies evolving from manufacturers of electronic equipment:
    General Electric (GE)
    Radio Corporation of America (RCA)
    Honeywell Corporation
3 New companies manufacturing only electronic data processing
    equipment:
    Control Data Corporation (CDC)
    Scientific Data Systems (SDS)

IBM

It is estimated that International Business Machines has cornered 70 to 80 percent of the computer manufacturing market. In 1953, after several years of indecision, the company changed itself from the world's largest punched card office machine manufacturer into the world's biggest electronic computer manufacturer. Though slow to enter the market, by January, 1961, IBM accounted for 71 percent of the 1.8 million dollars worth of general purpose computers in use at that time. IBM has since maintained this position and unquestionably dominates the industry.

IBM has several "families" of computers ranging in rental from small ones ($1,500 per month) to its largest models, which may rent for as much as $300,000 per month. The first IBM computers were all scientific computers; the initial machine was the IBM 701, which was installed in April, 1953. This was followed by the IBM 704, whose first installation date was December, 1955, and by the IBM 7090, a family of scientific machines, the first of which was installed in November, 1959. The last of the scientific computers to be announced was also a member of this family: the IBM 7094 II, which rented for about $78,500 per month and was installed in April, 1964.

In February, 1955, IBM installed its first commercial business processing machine, two years after announcing that it was entering the commercial market. The computer was the IBM 702, which rented for $6,900 per month. Only seven of these machines were ever installed before IBM upgraded it to the 705 (first installed in November, 1955, at a rental of about $38,000 per month); IBM did very well with this model, installing 60 machines.

In August, 1961, the 7080 made its appearance; this machine was one of the most influential and complex that IBM developed for commercial purposes. It was a large machine which rented for about $55,000 per month, and although there were only 80 installations, it was a definite success for IBM.

IBM actually became a formidable competitor with the 1400 series of computers. They began to flood the market with the IBM 1401 in September, 1960. Over 6,000 of these very commercially useful machines were installed, as well as an equivalent number of the other members of this family. Until the advent of the IBM System/360 series, the 1401 was the most popular machine ever produced, i.e., more of them were rented or sold than any other commercial computer.

Other popular early IBM computers were the 650, first installed in November,

1954; the 7070 family, which appeared in early 1960; and the 7040 family, which was installed in mid-1963.

In 1964 IBM announced a new line of "compatible" computers, the System/360. This computer, which other volumes in this series will teach you to program, incorporates many technical advances and greatly improved accessory devices. This line lowers IBM's manufacturing costs and also increases the computer's speed and "computation per dollar." None of these machines or those of any other manufacturer to date has been introduced with quite the impact of the IBM System/360 series. So radical was the decision to produce this series that it made nearly all other IBM machines obsolete. Except for two small models, the 1130 and the 1800, IBM has discontinued production of all other machines and now provides only a maintenance service for customers who have any but a System/360, 1130, or 1800.

What is so radical about System/360 that makes it unique in computer history? The first, and most obvious, aspect is the sheer bravado of IBM in using *one* machine to replace all others. IBM risked losing millions of dollars and its position in the industry if System/360 was not a successful venture. Secondly, System/360 is a coalescent machine. In other words, IBM has merged its scientific and its commercial computers into this single device. System/360 has a single basic design, but each model has a different implementation and is made in a different plant.

System/360 is a series of machines that are upward and downward compatible, i.e., a program which will run on a fast, expensive model of System/360 can be run on a slow, inexpensive System/360 as well, and vice versa. However, no 360 model is compatible with any of the old IBM computers, although IBM supplies many aids to customers to help ease the conversion to the System/360. Another interesting aspect is the enormous amount of software System/360 computers demand, since machines of this type require very complex programming systems in order to operate effectively. About half of the cost of the machines has been devoted to developing these systems.

The computers in the IBM 360 line are identified by model number, the lowest model numbers being assigned to the smallest and lowest-priced computers in the line. The least expensive computer, the model 20, called the 360/20, rents for about $1,500 per month. The highest model numbers are assigned to the largest and most expensive computers—for example, the 360/91, which rents for more than $300,000 per month. The model numbers run 20, 25, 30, 40, 44, 50, 65, 67, 75, 85, and 91. Of these the model 20

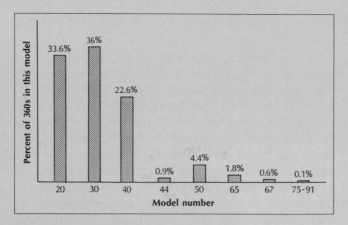

ADAPTED BY PERMISSION FROM ADP NEWSLETTER.

(economy class), model 44 (scientific), model 67 (time sharing), and model 91 (supersize) are not fully compatible with the rest of the line or with each other. About 80 percent of all computers in the United States are IBM System/360, the bulk of them being the smaller models 20 and 30. The diagram shows an estimate of the percentages of IBM 360s in each model class.

Over 300 separate devices have been presented with the 360 system. This equipment can be arranged in the widest variety of ways so that a use can begin with a small installation and grow larger as its individual needs increase. This possibility is due primarily to the systems control programs.

The IBM System/360 computer is adaptable to business or science, and in addition, the larger models are available for the time sharing market to compete with similar models of other manufacturers. The only IBM computers not in the 360 line are quite small; they are the 1130, which is intended to be used by small engineering offices, and the 1800, a very similar computer, which is designed and priced for process control applications. Even though IBM is presently the undisputed leader in the computer manufacturing field, it cannot afford to rest for a moment on past or present laurels.

SPERRY RAND'S UNIVAC DIVISION
About fifteen years ago, Remington Rand's computer division (now Sperry Rand's UNIVAC division) had close to 100 percent of the computer

installations. From the top position UNIVAC has fallen into second place / in the industry, and its installations account for less than 10 percent of the market.

UNIVAC's first commercial computer was the UNIVAC I, which was first installed in 1951 at a monthly rental rate of $25,000. This machine was followed in 1957 by the UNIVAC II, a faster, more advanced model. To date, UNIVAC's largest-selling machine has been the UNIVAC 1004. This is a small-scale machine used for punched card applications. The UNIVAC 9000 series computers are the third-generation replacements for the 1004s. Other UNIVAC computers that have been notable include the 1107 computer, which was first installed in late 1962, and the UNIVAC 1108, another large-scale computer, which was first installed in 1965.

Sperry Rand is a company having the technical expertise to develop new models; it has been extremely effective in its use of large magnetic drums and in its work involving real time computing. The company has been particularly successful in selling to government agencies which find it politically advisable to minimize their IBM business.

BURROUGHS CORPORATION
Burroughs Corporation installed its first computer in July, 1954. The machine was the Burroughs 205, with a typical rental of $8,000. This rental varied, as is the case with any computer, depending on the peripheral equipment ordered. The actual range in rent was from $2,000 to $17,000 per month. Forty-nine of these computers were installed before the company discontinued manufacturing this model.

In March, 1963, Burroughs installed the first B5000 computer. This unique machine (and its improved version, the B5500) was one of the boldest computers ever produced. It was quite controversial owing to its unconventional design, which can be attributed to the fact that for the first time the design team included software specialists as well as hardware specialists. Burroughs claimed that it was the first commercial computer built for multiprogramming and parallel processing under control of a comprehensive operating system, and the first computer to be programmed exclusively in higher-level languages. Unfortunately the B5000 did not sell well, partly because of inadequate sales effort and support and partly because of the choice of Algol instead of Fortran as the programming language.

In the late 1960s Burroughs introduced its third-generation systems: the B2500/3500 small to medium machines, the large scale B6500/7500 series, and the very large B8500. Burroughs has only a very small part of the total commercial computer market but has had continued success with government sales. In 1968 Burroughs won a 60 million dollar Air Force contract for more than a hundred computers, in spite of the spirited efforts of IBM, RCA, and Honeywell.

NCR

NCR is not primarily a computer manufacturer but a producer of cash registers and bookkeeping and accounting machines, the utility of which is greatly added to by certain types of computers. These are made by NCR, of course, and include peripheral equipment. Thus far NCR has been very successful in the computer business. Its net installations rose from a mere 20 million dollars in 1961 to 300 million dollars in 1968. About a quarter of NCR's new equipment orders are for computers.

NCR's first computer installation was an NCR-304, installed in 1960. This was the company's most expensive computer and is no longer being manufactured. NCR's most popular machines have been the NCR-390—first installed in 1961—and the NCR-500, which was first installed in 1965.

In 1968 NCR introduced a new family of computers, the Century Series. It is the most extensive line of EDP equipment yet offered by NCR and indicates that the company intends to maintain a position in the industry.

RADIO CORPORATION OF AMERICA

After some years of dabbling in computers, in 1958 under General David Sarnoff RCA determined to become number two in the computer manufacturing industry. It has since expended more than 150 million dollars in an attempt to accomplish its goal.

RCA's first major commercial venture was the RCA-501, initially installed in June 1959. This machine was followed by the popular RCA-301 in 1961 and later by the RCA-3301 in 1964. Each of these models was based upon the preceding machine but was a decidedly improved piece of equipment. All of them were medium-sized business data processing computers.

RCA has one major advantage; it produces more than 90 percent of the electronic components incorporated into its computers (this is not equaled by any other computer manufacturer).

After having some early marketing problems, RCA decided to aim at a selective market and has developed the Spectra 70—a line deliberately compatible with the IBM System/360 but lower in price.

The Spectra 70 series is a family of six computers:

Small-sized	70/15
Medium	70/25
In-between	70/35
Large-sized	70/45
Time sharing	70/46
Very large	70/55

They are all aimed directly at their opposite numbers in the IBM System/360 series. In a sense, RCA has linked its future success to directly competing with the major product of its chief rival. It is a bold marketing step.

GENERAL ELECTRIC
General Electric is the company that many experts consider as the greatest potential competitor for the number one position in the market. The company entered the field in 1956, but was already the world's first and biggest commercial *user* of computers. It has a large captive market, employing almost 300 computers in its own operations, and vast experience with computers in addition to the financial and technical resources with which to back its venture.

General Electric originally concentrated in three areas:

Process control applications
Banking applications
Communications applications

Now, however, the company provides a full spectrum of general purpose computer equipment in addition to its 4000 series of process control computers and its Data-Net series of communications controllers. The commercial computers range from the small-scale 100 line through the 200 and 400 medium-sized computers up to the 600 series large-scale multiprogramming systems. The very large GE-645 time sharing system is a specialized computer depending on an advanced software system created jointly by MIT, Bell Telephone Laboratories, and General Electric.

GE has three major computer associates abroad, making GE the second largest European computer manufacturing interest. (IBM, through its World Trade Corporation, controls the largest foreign interest.)

In spite of its size and obvious advantages, General Electric's progress as a computer manufacturer has been stumbling and profitless. It has often been said that according to the GE philosophy, a good manager can manage anything. The successive changes of management and organization that have been imposed on the GE computer operation may reflect a need for an understanding of the rather special computer industry if even good managers are to succeed in this field.

HONEYWELL

Honeywell's electronic data processing division was founded in 1955 with the Raytheon Corporation as its partner. Two years later it bought out Raytheon, but the division retained a nucleus of top scientists who had worked on early machines such as Harvard's series of Mark Computers. In 1960 Honeywell installed the first successful multiprogrammed computer. This machine, the H-800, could run up to 8 programs at once. By early 1964, Honeywell had more than 100 million dollars worth of machines operating in the commercial market.

Like RCA, Honeywell directly attacked an IBM product. The Honeywell Series 200 computer system was advertised as "superior to" and "cheaper than" IBM's highly successful medium-sized 1400 series, particularly the IBM 1401 computer. Honeywell supplied a program named Liberator which translated IBM 1401 programs to H-200 programs. The success of this program was responsible for switches from 100 million dollars worth of IBM equipment to Honeywell equipment.

Although the Honeywell product line includes computers ranging from the small model 110 to the large model 8200, Honeywell has been uncertain how to attack the IBM 360 line in the commercial field. Like UNIVAC and Burroughs, Honeywell depends strongly on the government market, where IBM is at a political disadvantage.

CONTROL DATA CORPORATION

CDC is one of the most aggressive and fastest-growing companies in the industry. Its growth has been interesting. CDC was founded in 1957 by William Norris, an ex-vice-president of UNIVAC. It began with revenues of almost zero in 1958 and soared to 121 million dollars in June, 1964, showing a 6 million dollar profit. At that time it was the only company other than IBM to make a consistent profit on its computers.

Particularly interesting is the fact that CDC made money by selling, not leasing, the machines to sophisticated scientific users such as research institutes and government agencies, who need almost no software, service, or education—all of which commercial customers require. (UNIVAC's 1108 owes its success to its position with similarly sophisticated users.)

CDC's first major machine was its 1604 computer, which was installed in January, 1960. It has since come out with three families of computers, the 3000, 6000, and 7000 series. CDC's 6800 computer, priced between 5 and 7 million dollars and first installed in 1967, is one of the world's most powerful computers. The even larger 7600 was announced in late 1968.

SCIENTIFIC DATA SYSTEMS

It has been reliably reported that SDS, the newest member of the computer manufacturing industry (founded in September, 1961) is probably the most successful of the computer makers next to IBM.

SDS's first computer was the SDS-910, which hit the market in late 1962; this was the first of a family of general purpose computers aimed at various weak points in the computer market, particularly that market represented by the small to medium-sized scientific real time and process control computers. The largest member of the 900 series is the SDS-940, first installed in 1966 and renting for $10,000 per month. This machine has been specifically designed for time sharing. Most SDS machines have been used in real time applications such as telemetry systems rather than in commercial work.

The Sigma 7 is the first computer in the SDS line to be compatible with the IBM System/360. Specifically, the company announced that the Sigma 7 was designed for time sharing in a real time environment. Theoretically this would mean that the machine can process inventory control programs (as an example) while servicing as many as 200 or more nationwide users at remote consoles.

☐ COMPUTERS THAT DESIGN AND BUILD COMPUTERS

At IBM and in most other computer companies, computers are running numerically controlled machine tools, chemical processes, and mechanized assembly and testing divisions.

In 1961 IBM decided to make its own semiconductor circuits rather than continue to buy them. As it could not make enough usable circuits by hand, IBM equipped its plants with the type of highly advanced machinery it was selling to others in order to build these semiconductor circuits. The importance of the circuits lies in the fact that they are the basic building block of the central processing unit of a computer. An average computer has 20,000 to 30,000 transistors or diodes, which are usually arranged in patterns on ½-inch-square white bases called substrates. The substrates are then mounted on printed circuit cards that are installed in the computer. IBM has had to manufacture these circuits in the tens of millions per year to keep up with its computer delivery schedules.

In order to justify the use of computers and automated equipment for an operation of this level, both volume and standardization are absolutely necessary. In the past, the mechanization of this process had been limited because of a lack of volume. IBM's commitment to automated process control will, of necessity, hold it to the basic system design of its System/360 series for the next several years because of the large financial investment in the complicated automatic machinery.

The IBM engineers who designed this system for six plants, four in the United States and two in Europe—forming possibly the world's most highly

MANUFACTURER OF COMPUTER COMPONENTS UNDER COMPUTER CONTROL. AUTOMATIC FABRI-CATING EQUIPMENT IS DIRECTED BY SIGNALS FROM THE COMPUTER SYSTEM.

automated manufacturing operation—claim they have offset the implied hazards of the situation. In other words, they feel they have counteracted the dangers involved in standardizing the design for a fast-changing product like the computer. They have done this by providing enough flexibility in the basic combination of product planning engineering and automation by programming computers to control the entire operation.

☐ FUTURE DEVELOPMENTS IN THE COMPUTER MANUFACTURING INDUSTRY

Much of what lies ahead for the computer manufacturing industry is impossible to either predict or conceive. It should be obvious to all that as advanced as it is, the industry is still in its infancy. It is not difficult to predict that if the present rate of growth continues, and it is certainly expected to, 1975 will find the industry doing several times the volume of business that has yet been done.

The most advanced computers of the mid-sixties will appear far from advanced if computers that recognize handwriting and understand English become commercial realities, as has been predicted.

The growth and advancement of this one industry seems destined to change the face and character of the world we know.

☐ QUESTIONS

1   Make a table showing the principal computer companies, the year of their first commercial computer, and the names and numbers of their current computers.

2   Suggest a business strategy for entering the computer market as a manufacturer. Should you attack IBM directly on all fronts or concentrate on a small specialized area? Should your equipment be fully compatible with IBM's, or should you emphasize your design advantages by being totally different? Should your efforts be greatest in the government or commercial market? Should you put your major initial investment in manufacturing facilities or in a sales organization? Why?

3   Reread the Prose Glossary in preparation for the next chapter.

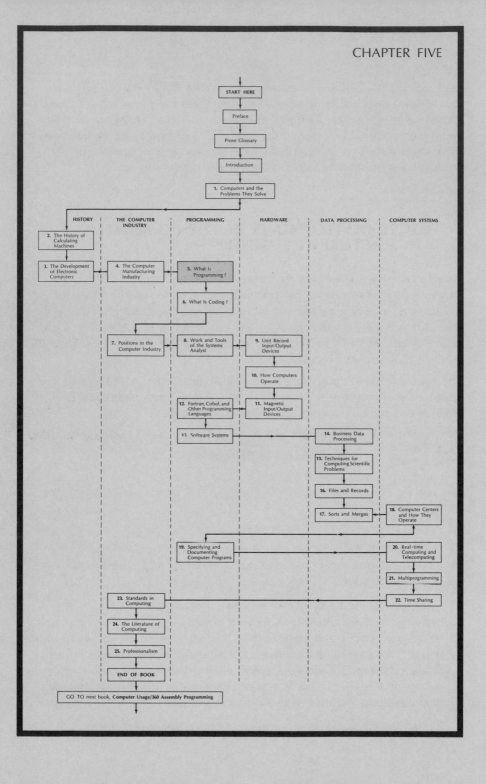

CHAPTER FIVE

WHAT IS PROGRAMMING?

Every different use (application) of each computer requires a separate program (an explicit sequence of instructions) to be developed. Computers without programs can do nothing. Therefore all their contributions in building modern technology have come through programming. Nothing is more essential to the use of computers than programming, because every electronic computer requires programs to direct each different task it must do. Conversely, a computer without a program is truly an "electronic idiot," because it can do nothing constructive.

What is a program? A program is primarily a written plan of action or, more specifically, an explicit sequence of instructions to be carried out by a computer.

Since a program operates only on computers of the type for which it was written, one generally learns the detailed characteristics of that computer. Equally popular are "machine-independent" programming languages (such as Fortran) which will operate on a large variety of computers.

In this book, you will learn the fundamental principles of programming. Later books in the series will take up the details and give you programming practice.

☐ THE NEED FOR COMPUTER PROGRAMMERS

The times we live in have been variously called the Atomic Age, the Electronic Era, and the Computer Age. Because more and more people with very specific skills are required, this could also be called the Age of the Specialist. One of the most sought-after specialists these days is the computer programmer. The Sunday want-ad section of any large-city newspaper may contain as much as a full page of advertisements for programmers. It seems harder to find men and women to program computers than to build them. According to one estimate, more than 200,000 additional programmers will be needed in the next five years.

What kind of person makes a good programmer? There is no single computer "programmer type," but a person who has an orderly, logical mind and who is also imaginative and creative has the makings of a good programmer.

How about educational requirements? Here, too, there are no standard prerequisites, but a high school graduate with the right motivation and aptitude can make an excellent programmer. When one is working in a professional environment, though—for example, a nuclear laboratory—a higher education is useful.

It is a common misconception that a mathematical background is necessary to become a programmer. If you are going into scientific programming, a good knowledge of mathematics would certainly be helpful. However, for

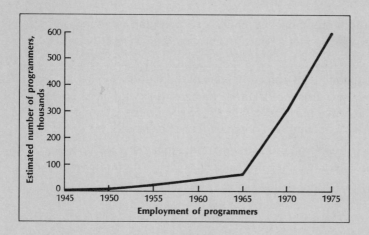

the majority of programming jobs, useful backgrounds are business administration, accounting, or indeed, any subject that deals with some aspect of the area with which your future computer career will be involved.

It may surprise you to know that many excellent programmers come from completely unexpected backgrounds; for example, they are secretaries, musicians, and linguists. *What is most important for success as a programmer is not what you are doing now, but what you want to do from now on, and how well you want to do it.*

Despite the shortage of programmers, there is no shortcut to programming. Training takes time. The study of this book will prepare you for the detailed lessons and practice in programming that the later books in the series will provide.

Once you've obtained a position as a computer programmer, if that is your goal, you'll find that your programming skills must be tempered to meet your employer's specific needs. If you're working for a computer manufacturer, it will soon become apparent that he must provide a large variety of programs to users of his equipment. Computer sales are presently increasing at the rate of 15 to 20 percent a year, meaning that more and more programmers will be needed in the future and that they can expect an economically secure career.

If you're working for a computer user (and there are five or six times as many programmers working for users as manufacturers), you'll soon see that the user may not be able to use his computers to maximum advantage until they have been programmed to perform all the major tasks they can handle.

If you're working for a programming firm, such as Computer Usage, you'll find that the company must be able to prepare a full range of programs, and therefore must have programmers who are readily adaptable to changing from one type of program to a radically different one.

Whether you're working for a manufacturer, user, or programming company, you'll find that programs take time to write because you must specify every single step a computer takes in solving a problem. This means that a great deal of time must be spent by the programmer in getting to understand the problem in all its details. Before the program can be written, he must also take more time to figure out how to attack the problem. Once written, the program must be tested on a computer, and the process of getting the program to work, or "debugging" it, can often be a lengthy one.

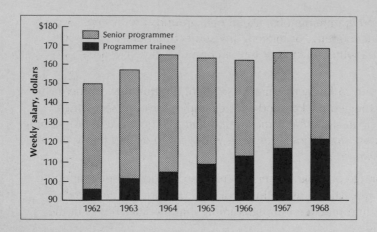

☐ THE PROGRAMMER'S JOB

Exactly what a programmer does depends a great deal on where he works. Rather than inspecting job titles, of which there is a great and often confusing variety, let us look at functional job descriptions:

1 *Analysis*
2 *Programming*
3 *Operation*

You may eventually be involved in only the first two, perhaps in only the second. In a smaller organization you may find yourself performing all three. In larger organizations, you'll be part of a team working in only one of these areas.

There are two aspects of analysis. *Applications analysis* may not require a deep knowledge of computers, but it does require a full knowledge of the particular type of application to be programmed. It includes working out methods, equations, references, paper flow, etc. *Computer oriented analysis,* on the other hand, requires thorough knowledge of the computer's capabilities, capacity, and speeds, and of the ways to use it most efficiently, given a good description of the application.

Programming consists principally of writing down the symbols, in a carefully prescribed format, that tell the computer exactly how to perform the detailed steps of the application.

Operation consists of putting the program on a computer, setting up the required input/output devices, and running the program through to completion.

Looking further into the programmer's role, it can be broken down into these steps:

1   *Specifying the task*
2   *Planning*
3   *Flowcharting*
4   *Coding*
5   *Debugging*
6   *Testing*
7   *Documentation*

In *specifying the task,* you collect every piece of information that will help you fully define the job to be done, including all its ramifications.

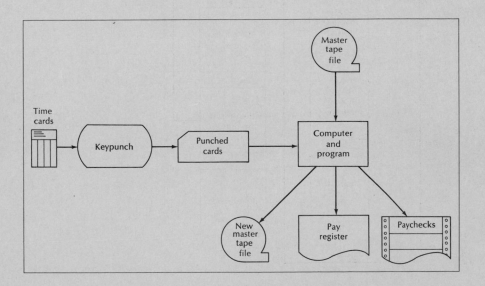

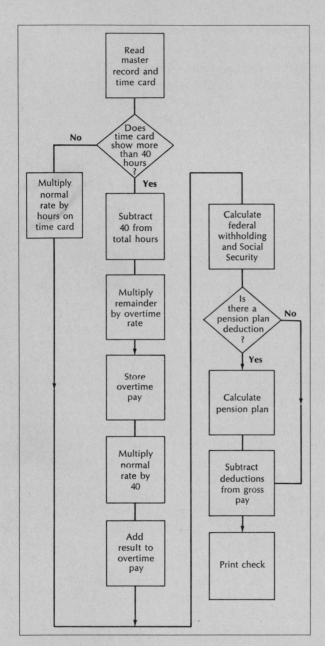

PAYROLL FLOWCHART.

In *planning,* you break the problem down into its components and work out the best approach to the solution.

Part of planning consists of constructing a *processing-flow* diagram and a program *flowchart.* The processing-flow diagram shows each part of the total problem, including data sources, computer components, operations to be performed, and the logical relationship of each part to the others. A program flowchart is a diagramed representation of the major steps performed by the computer within a single program.

Coding, the heart of programming, is the process in which you write the step-by-step instructions that take the computer through its operations. The next chapter will show you some details of this work.

After a program is coded and then keypunched into cards, it must be checked for accuracy or *"debugged."* First you perform *desk debugging,* checking out every step by hand using pencil and paper. In machine debugging, you will put the program on a computer and check its accuracy in actual operation.

Although debugging ensures that a program will run as planned, the program still has to be *tested* with real data to make sure that all the possibilities and variations have been covered, that all loopholes have been plugged. In a computer installation, *parallel running* is an often-used testing method. In this procedure, both the new computer operation and the old operation are performed, to check that the same results are obtained by the computer. If so, the old operation is then phased out.

In *documenting* a program, you put together all the information needed for a complete understanding of that program. This is a reference record that includes processing-flow diagrams, flowcharts, a narrative of what the program does, a description of the operator's actions required, the configuration of equipment, types of input/output devices, cross references, and whatever else is required to enable another person to use the program without having to refer back to the original programmer.

By now, you may realize that whether a programmer is writing a business program for predicting market trends or a scientific program for guiding a manned rocket to the moon, he is becoming the key man in the entire computer field. Without a programmer, the computer is only a dead machine, waiting to be brought to life.

☐ QUESTIONS

1 Writing a program consists of writing out detailed instructions. Write out the detailed instructions for some common activities: (a) How to boil water; (b) how to tie a shoelace; (c) how to dial a telephone number. Be sure that you have described every step and not left anything unsaid or to be understood. Did you provide instructions on what to do if something went wrong?

2 Try using the instructions that were written by another student for one of these activities.

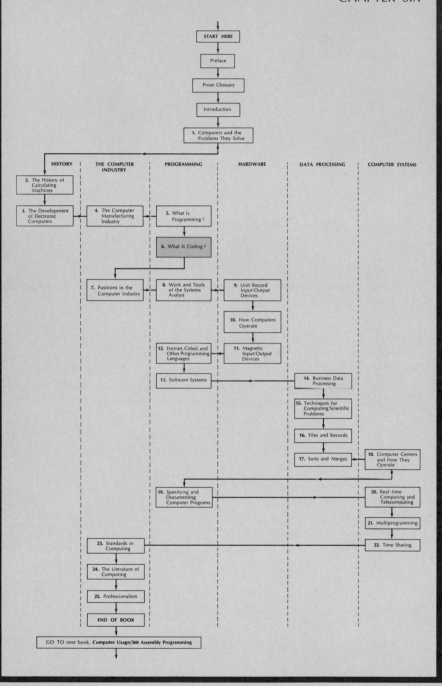

CHAPTER SIX

START HERE

Preface

Prose Glossary

Introduction

1. Computers and the Problems They Solve

HISTORY | THE COMPUTER INDUSTRY | PROGRAMMING | HARDWARE | DATA PROCESSING | COMPUTER SYSTEMS

2. The History of Calculating Machines

3. The Development of Electronic Computers

4. The Computer Manufacturing Industry

5. What Is Programming ?

6. What Is Coding ?

7. Positions in the Computer Industry

8. Work and Tools of the Systems Analyst

9. Unit Record Input/Output Devices

10. How Computers Operate

12. Fortran, Cobol, and Other Programming Languages

11. Magnetic Input/Output Devices

13. Software Systems

14. Business Data Processing

15. Techniques for Computing Scientific Problems

16. Files and Records

17. Sorts and Merges

18. Computer Centers and How They Operate

19. Specifying and Documenting Computer Programs

20. Real-time Computing and Telecomputing

21. Multiprogramming

23. Standards in Computing

22. Time Sharing

24. The Literature of Computing

25. Professionalism

END OF BOOK

GO TO next book, **Computer Usage/360 Assembly Programming**

WHAT IS CODING?

The central skill, the one ability that every programmer must have, is coding. This is the heart of programming. A programmer must be able to write down the step-by-step instructions that take the computer through its operations. Specifying the task, planning, and flowcharting lead up to the coding, while debugging, testing, and documentation are the steps that follow. A programmer trainee will almost always start his computer career as a coder; and while a senior programmer may seldom have to do any coding, his position will require that he be able to review and judge the quality of coding done by his subordinates.

This chapter will introduce you to a little bit of coding. To do this, we must be very specific and deal with the details of the instructions for a specific computer—in our case, the IBM System/360. An understanding of coding requires both an understanding of the way that the code is written and an understanding of the part of the computer affected by the code.

In this chapter you will study:

1 A review of the overall picture of the IBM System/360
2 The use of one part of the computer—the general registers
3 Instructions that use the general registers
4 The characteristics of the main memory of the IBM System/360
5 Instructions which operate with one register and one unit of main memory
6 The way to direct the computer to place a number in main memory

This will give you only a first taste of coding. Other books in the series present the more extensive details that are needed in order to actually write code and do programming for a computer. But this is a necessary beginning.

☐ A REVIEW OF THE IBM SYSTEM/360

In Chapter 1 some introductory remarks were made about this computer. To get us off to a running start, some of these remarks will be repeated here. System/360 is a general purpose, stored program, digital computer. Below is its block diagram.

The *I/O devices* and the *data channels* provide the means of transmitting information between the computer and the people who use it. (I/O means *input/output*.) Some input/output devices, like the card reader, put data into the computer; some, like magnetic drums or magnetic tape, store it; and some, like a printer or card punch, supply the computed results in a form that can be followed by the user. The *registers* assist in performing the

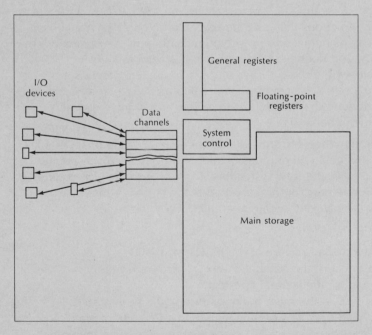

BLOCK DIAGRAM OF SYSTEM/360 COMPUTER.

various computational operations on data in main storage. The *main storage* block is sometimes called the *memory*. The *system control* coordinates all the equipment as directed by the program.

☐ HOW A PROGRAM IS EXECUTED BY SYSTEM/360

In the simplest case, the program is loaded into *main storage* from one of the *input devices*. The data to be operated on is also read from a device such as a punched card reader or a magnetic tape unit into the main storage. When the program is ready to start work, the instructions that make up the program are automatically fetched from their places in main storage, one by one, and placed in the *system control* section.

According to the nature of the instruction, the various parts of System/360 perform the required operations. For instance, arithmetic operations may be performed in the *registers*. When the operations required by one instruction are completed, the next instruction to be executed is brought to system control. When it is time to write out results, either at the end of the program or, more usually, at a variety of points through the program, data is written out from main storage through a data channel to an output device such as a line printer or magnetic tape unit.

☒ HOW TO USE THE GENERAL REGISTERS

In another book in this series, *Computer Usage/360 Assembly Programming*, you will learn all the parts of System/360. But you must learn them one by one. Here we will introduce the first part, the set of 16 general purpose registers (henceforth called *general registers*). They are an indispensable part of System/360. These registers are involved in some way in every operation performed by the computer. They are the computer's calculating or arithmetic unit. They act on the same principles as a desk calculator; that is, with them the computer can add, subtract, multiply, and divide, or perform other data manipulation functions.

Registers both enable operations to be performed and hold the information to be operated upon. Information in a register may consist of numbers, alphabetic characters, or code having special meaning to the programmer. We say that a register *contains* information or that the information is the *contents* of the register.

With few exceptions, the 16 general registers are not committed to any specific functions but are available to the programmer for a variety of purposes. The programmer usually makes his own choice as to which registers he will use. At one point in his program, he might use a register to contain a number, and later in the same program, he might decide to use the same register to contain a code for an alphabetic character. A number in a register might represent the sum of a series of additions, or it could be a number used in division. It is up to the programmer to keep track of what the information in a register means in terms of his program.

We will begin our study of the registers by concentrating on their arithmetic functions. When performing arithmetic functions, the contents of registers are always considered to be a number. This number is always accompanied by either a plus (+) or a minus (−) sign (the number zero is assumed to have a plus sign).

Later we will discuss ways in which numbers are brought into the general registers. For the time being, we will be concerned only with some of the ways of manipulating numbers already in the registers.

REGISTER NUMBERING
In order to use a register, the programmer needs some means of designating which of the 16 possible registers he is referring to. That is, he needs a name for each register. For this purpose, the computer designer assigned a *number* to each register. The general registers are referred to by the numbers 0 through 15. (Most computer numbering schemes start with the number 0 instead of 1.)

| 3 | +5885 |

If we say that general register 3 contains the number +5885, we mean that the "3" is the *number* of the register and the "+5885" is the *contents* of the register. Confusion about this distinction is common and dangerous. At some time, nearly every programmer confuses the two. Make sure you understand the difference between the number of a register and the contents of a register before continuing further.

□ **INSTRUCTIONS**

Now you are prepared to instruct the computer to perform operations upon the contents of the general registers. This is done through the use of *instructions.* An instruction tells the computer what operation to perform (such as add or subtract) and where the information to be operated upon is located (such as the number of a register).

Here we will deal with three different instructions which direct the computer to (1) add the contents of one register to the contents of another register, (2) subtract the contents of one register from the contents of another register, and (3) replace the contents of one register with the contents of another register.

THE "ADD REGISTER" INSTRUCTION

The first instruction to be examined is the one called Add Register. The symbolic code for Add Register is AR. Most communication between the programmer and the computing system is done in this symbolic code (known technically as the *assembly language*). As you learn to program the System/360, you will learn the symbolic codes for the instructions of the System/360.

The instruction AR is always followed by two numbers, separated by a comma, which are the numbers of two general registers. AR is called the *operation code*. The two numbers that follow are the *operands*. The following is a detailed description of what the computer does when it executes the AR instruction:

The contents of the second-named register are added to the contents of the first-named register. The sum is left in the first-named register, replacing the previous contents. The contents of the second-named register are left undisturbed.

In the example below, suppose general register 2 contains +37 and register 4 contains +22. After the following instruction is executed:

```
AR   2,4
```

register 2 will contain +59. Register 4 will contain +22, its original contents.

BEFORE: GENERAL PURPOSE REGISTERS

REGISTER NUMBER	CONTENTS
2	+ 37
3	+5885
4	+ 22
5	+ 31

AFTER: GENERAL PURPOSE REGISTERS

REGISTER NUMBER	CONTENTS
2	+ 59
3	+5885
4	+ 22
5	+ 31

The first- and second-named registers in an instruction may be exactly the same register number. In this case, the content of the named register is added to itself. For example, suppose general register 5 contains +31. After the following instruction is executed:

```
AR   5,5
```

register 5 will contain +62.

The contents of a register need not be a positive number for the AR instruction. Two negative numbers, a negative and a positive number, or two positive numbers may be added. The sign of the result is determined by the usual rules of algebra:

RULES OF ALGEBRA FOR ADDITION

Positive	+4
added to positive;	+5
result is positive.	+9
Negative	−4
added to negative;	−5
result is negative.	−9
Positive	
added to negative;	−4 +4
result has same sign	+5 −5
as the greater number	+1 −1

You may test your understanding of the Add Register instruction with the following examples:

```
AR   3,4
```

REGISTER NUMBER	CONTENTS BEFORE	CONTENTS AFTER
3	+100	+90
4	− 10	−10

AR 0,13

REGISTER NUMBER	CONTENTS BEFORE	CONTENTS AFTER
0	+21	+40
13	+19	+19

AR 1,5

REGISTER NUMBER	CONTENTS BEFORE	CONTENTS AFTER
1	−11	−39
5	−28	−28

AR 14,14

REGISTER NUMBER	CONTENTS BEFORE	CONTENTS AFTER
14	−22	−44

THE "SUBTRACT REGISTER" INSTRUCTION

The next instruction you will learn is Subtract Register, which is known by its symbolic code SR. Like AR, the operation code SR must always be followed by two register numbers. The following is a detailed description of what the computer does when it executes the SR instruction:

The contents of the second-named register are subtracted from the contents of the first-named register. The result is left in the first-named register, replacing its previous contents. The contents of the second-named register remain undisturbed.

For example, suppose register 11 contains +22 and register 3 contains +37. After the following instruction is executed:

SR 11,3

register 11 will contain −15. Register 3 will still contain +37, its original contents.

To increase your understanding of the Subtract Register instruction, observe how this instruction would affect the same numbers that were used previously for the Add Register instruction.

SR 3,4

REGISTER NUMBER	CONTENTS BEFORE	CONTENTS AFTER
3	+100	+110
4	− 10	− 10

SR 0,13

REGISTER NUMBER	CONTENTS BEFORE	CONTENTS AFTER
0	+21	+ 2
13	+19	+19

SR 1,5

REGISTER NUMBER	CONTENTS BEFORE	CONTENTS AFTER
1	−11	+17
5	−28	−28

In the Add Register instruction, the first- and second-named register of the instruction may be the same. This results in *doubling* the contents of that register. If both registers are the same in the Subtract Register instruction, the effect is quite different. Instead of adding a number to itself as in the Add Register instruction, the Subtract Register instruction, with both operands the same, causes the number to be subtracted from itself. Any number (whether a positive or a negative number) subtracted from itself will result in zero. Setting a register to zero is also referred to as *clearing* a register.

SR 14,14

REGISTER NUMBER	CONTENTS BEFORE	CONTENTS AFTER
14	−22	+ 0

☐ INSTRUCTION SEQUENCES

You now know enough to write a useful sequence of instructions. A program is simply an explicit sequence of instructions. In the System/360, as in most computers, instructions are executed sequentially, that is one after another in the order in which they are written. Special instructions, called *branch* instructions, can break the sequence and change the flow of the program.

The simple problem of adding three numbers together would call for the use of a sequence of instructions, since no single instruction exists in the System/360 which would do this.

Suppose the numbers in registers 7, 8, and 9 are to be added together. The sequence of instructions

```
AR   7,8
AR   7,9
```

will add the contents of all three registers, leaving the sum in register 7.

Suppose you wish to subtract the sum of the contents of registers 3, 4, and 5 from the contents of register 8. The following sequence of instructions will do it:

```
SR   8,3
SR   8,4
SR   8,5
```

Here is a specific example using this sequence:

Register Number	Contents before 1st Instruction	Contents after		
		1st Instruction	2d Instruction	3d Instruction
3	+ 43	+ 43	+ 43	+ 43
4	− 17	− 17	− 17	− 17
5	+100	+100	+ 100	+100
8	+ 50	+ 7	+ 24	− 76

One fact immediately apparent about programming is that there are many ways of solving the same problem. Assume the same original contents of registers 3, 4, 5, and 8 and the same objective as above. The following sequence of instructions will *also* meet the requirement:

AR   3,4   Produces + 26 in register 3.
AR   3,5   Produces +126 in register 3.
SR   8,3   Produces — 76 in register 8.

Register Number	Contents before 1st Instruction	Contents after		
		1st Instruction	2d Instruction	3d Instruction
3	+ 43	+ 26	+126	+126
4	— 17	— 17	— 17	— 17
5	+100	+100	+100	+100
8	+ 50	+ 50	+ 50	— 76

Notice that this program gets the same desired result in register 8, although the contents of register 3 were altered in the second sequence but not in the first sequence.

Suppose you wanted to evaluate the formula B—4A, when the value of B is in register 10 and the value of A is in register 11. The computation could then be programmed as follows:

AR   11,11   This doubles the contents of register 11, so that register 11 now contains the value of 2A.

AR   11,11   This quadruples the original contents of register 11, so that register 11 now contains the value of 4A.

SR   10,11   This value of B—4A is now in register 10.

If we wanted to place the contents of register 5 into register 3, we could write the sequence

SR   3,3   Clears register 3.
AR   3,5   Puts the contents of 5 into 3.

THE LOAD REGISTER INSTRUCTION

The next instruction you will learn is Load Register, or LR. LR has the following effect:

The contents of the second-named register are placed in the first-named register. The contents of the second-named register are left undisturbed. The original contents of the first-named register are, of course, destroyed.

If we again take up the problem of setting the contents of register 3 equal to those of register 5, we see that we can now accomplish this with only one instruction:

LR   3,5

You may ask why this instruction is needed, since we could always achieve the same result with a sequence of two instructions, as above. The answer is that LR does it in one step less, allowing the program to be shorter and faster.

The instructions built into a computer are those that the designers believe to be useful, but few are indispensable. It's possible, in fact, to design a computer that has only three or four instructions but can be programmed to perform all the operations of all other computers. Such a computer, however, would require programs of enormous length to solve even simple problems. (The Turing Machine described in Chapter 2 is the classic example of a computing device with the minimum number of instructions.)

Here is a sequence of instructions using LR. The given problem is to place three times the contents of register 7 into register 10,

LR	10,7	Register 10 now contains whatever is in 7.
AR	10,7	Register 10 now contains twice what is in 7.
AR	10,7	Register 10 now contains three times what is in 7.

Check your understanding of the operations of the LR instruction by following the examples below very carefully.

LR   10,3

REGISTER NUMBER	CONTENTS BEFORE	CONTENTS AFTER
3	+ 5	+5
10	+25	+5

LR   2,8

REGISTER NUMBER	CONTENTS BEFORE	CONTENTS AFTER
2	+25	−5
8	− 5	−5

LR   1,2

REGISTER NUMBER	CONTENTS BEFORE	CONTENTS AFTER
1	−25	+0
2	+ 0	+0

Notice that in every previous case, the orginal contents of the first-named register are destroyed. Here is a special case where this does not happen:

LR   15,15

REGISTER NUMBER	CONTENTS BEFORE	CONTENTS AFTER
15	+100	+100

□ MAIN MEMORY

Before dealing with the next class of instructions, we must consider the characteristics of another part of the computer: the main storage or main memory. The main memory of a computer is that portion in which both instructions (programs) and data may be stored. The main memory can contain data, instructions, tables, and everything else that will be needed in the course of a computation. Indeed, the large System/360 main memories can hold all that is required for a group of programs.

The registers, on the other hand, are not intended for storage. Their use is limited to data *currently* being manipulated. By containing *the minimum of data*, the registers are able to operate at maximum speed. Register storage is much more expensive than main-memory storage. Because computers must be sold at competitive prices, the designers allow for relatively little storage space in registers, as compared with storage space in main memory.

Physically, the main memory consists of hundreds of thousands of tiny metallic ring-shaped "cores" that are capable of being magnetized in either a clockwise or a counterclockwise direction. Connected to electronic circuits (to be described in Chapter 10), the cores are made to represent the numbers and characters that the computer is dealing with. This representation of information is accomplished by making the magnetization directions of the cores (clockwise or counterclockwise) correspond to a sequence of 1s and 0s. That is, the numbers and letters are represented in a special code

64 bits). It is this variety that permits a lot of flexibility and power when working with System/360 main memory.

At this time, we will consider only two of the eight ways in which the main-memory cores may be grouped: the *byte* and the *word*. Remember that a unit of 8 bits (which means binary digits) is called a byte, and a unit of 32 bits is called a word. As you may have noticed, *each word contains 4 bytes*.

Bytes are used in describing total capacity and in addressing memory. System/360 main memories are available in units of constantly doubling size: 4,000 bytes, 8,000 bytes, 16,000 bytes, etc., on up to 4,096,000 bytes —although this size is quite rare.

Because large memories are expensive, small installations generally have 16,000 bytes or less, and medium-size installations generally have 128,000 bytes or less of memory. Because the symbol "K" is used as shorthand for one thousand, you'll probably hear System/360 people asking questions such as, "We have a 128K machine—what do you have?"

The machine sizes just quoted are approximate, since, as in many concepts in the computer field, K actually refers to a power of 2, in this case 1,024, which is the power of 2 closest to 1,000. 64K, for instance, is really 64 times 1,024, or 65,546. You can see that most people are not likely to remember a number like this, and it is not particularly important that they do, since they can look it up in a table when necessary.

Although capacity varies, the *addressing* principle remains the same—always by *byte*. Therefore, when visualizing the memory, it is helpful to see it as a sequence of bytes ranging from the first address (0), to the highest address (one less than the capacity of the memory).

This is a good place to reemphasize a point that was briefly noted in dealing with the general registers. Every byte in the System/360 main memory is identified by a number. The first byte is 0, the next byte is 1, the next byte is 2, and so on to the last byte, which would be 65,545 in a 64K machine. This identifying number is the *address* of that byte; like a house address, it tells the computer where the byte is located. That byte always has that address. The address of the byte never changes.

But a number is stored in the byte. This is the *contents* of that byte. The contents of the byte will be changed from time to time as the calculation proceeds. It is the contents of the byte that represent the information we are manipulating with the computer.

Just as each register has a number which tells us which register we are

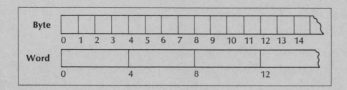

dealing with, each byte has an address (which is a number). And just as the register always has the same number, so the address of each byte never changes. But each register *contains* a number, the *contents* of the register; and the instructions can change these contents. In the same way, each byte in main memory will contain a number, and the contents of the bytes will be changed by the computer instructions.

The distinction between an *address,* a location in the main memory, and the *contents* of that location is basic to all computing. If you do not see the difference and understand it, go back to the beginning of Chapter 6 and reread it to this point.

Because every word is made up of 4 adjacent bytes, and the address of the first byte is used to address the whole word, word addresses are 0, 4, 8, 12, 16, etc. (see the figure above).

Some instructions—primarily those which transfer data between registers and main memory, including three that you will learn in this chapter—require that the location in main memory addressed by the instruction must be a word address. If you write such an instruction using an address that is not a multiple of 4, such as 5 or 14, it will be recognized as an error by the automatic procedure used to prepare your program for use.

☐ THE ASSEMBLER

However, such word addresses as 4, 8, or 16,000 are rarely used. When writing programs on the coding sheet, you will give made-up symbolic names to the main-memory addresses. They should be meaningful and must be distinct. The first step in computer processing of your program converts your *symbolic addresses* into *machine addresses, using an assembler program.*

The programmer thus does not have to assign machine address locations for symbolic addresses; this task is performed under the supervisory control of

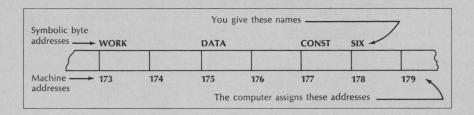

the *assembler*. An assembler is a special computer program that translates the programmer's symbolic operation codes into computer operating instructions, assigns locations in storage for successive instructions, and computes memory addresses from symbolic addresses, such as LOCN, A, B, C, DATA, and DATA2, which are in the examples on the following pages. An assembler translates input symbolic codes into machine instructions, item for item, and produces the object program that is then run on the computer to produce output data.

Although both the *instructions* (that comprise the program) and the *data* are stored in main memory, we will be concerned only with data storage at this time.

☐ FOUR NEW INSTRUCTIONS: ADD, SUBTRACT, LOAD, STORE

Corresponding to AR, SR, and LR are three main-memory instructions: A, S, and L. The R in the first three indicates that the operations are to take place *between registers;* for instance, that the contents of one *register* are to be added to the contents of another *register*. These three instructions, AR, SR, and LR, are known as register-to-register or "RR" instructions.

Instructions A, S, and L are used when operations are to take place between *main memory* and a *register;* for example, when a number from main memory is to be added to the contents of a register. These instructions are called *register-and-indexed-storage* or "RX" instructions. For the moment it is enough to remember that this instruction format is called RX, as compared with the RR format described before. Another book in this series, *Computer Usage/360 Assembly Programming*, describes many more instructions in both formats, other instruction formats, and indexed storage, as well as providing the other details needed to program the System/360.

As in the RR format, the operand field of an RX instruction consists of two parts separated by a comma. The first field designates a general register. The second field, unlike the RR instructions, is a *symbol for the address of a word* in main memory.

THE ADD (A) INSTRUCTION
The Add instruction, A, operates as follows:

The contents of a word in main memory are added to the contents of a register, and the sum replaces the contents of that register. The contents of the word in main memory remain unchanged.

In the example below, register 2 contains +27 and memory location DATA contains −13. After the following instruction is executed:

A   2,DATA

register 2 will contain +14, and memory location DATA will contain −13.

	BEFORE	AFTER
Register 2	+27	+14
Memory location DATA	−13	−13

THE SUBTRACT (S) INSTRUCTION
The description of the Subtract instruction, S, is similar:

The contents of a word in main memory are subtracted from the contents of a register, and the difference replaces the contents of that register. The contents of the word in main memory remain unchanged.

If, for example, register 12 contains +1094 and memory location LOCN contains +90, the following instruction:

S   12,LOCN

will put +1004 in register 12 and leave +90 in memory location LOCN.

THE LOAD (L) INSTRUCTION
The Load instruction, L, has the following effect:

The contents of a word at a memory location replace the contents of a register. The contents of the memory location are left undisturbed.

If general register 9 contains +66 and memory location XXX contains −45, this instruction:

```
L  9,XXX
```

replaces the +66 in register 9 with −45, and still leaves −45 in memory location XXX.

Thus, assuming that main-memory locations A, B, and C contain the same values as registers 1, 2, and 3, the following instruction sequences produce equivalent results in register 6:

RR	RX
LR 6,1	L 6,A
AR 6,2	A 6,B
SR 6,3	S 6,C

THE STORE (ST) INSTRUCTION

The Load (L) instruction places the contents of a main-memory word into a register. There is a corresponding instruction, Store (ST), that places the contents of a register into a main-memory word.

The contents of a register are placed in the main-memory word location indicated by the second address. The register contents remain unchanged.

The following sequence:

```
L   6,DATA
ST  6,DATA2
```

places the contents of word DATA into register 6 and also into main-memory location DATA2, by first-placing the contents of main-memory location DATA into register 6, and then placing the contents of register 6 into main-memory location DATA2. The previous contents of register 6 (before the Load operation) and of DATA2 (before the Store operation) are lost. The contents of DATA remain the same as before the Load operation.

	BEFORE	AFTER L 6,DATA	AFTER ST 6,DATA2
Register 6	anything	2500	2500
Memory word location DATA	2500	2500	2500
Memory word location DATA2	anything	anything	2500

☐ PREPARING A PROGRAM FOR THE COMPUTER

As you have already learned, the computer is unable to solve a problem unless it is given an explicit sequence of instructions. The computer follows these directions step by step until a job is done, whether the problem is adding a column of numbers or solving complex equations necessary to track a missile. These detailed instructions are called a *program*.

THE CODING SHEET

The first step a programmer takes after analyzing his problem and planning

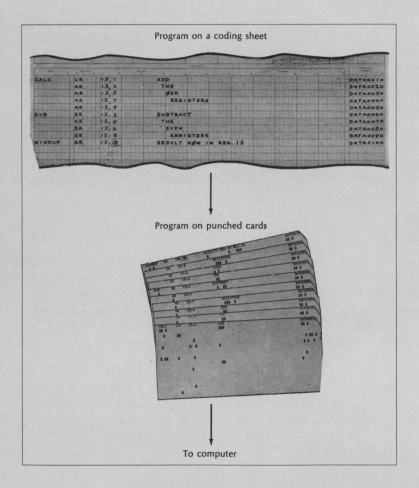

Program on a coding sheet

Program on punched cards

To computer

and flowcharting his solution is to write the step-by-step instructions which form his program on a standard coding sheet. On it he writes not only his program but identifying labels, comments, and sequence numbers as appropriate.

The coding sheet is ruled into columns, which are numbered across the top of the page. Each column corresponds to one of the 80 positions on a punched card, and one character should be written in each column. Each character coded, including the comma, requires a column on the coding sheet.

The completed coding sheet is sent to a keypunch operator, who punches the program into IBM cards. These punched cards are a representation of the program which the computer can process.

FIELDS OF THE CODING SHEET
There are five parts (or fields, as they are called) available to the programmer on each line of the coding sheet. Only two contain the actual computer instruction itself. We have already been using these two: the *operation* field, which contains the symbolic code for the instruction (for example, AR or SR), and the *operand* field. This last generally contains two operands (for example, two register numbers).

The other three parts are the *name*, the *comments*, and the *identification sequence fields*. Here is an example:

NAME FIELD
The name field, which starts in column 1 of the coding sheet, allows a point in the program to be given a symbolic name, permitting the programmer to refer to this instruction in other parts of the program.

You may use any combination of letters and numbers in making up a name or label, subject to these restrictions:

The name must begin with a letter.
The name may not contain more than eight characters.
The name may not contain blank areas.
No two points in the program may be given the same name.

Normally, only a small percentage of the lines within a program are named.

COMMENTS FIELD

The comments field is available to the programmer for any pertinent remark he wishes to write. What is written in this field has no effect on the computations at all; but when a reference copy of the program is printed out by the computer, these comments will appear on the listing at the points they were written.

The value of comments is twofold: First, they are a way of annotating your program so that *others* can understand it. This is important, since most programmers work in conjunction with other programmers; most large programs are produced by a team of programmers. Second, comments are a way of explaining to *yourself* what you have done. For instance, you write a program and it is put into production. Several months later, after you have been working on another project, you are called back to make changes in your program. At this time, you may find you have forgotten some of the reasons why you took that approach, and only a good set of comments will allow you to understand the workings of your own program.

You should always use enough comments to fully explain everything you do in your future programming assignments. Comments serve as an excellent means of communication with your instructor or your supervisor.

	CALC	LR	15,1	ADD		DATA0010
●		AR	15,3	THE		DATA0020
		AR	15,5	ODD		DATA0030
●		AR	15,7	REGISTERS		DATA0040
●		AR	15,9			DATA0050
	SUB	SR	15,2	SUBTRACT		DATA0060
●		SR	15,4	THE		DATA0070
●		SR	15,6	EVEN		DATA0080
		SR	15,8	REGISTERS		DATA0090
●	WINDUP	SR	15,10	RESULT NOW IN REG. 15		DATA0100

PROGRAM ON PRINTED OUTPUT.

Notice that there is no line to indicate the start of the comments field. Comments can be started in any column after the operand, as long as one or more blank spaces separate the comments from the operand. It is good practice, however, to start all comments in the same column—one that is far enough to the right on the coding sheet to allow for the longest of your instructions. Columns 30, 35, or 40 are good places to start writing comments.

There will be times when you will want to write a comment on a line by itself, without an accompanying instruction. You may do this by placing an asterisk in column 1 of a comments line.

IDENTIFICATION SEQUENCE FIELD

Early in your computer career you will learn that you may clumsily drop your deck of keypunched program cards, thus getting them out of sequence. This is one reason for the use of the columns on the coding sheet marked *Identification Sequence;* they allow you to use some system of numbering your cards so they can be put back in their original order.

This field is also useful as a means of finding a particular line on a program listing and, if necessary, of directing you to the card in your program deck that was punched for the line of coding in question. Most programmers have their program decks on their desks until the programs are completely checked out. They often make changes in the cards, so that they not only must be able to identify a particular card within a deck, but also need to distinguish one deck from another. For this reason it is a good idea to use the alphabetic part of the identification sequence as a method of identifying the program—like LESI, TAXC, or PAYR.

As with comments, these columns do not affect the computations, but they allow you to use some system of numbering your cards so they can be put back in their original order. Single out-of-sequence cards can be put in their correct place using these numbers. Some computer systems will automatically check the sequence for you and notify you if any out-of-sequence cards are found. Effective computing organizations will *require* that their programmers make proper use of the Identification Sequence columns.

In the preceding illustration a combination of letters and numbers are used in the sequencing. The letters identify this program and the numbers specify the sequence. Notice that these numbers increase by ten. If changes are made in the program and new cards inserted, these new cards can still be numbered in sequence. For example, a card numbered DATA0035 can be inserted between DATA0030 and DATA0040.

SUMMARY OF THE FIELDS OF THE CODING SHEET

FIELD	STARTING COLUMN	PURPOSE
Name	1	To provide labels for referring to an instruction
Operation	10	To give the instruction code
Operand	16	To give the operands of the instruction
Comments	On the coding sheet, start all comments in the same columns after at least one blank	To allow the programmer to make pertinent remarks
Not used	72	
Identification sequence	73	To verify card deck sequence and allow insertion of changes

RULES FOR USING THE CODING SHEET

1   Each character, including commas and other punctuation, should occupy one space on the sheet.
2   When using a name field, the first letter of the label must be in column 1.
3   Write the operation code (such as AR) starting in column 10. There must be no blanks within the operation code (for instance, do not write A R).
4   Start writing operands in column 16. Commas are used to separate operands.
5   Comments can start in any column after the operands, provided one or more blank spaces have been left between the operand and the comments. Start all comments in the same column.
6   Be sure your letters I, Z, and O can be distinguished from the numbers 1, 2, and zero.
7   USE *ONLY* CAPITAL LETTERS so the keypunch operators will not make errors. Keypunch operators expect to find slashes through the letters Ø and Ƶ and bars across the top and bottom of the letter I (so that it won't look like 1). Write the numerals 0, 1, and 2 as you always do.

☐ CONCLUSION

This chapter has given some of the details of coding for the System/360. In order to really code for the computer, you would have to learn a good deal more of the same kind of material and then actually practice coding. These additional details are treated in other books in the series. The intent of this chapter is not to teach you to code but to give you a taste of the nature of the detail involved in coding, so that you can better understand the material in the remainder of the book.

☐ QUESTIONS

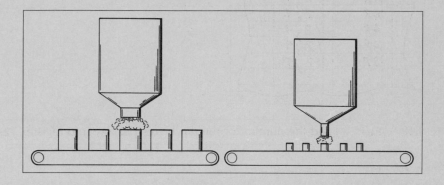

1 **Statement**   Two container-filling machines in a cosmetics plant package talcum powder. One machine packages only regular (10-ounce) size boxes, while the other packages trial (1-ounce) size boxes. The machine that packages the regular boxes turns out many more ounces of product than the one packaging the trial boxes. Given the number of each kind of box produced in a day, write the program to compute how many more ounces the regular machine fills than the trial machine.

EQUATION
Difference in ounces =
                 (number of regular boxes × 10 − number of trial boxes)

REGISTER USAGE
Register 4   Number of regular boxes per day
Register 5   Number of trial boxes per day
Register 12   Calculated difference in ounces

PROGRAM 1

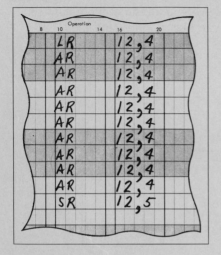

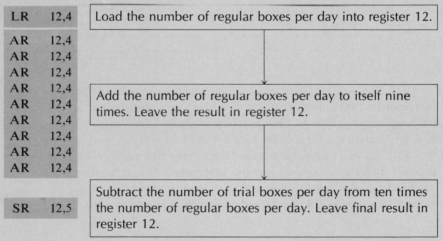

LR	12,4	Load the number of regular boxes per day into register 12.
AR	12,4	
AR	12,4	
AR	12,4	
AR	12,4	Add the number of regular boxes per day to itself nine times. Leave the result in register 12.
AR	12,4	
AR	12,4	
AR	12,4	
AR	12,4	
SR	12,5	Subtract the number of trial boxes per day from ten times the number of regular boxes per day. Leave final result in register 12.

Of course, this problem is really too simple to run on a computer. However, it was selected in order to state a problem solvable with only three of System/360's 141 instructions.

To illustrate the great freedom of choice in computer programming, we show you two of the many other ways of treating the same problem— Program IA and Program IB. Note that these are increasingly compact, requiring 7 and 6 instructions respectively, as contrasted with 11 in Program I.

PROGRAM 1A

| LR   12,4 | Load the number of regular boxes per day into register 12. |

| AR   12,12 | Double the number in register 12. |

| AR   4,4
AR   4,4
AR   4,4 | Double the number in register 4 three times. Result now equals eight times the original number. |

| AR   12,4 | Add the number in register 4 to the number in register 12. Result now equals ten times the number of regular boxes per day. |

| SR   12,5 | Subtract the number of trial boxes per day from ten times the number of regular boxes per day. Leave final result in register 12. |

PROGRAM 1B

| AR   4,4 | Double the number of regular boxes per day (in register 4). |

| LR   12,4 | Load the doubled number of regular boxes per day into register 12. |

| AR   4,4
AR   4,4 | Double the number in register 4 twice, to equal eight times the original number. |

| AR   12,4 | Add the number in register 4 to the number in register 12. |

| SR   12,5 | Subtract the number of trial boxes per day from ten times the number of regular boxes per day. Leave final result in register 12. |

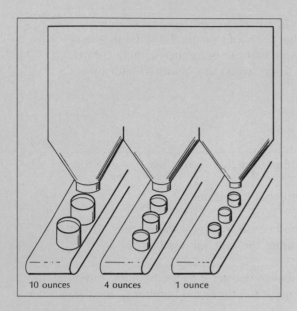

10 ounces   4 ounces   1 ounce

2 **Statement** Consider the following change in the cosmetics plant. An improved package filling machine replaces the two described in question 1. It can fill regular (10-ounce), junior (4-ounce), and trial (1-ounce) packages. Given the daily requirements in terms of number of each type of package to be filled, write the program to find the total weight in ounces to be packaged.

EQUATION
Ounces required = (number of regular boxes × 10)
        + (number of junior boxes × 4)
        + number of trial boxes

REGISTER USAGE
Register 2 Number of trial boxes required
Register 7 Number of junior boxes required
Register 8 Number of regular boxes required
Register 12 Total ounces required

3 Which computer has the larger memory in terms of the number of bits: one having 64K bytes, or one having 16K of 32-bit words? How many double words can be stored in the 64K-byte memory?

4 Write the program to put whatever number is in main-memory location COUNT into registers 1 through 6 inclusive. Do the same thing using different instructions.

5 Write the program to add up all the numbers in registers 1 through 6 inclusive, and put the total in main-memory location TOTAL. Do the same thing without disturbing the contents of any of the registers and without using any other register or main-memory location.

6 Write the program to add up all the numbers in registers 1 through 6 inclusive, and put the total *with sign reversed* in main-memory location NTOT.

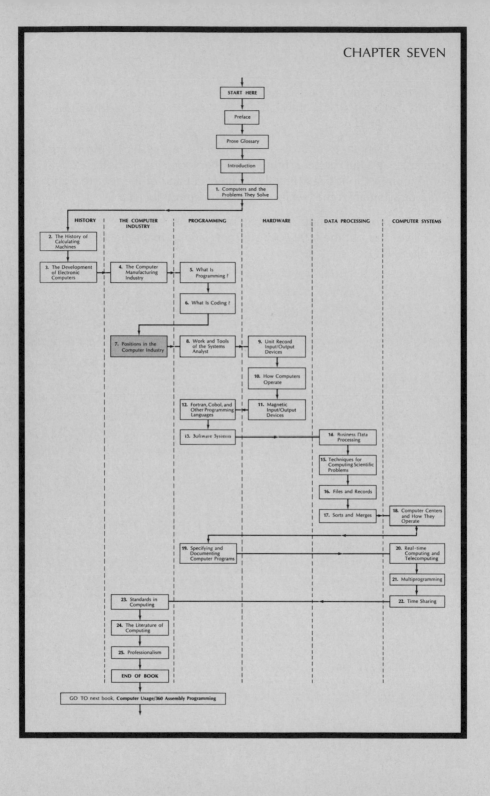

CHAPTER SEVEN

Here various key positions in the computer industry will be explored and reviewed. Although the chapter will acquaint you further with certain facets of the industry, it is important to remember that *people* are unquestionably the lifeblood of the computer field. Not only is the computer an "electronic idiot box" without the programmer and his program, but also there would obviously be no electronic "brain" at all without the brain of man.

From reading the business section of a newspaper, you know of the demand for trained personnel at all levels of the computer industry. The range of employers is almost as wide as the range of available positions in the industry. There are five major categories of employers of computer personnel:

1 *Commercial users*—Banks, insurance companies, stock brokers, manufacturers, department stores, etc.
2 *Scientific users*—Research scientists, aircraft designers, medical researchers, astronomers, aerospace scientists, etc.
3 *Commercial service centers*—Any of the many computer centers leasing machine time to outside users
4 *Contract programming companies*—Companies like Computer Usage which contract to design, develop, program, and install systems for their customers

5   *Manufacturers of computers*—Any company that designs and builds computers and component parts, including software and peripheral equipment

☐ COMPUTING AND PROGRAMMING RESEARCH

Every major manufacturer of computers supports a research and development department comprised of their most creative and advanced hardware and programming specialists. These men and women are involved in creative research in significant areas that might affect the computer or that the computer might affect.

Most of the people in this department are required to have a B.A. or B.S., M.S., and Ph.D. degrees. These degrees should perhaps be in the field of mathematics, electrical engineering, or physics. In addition, two or three years of programming experience is required in order to help develop computers or software to be produced one to three years in the future.

The researchers in these companies are given freedom to explore possible areas of benefit. One man might be working on the perfection of a computer that understands the human voice. Another research scientist who has studied both medicine and electronics might be developing a new technique useful in diagnosing disease. A third person might be working on the future use of computers in education to help overcome the teacher shortage with which we are faced. Fortran, the programming language discussed later in this book, developed from a project undertaken by a research group.

☐ COMPUTER DESIGNER

Computer designers are the one group that must have a *total* logical concept of the computer. Members of this group must also have a knowledge of mathematics, engineering, and electronics, preferably at the Ph.D. level. Not only do they need the academic training required for their work, but they must be good logical thinkers as well as creative designers.

The computer designers are able to take ideas that the research group has developed and to incorporate these ideas, as well as their own creative thinking, into workable electronic realities, i. e., new computers slated for future production.

☐ ENGINEERING STAFF

Once the computer designers have formulated and designed a new computer, the design is handed over to the engineering staff, whose duty it is to implement the proposed computer. The positions in this area are:

1 Staff engineer
2 Senior engineer
3 Engineer
4 Associate engineer
5 Engineer trainee

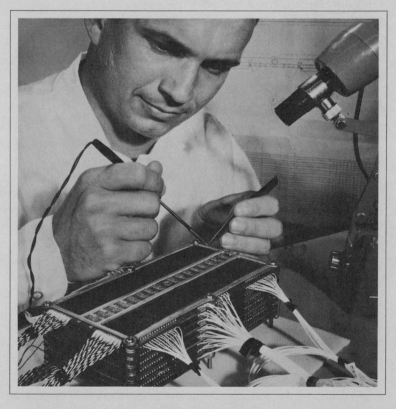

A NEW CORE MEMORY UNIT UNDER DEVELOPMENT BY AN ENGINEERING TEAM.

The minimum academic training required is a college degree, generally in engineering. Specialization is not generally a requirement for the trainee, as most large companies have their own training programs.

There is a wide range of possibilities for engineering specialization in the computer industry, including electrical, mechanical, and industrial engineering. Though the following list is by no means complete, it indicates areas in which specialization may lead to promotions as high as the staff engineer level. The areas of specialization include:

Input/output engineer
Display engineer
Memory development engineer
Systems designer
Mechanical designer
Product development engineer
Circuit designer
Microcircuit designer

Because of the rapid growth of the computer industry, the demand for engineers is certain to grow rapidly. The salaries for engineers in the computer manufacturing industry have increased at the average rate of 7 percent a year for the past ten years.

There is a personnel shortage in almost all areas concerned with hardware systems development, a shortage which is expected to continue well into the mid-1970s. This is aggravated by the major role the computer is playing in accelerating the government's military and space programs— impossibilities before the development of the computer. All our missiles, satellites, and rockets require electronic data processing equipment as components, and their development draws heavily on the limited supply of engineers.

☐ SOFTWARE DESIGNER

Working simultaneously with the engineering staff to build a new computer are the software designers, highly advanced programmers having a thorough knowledge of the hardware and an understanding of the possibilities and the limitations of the particular computer being developed.

It is the task of the software designers to develop *control programs* (i.e.,

SOFTWARE DESIGNERS SKETCH A CONTROL PROGRAM.

programs used by *other* programmers), compilers, etc., that complement the new computer being developed. Without this software the computer would be incapable of performing the tasks it will eventually be required to do.

The requirements for those doing the initial software for a new computer are quite stringent. The most important requirement is a number of years of on-the-job training in programming and software development.

It is essential that these designers have the ability to discuss problems and equipment requirements with other technical personnel, both engineering and software. Communication at this level is essential if a computer is to be successfully developed and operated.

As in all programming situations, there is in software design (even at the manufacturer's level) a need for analysts and programmers to help implement various portions of the system being developed.

☐ TECHNICAL WRITER

Once a computer is in the initial stages of development and production, a team of technical writers is called in. It is their responsibility to write technically descriptive manuals that give specifics of a particular computer, or describe the operation of peripheral equipment. They write operator's manuals, programmer's manuals, maintenance manuals—in fact, manuals of all kinds.

A technical writer would most typically be involved in the preparation of

FABRICATING COMPUTER COMPONENTS.

manuals, systems descriptions, computer program documentation, preparation of proposals, final reports, and all sorts of formal writing.

The educational requirements for a technical writer differ from company to company. The usual requirement is a college degree, though not necessarily one in science. Anyone having a flair for writing, logic, and organization has a good chance of becoming a successful technical writer. Although the technical writer has been described here as primarily a part of the manufacturer's staff, this is not his only role in the industry. Companies like Computer Usage have a number of technical writers attached to their staff, and trade magazines dealing with various aspects of the computer industry frequently have experienced technical writers on the writing and editorial staffs.

The salary of the technical writer varies, as do all salaries within the industry, but it is approximately comparable to that of a programmer. Like all salaries, it too increases as the levels of training and on-the-job experience increase.

☐ COMPUTER CONSTRUCTION PERSONNEL

The men and women responsible for fabricating and assembling the computer range from blue-collar to white-collar personnel. While it is the highly skilled blue-collar worker who assembles the computer, the demand for computer construction personnel is diminishing, owing to the increasing prevalence of automatic production techniques.

☐ POWERING UP THE COMPUTER

There is a special group of electronic technicians whose entire time is spent in testing and debugging the new computers. (*Debugging* may be a new word for you. All problems—in hardware, software, or programming—that prevent a computer from running properly are referred to as "bugs." Consequently, the work involving the discovery of the source of a difficulty and its subsequent removal is referred to as debugging.)

The powering up of the newly constructed computer is the term referring to the period from the initial application of electricity to the time when the machine runs perfectly and passes all acceptance tests. To learn powering up takes from one to three months; it consists of a number of sequential electronic connection tasks and tests which check every possible function of the hardware. This testing is not considered finished until a machine has been running perfectly for some time.

☐ MANUFACTURERS' FIELD MAINTENANCE MAN

There used to be an inside joke in the computer industry that said, "With every computer the manufacturer ships out for commercial installation, he ships out a maintenance man."

This, in a sense, is true. Most large commercial installations have an assigned maintenance staff who represent the manufacturer. They may also have been involved in the installation of a new computer. Because parts can be rattled about in transit and new bugs developed, retesting is necessary immediately after installation. With integrated and printed circuits, however, it is not uncommon to turn over a machine one to three days after arrival. Maintenance electronic technicians must be high school graduates with no less than two years of additional technical training in electronics or electrical engineering. This training is then supplemented by the employer, who will provide up to one year of classroom and on-the-job training. The training must usually include computer operating and programming techniques.

In addition to required repairs, preventive maintenance is an important part of the computer electronics mechanic's work. These duties include cleaning the unit, periodic replacing of certain transistors or tubes, and the constant testing of components. The work is exacting and challenging.

☐ SALES AND SALES SUPPORT FOR THE MANUFACTURER

Almost every level of the electronic data processing field is either directly or indirectly concerned with marketing and sales. Primarily, the *computer salesman* is product-oriented. That is, his goal is to sell specific equipment to a potential user. Behind the sales force is a large headquarters group involved in product management, product planning, market research, sales planning, competitive evaluation, advertising, sales promotion, etc.

The list of possible responsibilities is lengthy and depends very much on the way a company designates responsibility. The sales staff can be set up in a number of ways. A likely possibility is this:

1 Vice-president of marketing
2 Market research department
3 Advertising department
4 Sales promotion department
5 Regional sales managers
6 District managers
7 Sales representatives
8 Sales trainees

With some manufacturers, there are two more special sales designations: *national accounts salesmen and industry-oriented salesmen.* Each national accounts salesman handles only one account, but it is the account of a large national or international company. It is his duty to cover all possible areas of his assigned account's business.

The industry-oriented salesman is one that has received special orientation for selling to a specific type of user. Some of these salesmen are trained to sell only to banks, others only to medical centers, and still others only to insurance companies.

The educational requirements are unusually high for a salesman. As a minimum he must have a bachelor's degree, and preferably technical training as well, before entering sales. In addition, he should be well trained in software and applications in order to help the customer choose the equipment most appropriate to his goals.

☐ THE PROGRAMMING TRAINEE

A common, but not invariable, prerequisite for the programming trainee is a college background, frequently scientific. The minimum requirement is a high school diploma with additional training in the general principles of programming. It is also felt that a trainee should show evidence of the following aptitudes:

1   An ability to think logically
2   An ability to understand, analyze, and discuss oral or written statements
3   Numerical ability for understanding and interpretation
4   Attentiveness to details and the detection of errors in clerical work
5   Aptitude for problem solving
6   Aptitude for abstract thinking

The abilities and aptitude of the potential trainee are determined in several ways. He is, of course, interviewed by the employer and may be questioned about the knowledge of programming that he has. In addition, he may be asked to take one of several tests determining his programming aptitude or his ability to think in a logical manner.

If the applicant is hired, he becomes part of the training program. This may last anywhere from a week or two to six months or more, depending on the company policy and the trainee's individual qualifications. Any programmer who has not worked professionally is considered a trainee.

☐ PROGRAMMER

Advancement takes place, after a certain amount of time, from the trainee to the programmer level. Usually an individual will remain at the trainee level for only 6 months.

In hiring a programmer, the background requirements are the same as those for a trainee, but with the additional stipulation that he have six months of professional experience.

The type of work he is assigned depends on the individual. Usually he is

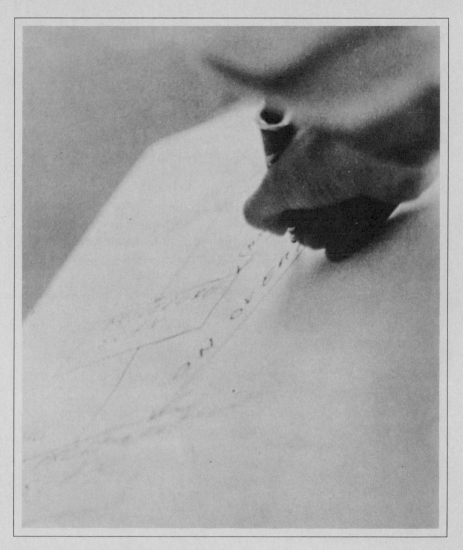

A PROGRAMMER PUTS NOTES ON A FLOWCHART.

given portions of systems or programs on which to work. He is expected to do both the flowcharts and the analysis of the program he is developing, but in most instances he will *not* have to provide his own test plan to test the program's accuracy. The programmer is usually provided with all test data by his supervisor.

VARIOUS TYPES OF PROGRAMMERS

The term "programmer" is the generic term used to designate those individuals who prepare and develop programs for computers. Just as there is a variety of computer applications, so too is there a variety of types of programmers. Once a programmer has developed his programming skills to a point where they have become second nature to him, he may begin to specialize in a specific area of programming.

If an engineer or a scientist decides to learn computer programming, it should be obvious that he would naturally seek to do programming in an area with which he is familiar. The end result would probably be a *scientific programmer* who will eventually do mainly scientific or engineering problems.

Another man may have been a pilot in the Air Force during his military service. It is quite possible that after he learns programming he might specialize in *air traffic programming* or perhaps *aircraft operational programming*.

A third person may not have had prior business or academic specialization. It is not unlikely that his primary interest is "just plain programming." His first jobs may have been for an insurance company, a manufacturer, or perhaps a bank. The result of this type of experience might well be a good *business* programmer. When joining a new company, prior work experiences might well be a decisive factor in determining a programmer's assignment.

Here is a list of the programming jobs available in *one* major firm's recent newspaper advertisement. The following programming positions were open and needed to be filled immediately:

1   Programmer trainees
2   Junior programmers
3   Systems programmers
4   Time sharing systems programmers
5   Scientific programmers
6   Business programmers
7   Mathematics programmers
8   Scientific/engineering programmers
9   Management information systems programmers
10   Applications programmers
11   Aircraft operational programmers
12   Real time programmers

13   Tactical development programmers
14   Air Traffic control programmers

As in almost all professions, there are no hard and fast rules determining a programmer's area of specialization or assignments. Each person's progress is determined solely in terms of the ability he has evidenced in his prior work and in terms of the extent of his actual experience as a programmer.

☐ SENIOR PROGRAMMER

A good programmer is usually advanced to the level of senior programmer. The actual programming techniques remain the same, no matter at which level the programming is done. The major difference is in terms of the

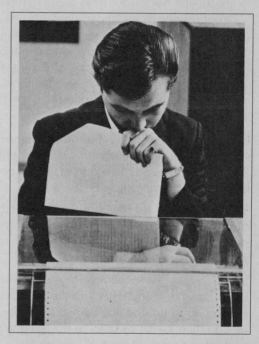

A SENIOR PROGRAMMER ATTENTIVELY WATCHES THE PRINTING OF THE RESULTS OF A CHECK-OUT RUN.

amount of independence and individual responsibility designated to the senior programmer by the project leader. He is given more analysis to do and is responsible to himself to get his portion of the job done.

☐ SYSTEMS ANALYST

The major function of the analyst is to analyze a user's requirements and then to design a system best meeting the needs of the particular application. Frequently, but not always, the term "analyst" also implies that the person in this job has more responsibility for other people, usually on a technical level, as well as some small administrative duties. The analyst analyzes and assesses the problems of his customer.

There are two specific types of analysts:

1 *Applications-oriented analyst*—Is not part of the computing staff. His particular responsibility is the development of systems for various applications in his department.
2 *Computer-oriented analyst*—As the name implies, this analyst is directly concerned with the actual working and capability of the computer, the peripheral equipment available, the software for the particular machine in question, and data storage methods. Specifically, his job is to determine how the computer may be most effectively used in handling a given application.

In order to accomplish a job most successfully, these two analysts must work together. Frequently no particular differentiation is made between the two categories, and often one man is expected to successfully accomplish both phases of the analyst's work.

It is not unusual for the *computer-oriented analyst* to work with a number of programmers under him. He is often designated to lead a particular project. If he is also the project leader, he is expected to take charge of a job and guide it to completion.

It is essential that he be able to discuss the project with the *applications-oriented analyst* and work out the problem in the most beneficial manner. He should in turn be able to work out the solution in a logical flow which he can then assign as tasks to his programmers. He should be able to follow through the work of his staff, devise test plans to make certain that the programs are correct, discuss the documentation of the project with the writer assigned to the staff, and remain in constant contact with his client.

☐ SCHEDULER

The scheduler designates activity in the computer room and schedules machine time for various jobs. To avoid delay and facilitate production, he assigns personnel and schedules work flow. He is also responsible for notifying maintenance and programming personnel in case of inability to locate or correct the cause of failure or error. In such instances he revises the operating schedule to adjust for delays. He consults with the manager about scheduling unanticipated runs or testing new programs. He also schedules time for preventive maintenance and coordinates the flow of work between shifts.

The requirements for the scheduler include a high school education and a minimum of one to three years of computer operating experience. It is also important that he know something about programming and coding techniques. Additional training in accounting, business administration, or mathematics is particularly desirable, though not necessary.

In terms of aptitudes and temperament, the scheduler should possess both verbal and numerical ability, though not at an advanced level. He should evidence clerical perception for the review of records and the recognition of pertinent details. He should also show a marked ability to perform a variety of tasks and to deal with people in a managerial capacity. This is particularly important when he is forced to change the job sequence or rechannel work flow.

☐ CODING CLERK

The job of the coding clerk is the preparation of data for a keypunch operator. Using a predetermined coding system, he converts routine bits of information from records and reports into codes for processing. He writes these codes by hand in a prescribed sequence on work sheets or coding sheets, which are then read and transferred by the keypunch operator.

A high school diploma is usually demanded by a prospective employer, who then provides several days of training in a classroom situation or gives on-the-job training under the direction of an experienced worker. The development of a high degree of accuracy and the achievement of great speed, however, takes from one to three months. This involves memorization of many of the codes used.

☐ KEYPUNCH OPERATOR

The keypunch operator uses the alphabetic and numeric keypunch machine to prepare programs and data for the computer. The machine is similar to an electric typewriter and demands the same motor coordination. The operator must read work sheets or coding sheets and simultaneously operate a keyboard with about 40 keys, set like those on a typewriter, which the operator presses. These in turn punch an appropriate hole in a card.

The primary prerequisites in the operation are manual dexterity, accuracy, speed, and the ability to comfortably perform repetitive duties without intense boredom or frustration, either of which may cause technical inaccuracy.

Requirements include a high school education, with proved ability in typing on an electric or standard typewriter. One week of paid training on a keypunch machine is usually provided by an employer or a manufacturer of equipment, though some high school or business school training in keypunch operations may be desirable.

Another task is that of verification using a special device called a *verifier*. The verifier operator checks the accuracy of the keypunch operator's work.

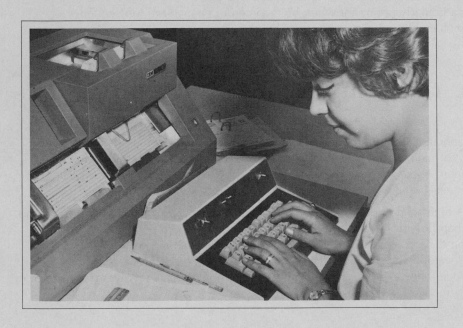

This is done by "repunching" the cards on a verifier and removing any incorrectly punched cards, which are then repunched on a keypunch machine. The verifier indicates mistakes by either showing a light or locking the key so that it will not depress.

☐ TAPE LIBRARIAN

After graduating from high school and receiving on-the-job training, a person can become a tape librarian. The primary work of the tape librarian is the *maintenance* and the *cataloging* of hundreds or thousands (depending on the size of the computer center) of reels of magnetic tape, punched paper tape, decks of magnetic cards or punched cards, and possibly files

AN OPERATOR PREPARES TO DISMOUNT A TAPE DESTINED TO BE STORED IN THE TAPE LIBRARY.

of program documentation and operating instructions for the computer center.

The tape librarian classifies and catalogs the various materials according to contents, the date the program was generated, the purpose of the program, and the required retention period.

It is also the function of the tape librarian to prepare index cards for file reference, to store materials in accordance with classification and cataloging, and to issue materials and maintain charge-out records. In addition, he must inspect returned tapes and cards for damage or wear and notify whoever the center has designated to handle such problems.

☐ COMPUTER OPERATOR

Although manufacturers have greatly simplified his tasks, the job of the computer operator still requires more than the ability to push a button or flip a switch. Not only does he stop and start the machine; he must also know enough about his equipment so he can monitor and control the computer according to prescribed operating instructions and detect a malfunction as soon as it occurs.

Here are the steps which an operator might take when running a program. The steps involved in running a job on a standard digital computer are interesting to observe:

1 *Sets* the control switches on the computer console and on the various pieces of peripheral equipment needed for the particular job run.
2 *Selects* and *loads* the input and output units with the various materials needed for running the program. These include tapes, punched cards, disc packs, etc.
3 *Moves switches* in order to clear the system and begin operation of the equipment.
4 At all times *observes* the machines and the control panel on the computer console for error light, for verification, for error messages printed out by the computer, and for equipment stoppage or faulty output.
5 *Types* alternate commands into the computer console according to predetermined instructions, to correct an error or a failure and to resume operations.
6 *Clears* unit at the end of a job run.
7 *Reviews* the schedule to determine the next assignment.
8 *Records* the operating time.

As you can see, the job of the computer operator is relatively simple but his responsibility is not.

Obviously, being responsible for operating a piece of machinery, worth on the *average* about one million dollars, necessitates some training and a great deal of trust.

The minimum education requirement is a high school education and three to six months of on-the-job training. Increasingly, however, employers are demanding additional education and training for operators. The prospective computer operator's training will then include courses such as accounting, data processing, mathematics, elementary programming, and of course, the operating of computers and peripheral equipment.

Usually, when an employer hires a new operator, he provides him with

COMPUTER OPERATOR AND SYSTEMS ANALYSTS DISCUSS EQUIPMENT STOPPAGE.

several weeks or more of formal instruction dealing specifically with the computer system on which the operator will be working.

☐ MANAGER

The role of the manager is the most demanding in the computer center. The manager should have had experience in systems analysis, programming, and computer operations. He also needs some business training, some experience in an administrative capacity, and a knowledge of accounting or engineering.

Usually a college degree with a major in one or more of the already mentioned fields is preferred, particularly in the larger installations. One final note in relation to training is that familiarity does not necessarily mean great skill, nor is it essential that the manager be an expert in all areas. He must, however, be capable of understanding all areas for, as you may have surmised, his work affects every person and department of the computer center. He deals with personnel problems and must be a good administrator, though his primary role is director and coordinator of planning and production activities in the computer center. In this capacity his role covers a variety of functions, including:

1   Determining the center's equipment needs
2   General assigning, scheduling, and review of work
3   Reviewing of all reports on usage and maintenance equipment
4   Directing the training program for new personnel
5   Establishing quality and performance standards
6   Consulting with all department heads to determine needs, goals, and problems within the center

☐ QUESTIONS

1   Prepare an organization chart of the sector of a company that is using a computer, and insert in the blocks the titles of the positions described in the chapter which apply to this computer use.

2   Prepare an organization chart of a company that is designing, building, and selling computers, and insert in the blocks the titles of the positions described in the chapter which apply to this activity.

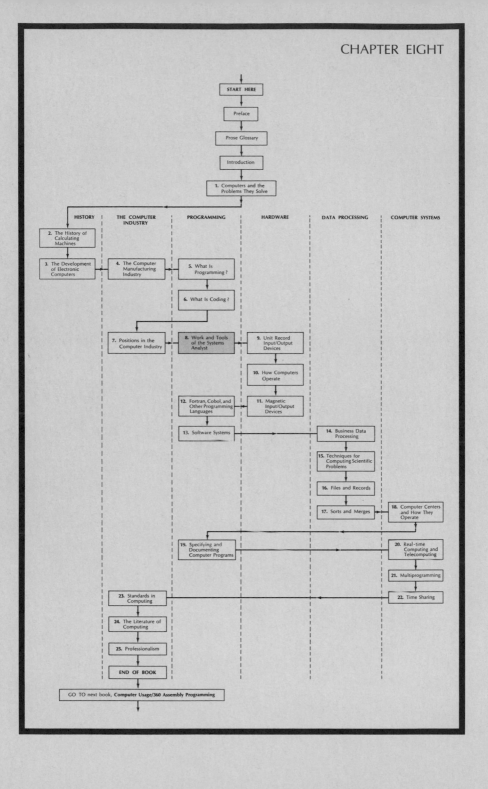

CHAPTER EIGHT

THE WORK
AND TOOLS
OF THE
SYSTEMS ANALYST

The systems analyst's working methods are determined by two factors that make it hard to be precise about how he does his work. The two factors are:

1 The nature of the *specific* application
2 The *particular* approach that the *individual* systems analyst takes to the specific application

Because every job is unique, there is a lack of regularity in the work of the systems analyst. It is often said to be more an art than a science.

From the previous chapter, you already know *who* the systems analyst is. You know that he can be either an application-oriented analyst or a computer-oriented analyst, and you have an *understanding* of what each term implies. Consequently this chapter will not be concerned with who the analyst is, but with the *nature of his work and the methods by which he does it.*

This chapter will not distinguish between the two types of systems analysts. The term "systems analyst" will refer to a combination of the two: both application oriented and computer oriented. But today and in the future, because of the extension of computers into every activity, it is becoming impossible for anyone to know all the aspects of the computing field. So the split between computer-oriented and application-oriented analysts will continue, and there will be further specialization by specific application.

☐ THE BEGINNING

Because the systems analyst is often the project leader having the responsibility of actually seeing that the job is done, it will be assumed in this chapter that he acts in this capacity.

The work of the systems analyst is started long before he ever knows of the existence of the problem. It may be that management has become dissatisfied with the present system and has decided to install a new system for the present computer. Or perhaps management has become convinced that a specific type and amount of information is needed more quickly to ensure success in the competitive race. Possibly the management of a small company has concluded that the volume of business demands and warrants the installation of a computer and the design of a new system to go with it. For these and many other reasons, the decision is made either to put in a new system or to redesign the present system. In any case, the *analysis* of the existing system and the determination of what will be required of the new one should be the first step.

☐ ANALYSIS OF THE EXISTING SYSTEM

It is the primary responsibility of the systems analyst to organize data handling in the best possible way for computer processing. This seems simple. It is not.

The computer has great capabilities; but if all information is not organized into a procedure which it is capable of accepting, it cannot perform properly. The systems analyst has the responsibility for determining this procedure. What this implies is not simply the mechanization of the existing system, but the ability to *replan* an old method or *design* a new system. A system must be patterned on an understanding of present needs and a grasp of the future plans and future requirements of the business. When a company assigns a systems analyst to develop a new system, it must open its operation to him for analysis. This is essential. The analyst must be told everything. The purpose of an analysis is to learn enough about the existing system and the demands on it so that the foundation can be laid for the design and implementation of a better system.

The work involved in the actual analysis of an existing system can be divided into six steps:

1 *Obtaining the facts*—Facts about the existing system are gathered in various ways and from a number of sources. Initially they are gathered through a series of meetings with the highest level of management that is concerned with the system. In these initial meetings the systems analyst should begin to identify and record management's concept of the problems in the present system. He should be on the lookout for problems which are present but are not recognized by management. At this time, he should also meet and arrange for the cooperation of the lower-level managers involved.

Much of his initial work is as an intelligent recording observer. The systems analyst observes and notes all activities that occur in all the events which originate and create each document. He pays special

attention to the various input/output procedures in the existing system. The analyst observes the maintenance of files and the issuing of reports, as well as all processing steps and the flow of all documents. He notes all his observations and makes a comprehensive and coherent record of the procedures as he understands them.

2   *Collecting sample documents*—The analyst then collects for study, analysis, and record filled-in sample copies of all paper work. These include reports, file papers, documents of all descriptions, interdepartmental memos, messages generated by the system, and any other material essential to the operation.

3   *Studying the processing operations*—The analyst must discover:
    Why each document originates
    How each document originates
    Who issues the document
    Who receives the document

It is also important that the systems analyst know what processing steps each person performs, the contents required in all reports that a person prepares, and the nature of all files that each person keeps or uses.

4   *Organizing the facts*—The organization of the facts is probably the most important part of the process of systems analysis. Organizing facts about the present system's flow of data into narratives, charts, lists, or diagrams gives the systems analyst a visual picture of the data flow, enabling him to grasp the problem more quickly.

The analyst charts the path of the data from origin, through every stage of communication, all stages of process, into files, out of files, and finally into reports or any other output.

5   *Interviewing each user*—The next to last step in the analysis of an existing system is the interview of each person issuing or receiving documents and reports. This is done to learn what information the individual uses in his work and what additional information he believes he requires. At this point, dissatisfactions with and shortcomings of the system should be noted. This is also the time to seek out the informal communication links on which all systems depend for quick action and corrections of error.

6   *Review*—In the final step, the systems analyst reviews his now complete and detailed picture of the existing procedure with the managers of the system in order to ferret out missing details and confirm his conclusions.

☐ TECHNIQUES OF THE ANALYSIS

Each step of the analysis requires that the systems analyst get information about the existing system from all organizational levels. He must use a variety of techniques and approaches to accomplish his task.

The *ability to observe* is of major importance. A systems analyst who has trained himself to watch for small, unmentioned details has a great advantage when analyzing a system. This valuable skill is generally developed during his years as a programmer.

There are, however, techniques of a more definite nature that comprise the the tools of his trade and that are used by all systems analysts.

INTERVIEWS

One of the most valuable information-collecting techniques is the interview. A good analyst is able to conduct a successful interview at all levels of the organization. From *top management* he must learn the company's objectives and goals; from *department heads* he must have cooperation and an assessment of departmental performance and difficulties; and from those doing the work (branch office, clerical, and factory personnel) he must learn the factual data.

A serious problem encountered in the interview is the employee's fear of automation and the consequent loss of his job or status. (Often an unfounded fear, as the installation of computers usually increases, rather than decreases, the payroll.) The systems analyst must learn how to overcome these fears. He must be particularly careful about the use of computer jargon which laymen do not understand. *Organization, brevity,* and *clarity* are the ground rules of a successful information-getting interview.

DOCUMENTATION

Documentation is an essential tool in analyzing and designing a system. Documentation is the written record of each step in the analysis. Unless the systems analyst documents his findings, it will be impossible for him to remember in detail all the information he has collected.

When, for example, the systems analyst is documenting a specific activity in the existing system, the following information should be recorded:

1   *Functions* of the activity
2   *Input* required for the activity
3   *Output* generated by the activity
4   *Files* used to complete the activity
5   *Feedback* resulting from the activity
6   *Full narrative* of the activity

Obviously there is a lot of information to be recorded, and it may be recorded in one of several ways. Each systems analyst has his preferences, which may include one or all of these methods. Some use yellow pads on which they write down information; others use charts, diagrams, tables; some use special forms. Notes and the initial informal records may be kept according to the preference of each individual, but the final documentation must meet the standards of the organization.

Good documentation (in addition to providing a clear description of a process, a problem, or a solution) is essential for ease of communication between the systems analyst and management, and between the systems analyst and his programming staff. An effective organization will have established standards for this documentation so that everyone knows what to expect and how to understand what is recorded.

There are a number of areas in an analysis and design project that the systems analyst must document. Areas of documentation include:

1   Statistics important to the system
2   The flow of data in both the old and the newly designed system
3   Descriptions of files and documents
4   All general information that pertains to a process or activity

BLOCK DIAGRAMS
Block diagrams are a type of documentation used frequently by the systems analyst. The block diagrams may look like the flowcharts written by programmers, but they are *not* like them except in form. A block diagram of a system is a chart consisting of blocks describing each element of the system and how the work flows from one system component to another.

DECISION TABLES
Decision tables are a specific technique sometimes used for problem solving, for documentation, and in special instances as a programming

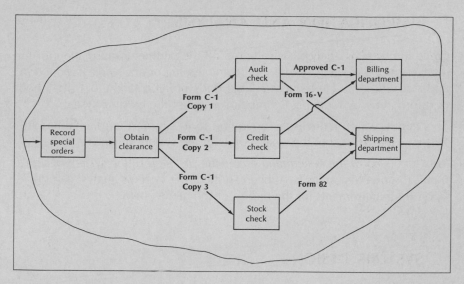

SECTION OF A BLOCK DIAGRAM.

language. There are a number of variations of the basic decision table format that the systems analyst may use. Decision tables are a compact and convenient shorthand notation for certain situations.

The basic concept behind a decision table is one of *condition* and *response* using an IF . . . THEN arrangement. For example, in analyzing a credit check for a retail sale:

CONDITION . . . IF	1	2	3	4
Customer has charge	Yes	No	Yes	Yes
Credit is O.K.	Yes		No	No
Payment experience is O.K.	Yes		No	Yes
Special clearance is granted			No	Yes
RESPONSE . . . THEN				
Approve order	√			√
Cancel order		√	√	

By following down each numbered column, you will see that the yeses and noes of the upper blocks (the CONDITION . . . IF) result in the appropriate actions of the lower blocks (the RESPONSE . . . THEN).

Decision tables similar to these are used by the systems analyst to analyze an existing system and to specify the behavior of a planned new system.

☐ SIMPLIFICATION AND ANALYSIS

Once the systems analyst has gathered all the pertinent information for his analysis of the existing system, he begins the important work of *reduction* and *simplification*. He reduces a large body of information to a small body of information by reducing the repetitiveness of the existing system.

This condensation reduces the operation to its simplest form, enabling the systems analyst to spot the weak points in the system quickly.

This final step of the system analysis is the first step of the system design. Once the problem areas have been spotted, the systems analyst can decide upon the requirements for the design of the new system.

☐ SYSTEMS DESIGN

Systems design is the formulation of a plan for processing data, based on the facts that the systems analyst has learned during the analysis stage.

The initial step in actually designing the new system is the selection of a design approach. This selection is based on these things:

1   The requirements of the system
2   The approach taken by the particular systems analyst to the particular problem
3   Capabilities and types of computer equipment available for the new system
4   Costs of devising, installing, and operating the new system

DETERMINING SYSTEMS REQUIREMENTS

In order to design a new system or redesign an existing system, the systems analyst must determine the system's requirements. He must find out exactly what the system is currently required to do. He must carefully assess how well the new system must perform these requirements. And lastly, the systems analyst must know what the future requirements of the system will be. These future needs are determined by factors such as:

1   Predictions of future markets
2   New services required of the systems
3   Design changes in the future

4 Advanced processes in the future
5 Changes in product volume
6 Changing business trends
7 Any projected management changes
8 Impact of changes in regulatory laws

APPROACHES TO SYSTEMS DESIGN

Human beings have individual ways of seeing the same picture, and systems analysts are no exception. Each analyst has his preferred methods of approaching a problem. Of course, the particular application influences the analyst's approach, but personal preference plays an important role in the decision.

There are five basic approaches that may be used in various combinations for systems design. Individually these five design approaches are:

1 *Input/output oriented*—In which the system is designed on the basis of input (data, raw materials, etc.) required by the system in order to produce the output (documents, products, etc.).
2 *Data file oriented*—In which the system design centers on the data contained in the files. These files then become the basis for all subsequent development of the system.
3 *Procedure narrative oriented*—This type of approach emphasizes the actions performed. It may lead the systems analyst to a decision to use Cobol, a business programming language (see Chapter 12) as the language for the particular application.
4 *Block diagram oriented*—This is an approach which emphasizes each unit within the system and the interconnections and flows between units.
5 *Decision table oriented*—The basis of this approach depends heavily on building decision tables for all aspects of the job.

☐ MAJOR TASKS INVOLVED IN INSTALLING A NEW SYSTEM

Once the systems analyst has developed a basic system design, he begins to determine the particulars of his system. He carefully analyzes the interaction of all the activities required by his new approach. This he does by reviewing his documentation, paying particular attention to procedures and data flow.

The final design must be submitted to management for approval, along with:

1 Estimates of costs of the new system
2 Staff required for implementation of the new system
3 Time required for implementation of the new system
4 Predicted date that implementation will be completed and operation begun

If management accepts and approves the system presented in the report and authorizes its installation, implementation and preparations for programming are begun.

After approval, the systems analyst prepares a plan for implementing the new system. This is a complicated step, as the word *implement* implies a great deal to the systems analyst. Implementing a system is the process of devising the procedures of the new system. These include:

1 Creating a detailed computer-oriented analysis and design of the new system
2 Programming the new system
3 Testing and debugging the new programs
4 Parallel-running the new system and the old system
5 Documenting the new system in detail
6 Preparing a run book containing
   Program documentation
   Flowcharts of computer runs and document flow

Along with the already mentioned tasks of implementation, the project leader is responsible for seeing that the equipment required by the new system is purchased and installed. He must also make certain that the necessary personnel are hired and trained so that they can handle their responsibilities in the new system. The latter tasks are usually handled by the manager of the computer center or some other responsible person, at the request of the systems analyst.

SYSTEMS IMPLEMENTATION

The systems analyst, if he is acting as project leader, is assigned his staff, consisting of a number of programmers and possibly several other systems analysts. The size of the staff depends on the extent of the work required by the new system.

Once approval is obtained on the new design, work can begin. The systems description now becomes the basis for all further work.

PREPARATION FOR PROGRAMMING

The programming staff can only begin work upon receipt of the proper specifications from the systems analyst. Owing to the complexity of the system and the number of persons working on it, the programmers must be careful to follow the project leader's directions, especially regarding common data formats, etc.

Programmers' specifications should consist of:

1   A copy of the design report prepared for management
2   A run description for each computer run in the new system
3   A file description for each file in the new system

RUN DESCRIPTION FOR EACH COMPUTER RUN

A run description indicates the required information for programming a computer operation or run. The description must include a *run requirements* model which shows:

1   The name of the particular run
2   Input for the run
3   Output resulting from the run
4   The use of the files in the run
5   A list of the functions of the run

There must also be a *narrative description of each function* for ease of programming. Decision tables might be included in order to correlate programming requirements. And to clarify the problem, an *outline block diagram* showing the sequence of processing must be included along with a summary of the new system's controls. Controls are mathematical checks which should be constantly maintained to ensure that no goods, cash, or records are lost or stolen in the data processing department or with the aid of someone in this department.

These controls are built into the system by the systems analyst; each program demands that the computer indicate with printed messages if anything is missing or incorrect in a computer run. For example, the sum of the value of every thousand items (depending on what is being processed) is recorded and checked against the value of the same items before processing. If the program is processing 87,000 items (not an impossibility), this control system would indicate that the mistake, if one has been made, is in the tenth group of one thousand—rather than in the twentieth group. This greatly simplifies correction of errors.

FILE DESCRIPTION FOR EACH FILE

Programmers must also have a file description of the new system in order to accomplish their task, for without a thorough knowledge of the files, programming becomes an impossibility. The file description includes a *layout record for each tape or disc file.* The layout record consists of:

1　Name of the application
2　Name of the particular file
3　Listing of the programs using this file
4　Name of the program creating the file
5　A layout of the file
6　A layout of each record indicating:
　　a　Field name
　　b　Field abbreviation or mnemonic
　　c　Field length
　　d　Any pertinent information, such as the location of decimal points
　　e　Field characteristics
　　f　Maximum and minimum values of this particular field

Also included in the description of the files is a cross reference indicating which program uses which file, and which files are used in each program. Up-to-date maintenance of this reference is important to ensure proper control of the files.

TESTING

Once the programming of the new system is begun, the systems analyst assigns tests to see that programs are as they should be. He constantly follows the work of the programmers in order to achieve programming cohesiveness for his new system.

At the same time, the systems analyst trains the clerical and the operating staff to begin work on the new system. Any operating or clerical instructions must be prepared under the supervision of the systems analyst.

If new equipment is required by the new system, the systems analyst discusses and plans installation and trial runs for it with management.

PARALLEL OPERATION AND CONVERSION

As the programs, files, and new equipment all become functioning realities, the work of conversion begins. This is the period of switching over from the existing system to the newly designed and newly implemented system. Before accepting a replacement system, both the old system and the new system are run at the same time using the same inputs. This is called "running in parallel." It is done for two important reasons:

1 To prove that the functions of the old and new system are the same (e.g., paychecks all correct and identical)
2 To continue using the output of the old system until the systems analyst is certain that all the bugs are out of the new system, and until management is certain that the system is doing the job it was designed to perform

This step, obvious as its requirements are, must be carefully planned and executed if the new system is to be a success.

FINAL DOCUMENTATION FOR THE RUN BOOK

The last formal step in the design and implementation of a new system is the preparation of a run book. This is a volume containing all program documentation and all flowcharts of computer runs and document flow. It should be formally transmitted to the manager responsible for operating and maintaining the system.

The careful documentation of the new system is for the purpose of future reference. This report covers in a specific and well-defined order such things as:

1 Scope of new system
  a Description
  b Departments supplying information
  c Departments receiving information
2 General description of new system
  a Aims
  b Functions to be performed
  c Method
  d Changes to existing system
3 Model of new system
4 Inputs of new system
  a Contents
  b Source
  c Frequency and average volume
5 Outputs of new system
  a Sample forms

b   Distribution
c   Frequency
6   Files of new system
a   Summary of contents
b   Volumes
c   Method of storage

MAINTENANCE

A system of any size will require maintenance. This takes two forms. The computer programs will have defects or bugs in them which no amount of testing will reveal. Some time after the system has been put into operation, real data and real operation will produce some combination of events that was never tested for and that will reveal a bug by some kind of system failure. The program must then be corrected to fix this defect so that the failure will not happen again. The activity of fixing the bugs as real operation reveals them is one part of the maintenance function.

The second part of maintenance is required by unanticipated external events. After the system has been in operation for some time, conditions will change, often only slightly; but the computer programs must then be altered to accommodate these changes. In a payroll situation, for example, the legislature may give counties the legal right to impose income taxes, so that all employees must have their county of residence added to their payroll records and appropriate taxes withheld, recorded, and remitted. Or in a marketing accounting situation, salesmen's commission rates may be changed so that special premiums are paid for volume sales of certain items. This means that information on such sales must be accumulated by salesman's number. The program must be changed to accommodate these new and unforeseen requirements. This is the second part of the maintenance function.

When the need for program maintenance arises, the systems analyst and the associated programmers who originated the system will be off on some new job. They will have lost touch with the details of this system. They cannot be constantly dropping the jobs they are working on to maintain the systems they created in the past. For this reason, the maintenance function is usually assigned to a specified individual in the group that is operating and using the system on a day-to-day basis. As an example, maintenance of the payroll system will be assigned to an employee in the payroll department.

Once the conversion is accomplished and the system is approved and accepted, the systems analyst is free to begin again—another new system!

☐ QUESTIONS

1 Prepare a decision table relating to the decision whether or not to attend a movie. The Responses would be "go" or "don't go." Among the Conditions might be "have money," "good movie," "have date," "assignments completed." Make a decision table on the subject whether to get out of bed in the morning or not.

2 Compare and contrast the qualifications of a systems analyst with those of a programmer. Include technical training, personal traits, and life objectives.

3 Compare and contrast the work and methods of a system analyst with those of a programmer-coder.

4 Compare and contrast the work and methods of a systems analyst with work and methods of any profession that you are familiar with: doctor, lawyer, engineer, teacher, clergyman, reporter.

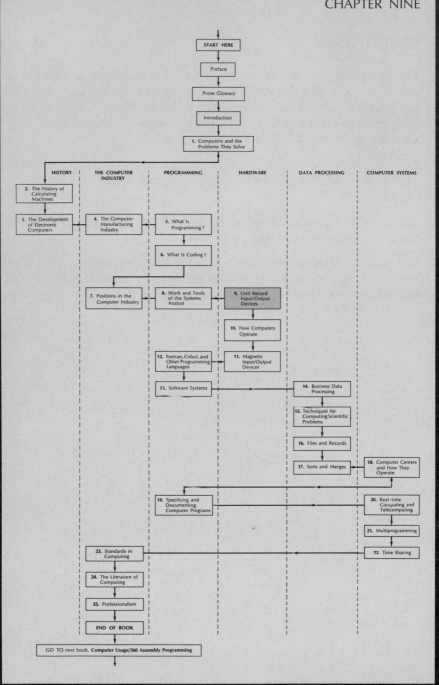

START HERE

Preface

Prose Glossary

Introduction

1. Computers and the Problems They Solve

HISTORY | THE COMPUTER INDUSTRY | PROGRAMMING | HARDWARE | DATA PROCESSING | COMPUTER SYSTEMS

2. The History of Calculating Machines

3. The Development of Electronic Computers

4. The Computer Manufacturing Industry

5. What Is Programming ?

6. What Is Coding ?

7. Positions in the Computer Industry

8. Work and Tools of the Systems Analyst

9. Unit Record Input/Output Devices

10. How Computers Operate

12. Fortran, Cobol, and Other Programming Languages

11. Magnetic Input/Output Devices

13. Software Systems

14. Business Data Processing

15. Techniques for Computing Scientific Problems

16. Files and Records

17. Sorts and Merges

18. Computer Centers and How They Operate

19. Specifying and Documenting Computer Programs

20. Real-time Computing and Telecomputing

21. Multiprogramming

23. Standards in Computing

22. Time Sharing

24. The Literature of Computing

25. Professionalism

END OF BOOK

GO TO next book, **Computer Usage/360 Assembly Programming**

UNIT RECORD
INPUT/OUTPUT
DEVICES

This lesson deals with punched cards and printed lines. You may not think they have much in common, but from the computer's viewpoint, they are very similar. Also covered is the equipment that handles such unit records. Particular emphasis is placed on the equipment supporting the IBM System/360, which is typical of modern computers.

One whole area *not* covered is the use of this equipment as part of a punched card accounting installation—the so-called "tab shop." Such operations are carried out as an *alternate* to computer processing and, consequently, do not fall into the area covered by this book. Some of the problems covered in this chapter, however, are very similar to those of a tab shop.

Technically, a unit record is a group of characters transmitted between the central processor and an input or output device. Although many different devices are available, only three types of unit records will be covered here:

A punched card that is to be read into the computer
A punched card that is to be punched as output from the computer
A line that is to be printed as output from the computer

□ READING PUNCHED CARDS INTO THE COMPUTER

The simple act of reading a program or data card "into the computer" is often misunderstood. Naturally, different computers handle input differently. The simplest scheme is employed by the old IBM 1401. When the computer encounters the READ instruction, it reads the card and places the contents of the 80 card columns into memory locations 001 to 080. Notice that there are several actions:

1 A physical mechanism moves the card through the card reader.
2 The information punched on the card is picked up.
3 This information is transmitted to specified locations in main memory.

The mechanism by which System/360 reads a card is considerably more complex. It involves two additional devices between the card reader and the computer: a *control unit* and a *channel*. When the SIO command (Start I/O) is given, the channel, control unit, and card reader must be designated (there may be many channels, control units, and card readers on a single System/360). *Channel Command Words* must be accessed to tell the channel where in main memory the information is to be stored. By means of what is

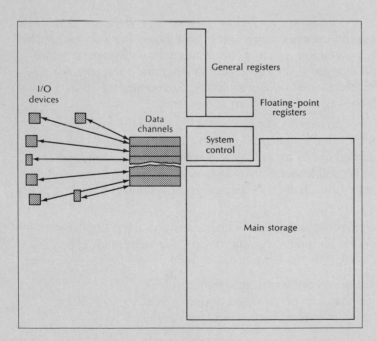

BLOCK DIAGRAM OF SYSTEM/360 COMPUTER.

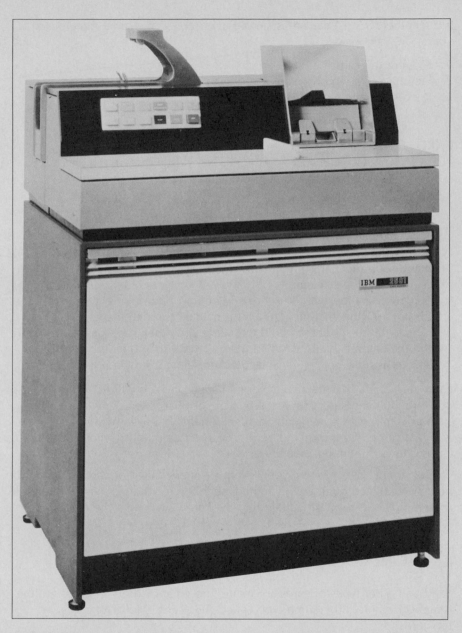

CARD READER.

called "scatter-read," the contents of a single card may be read into many
locations; the contents of 5 columns here, of 11 columns there, etc.

But whether the mechanism is simple or complex, the same three basic operations take place:

1 Moving the card
2 Picking up the information from the card
3 Recording it in main memory

CARD READERS
There are many card readers on the market. While there are individual differences, most have the same basic features:

1 A hopper (that part of a reader where cards to be read are placed) holding between 500 and 1,500 cards waiting to be read.
2 A device that picks one card at a time from the waiting stack and pushes it through a narrow space toward the transport mechanism.
3 A transport mechanism that carries the card through the reading station and toward the stackers.
4 A reading station with 80 sensors (wire contacts striking a brass roller, or phototransistors that pick up light projected through the holes).
5 One or more stackers to hold the cards once they have passed through the reading mechanism. When there is more than one, the normal stacker is used unless a special Stacker Select instruction is given.

Each card reader has its own maximum speed, which will lie in the range of 400 to 2,000 cards per minute. When the hopper is empty or when the stacker is full, card reading automatically halts. It also halts whenever there is a *jam* caused by a torn, creased, or warped card. Only regular reading of cards allows continuous operation.

Proper storage of cards to prevent warping is essential, for cards must not be bent or mutilated in any way. Immediately before loading, the operator will *joggle* the cards to make certain that they feed easily into the reader.

☐ THE 80-COLUMN CARD

Although other types of cards are made, the great majority of cards are the rectangular-hole, 80-column type called IBM cards, Hollerith cards, or tab cards.

There are twelve rows available for punching in each of the 80 columns. A fully punched card has 960 holes, but each column generally has one hole to represent a number and two holes to represent an alphabetic character. As a student you should familiarize yourself with the standard punches for

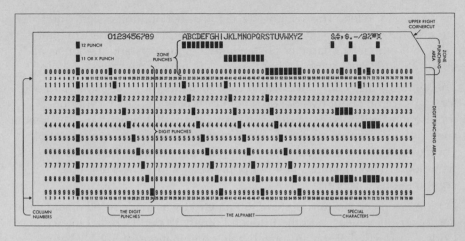

A STANDARD HOLLERITH CARD.

numbers and letters. Incidentally, the absence of a punch in a column is interpreted as the special character *blank*. This is a meaningful character— not the same as zero.

Three holes are usually punched to represent punctuation marks like parentheses, periods, commas, etc. Since System/360 allows a character set of 256 different characters, as many as six punches in one column may be valid, even though there is no simple interpretation of some such instances. If there are more than six, a validity check is signaled to the central processor by the card reader.

There is a special way of punching cards to cram a maximal amount of information into them: using *binary cards*. These are regular IBM cards which are interpreted differently; *every punch is a one or a zero*. In System/360, every column of a binary card is interpreted as if it had an upper and a lower half of six punches each. When one of these cards is read, 160 bytes of main memory are filled. Binary cards are never hand-punched with a keypunch; they are punched by a computer using an attached *card punch* (a unit record device which will be discussed shortly).

☐ CHARACTER SETS

Each computer is clearly going to have to handle the 10 decimal digits and the 26 letters of the alphabet. They all do this, and the Hollerith hole-punching combinations shown in the picture of a card are now universal. But input and output for a computer need other symbols in addition to the numbers and letters. The symbols for comma, period, dollar sign, and so on are also necessary. It is in the symbols which are included that computers differ. All computer character sets include the numbers and the letters and about 28 additional symbols, but they do not all use the same symbols.

The United States committee which tried to standardize the Hollerith code for cards found about two dozen different systems in use in 1968 for representing symbols. Even different computer models from the same vendor used different symbols and different representations for the same symbol. For example, some IBM machines will print the symbols # @ % & □, while other IBM machines will not print these but for the same hole combinations will print = ' (+).

During design of the IBM System/360 an effort was made to eliminate these and other differences, and the Extended Binary Coded Decimal Interchange Code was devised. The card-punch hole combinations of EBCDIC are shown below. They agree with the earlier IBM card codes in all the letters and numbers but only in about half of the symbols.

CHARACTER	CARD CODE	NAME
b	No punches	Blank
¢	12-2-8	Cents sign
.	12-3-8	Period or point
<	12-4-8	Less than
(	12-5-8	Left parenthesis
+	12-6-8	Plus sign
|	12-7-8	Vertical line
&	12	Ampersand
!	11-2-8	Exclamation point
$	11-3-8	Dollar sign
*	11-4-8	Asterisk
)	11-5-8	Right parenthesis
;	11-6-8	Semicolon
→	11-7-8	Logical "not"
-	11	Minus or hyphen (dash)
/	0-1	Slash
,	0-3-8	Comma
%	0-4-8	Percent
__	0-5-8	Underline
>	0-6-8	Greater than
?	0-7-8	Question mark
:	2-8	Colon
#	3-8	Number sign
@	4-8	"At" sign
'	5-8	Prime or apostrophe
=	6-8	Equals sign
"	7-8	Quotation marks

CHARACTER	CARD CODE	CHARACTER	CARD CODE
A	12-1	S	0-2
B	12-2	T	0-3
C	12-3	U	0-4
D	12-4	V	0-5
E	12-5	W	0-6
F	12-6	X	0-7
G	12-7	Y	0-8
H	12-8	Z	0-9
I	12-9	0	0
J	11-1	1	1
K	11-2	2	2
L	11-3	3	3
M	11-4	4	4
N	11-5	5	5
O	11-6	6	6
P	11-7	7	7
Q	11-8	8	8
R	11-9	9	9

Several years after the introduction of the IBM System/360 an industry-wide committee at last produced a standard code for information interchange. This will ultimately be accepted and used by the entire computer and communications industry. The code is called USASCII: USA Standard Code for Information Interchange. As far as card punching is concerned, USASCII agrees with EBCDIC in everything except the following symbols:

CHARACTER	USASCII CARD CODE	EBCDIC CARD CODE	NAME
`	8-1	none	Grave
!	12-8-7	11-8-2	Exclamation point
[	12-8-2	none	Left bracket
¢	none	12-8-2	Cents sign
{	12-0	none	Left brace
\	0-8-2	none	Reverse slash
		12-11	12-8-7	Vertical line
]	11-8-2	none	Right bracket
}	11-0	none	Right brace
^	11-8-7	none	Circumflex
~	11-0-1	none	Tilde
→	none	11-8-7	Logical "not"

Note that in only four cases (12-8-7, 12-8-2, 11-8-7, 11-8-2) do the same card codes represent different symbols. But there are other and more important differences between EBCDIC and USASCII in regard to the representation of the characters inside a computer. As described in Chapter

23, considerable effort at standardization is in progress which will in time eliminate the differences that exist between EBCDIC and USASCII, possibly by eliminating one of them.

☐ LAYING OUT A PUNCHED CARD

Program cards are punched according to the rules of the programming language. The layout of data cards must often be specified separately for each application.

In your work you may have occasion to lay out data cards. If you do, you should know some commonsense rules about layout:

1   Use a single card wherever possible, even if you must do a bit of crowding to get your data on one card.
2   Try to use only numerics or, if this is not possible, combinations of numerics and letters. This will allow easy punching, and easy interpretation of the punches.
3   Avoid giving more than one piece of information in a single column.
4   Where your data occupies less than a full card, keep all the fields of the card toward the left margin of the card.
5   Where the card will be used in sufficient volume, have an electroplate made which preprints on each card the various fields and their identifications.
6   Where sequence is important, and sufficient room permits, use a sequence field for serial card numbering.

☐ KEYPUNCHES AND VERIFIERS

Although some punched cards originate as output from a computer or another automatic device, the majority of cards come into existence by being keypunched.

A keypunch is a machine containing a keyboard, special controls, and a device for punching cards, one column at a time. In normal operation, there is a hopper which contains unpunched cards, a one-column punching mechanism, a one-column reader which permits duplication of one card's punches in the identical columns of the next card, and a one-column printing device that prints (*interprets*) the characters corresponding to the

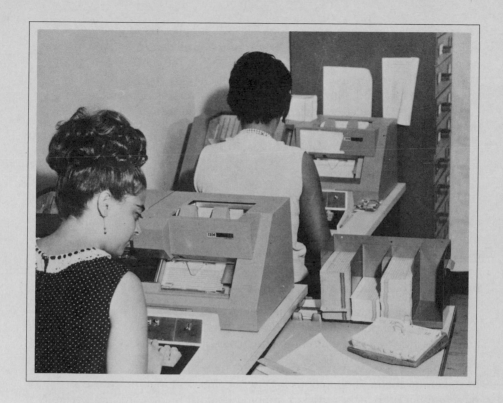

code on the card. Finally, there is a stacker which holds the punched cards.

Keypunches are electrically driven and contain extensive controls designed to speed the processing. Some of these controls are switches which select different modes—automatic feed, suppress interpreting, etc. Others are on a special drum around which is wrapped a *program card*. This controls the punching on a column-by-column basis, causing columns to be reproduced, skipped, punched numeric-only, etc. A program card must be prepared for each regular keypunching job.

Keypunch availability generally reflects the scope of character sets. Numeric only; numeric plus alphabetic; numeric, alphabetic, and the most common special characters (,.+=*—'); or a full set of all available characters. The price of the keypunch increases with the size of the character set.

Keypunch work is submitted on special forms or data sheets with the columns to be punched clearly marked.

There are other machines which look like keypunches but punch no holes! These are *verifiers*. The operation of the keys causes a comparison to be made between the depressed key and holes on the previously keypunched card. Disagreement causes a red light to go on and the keyboard to lock and allows the operator of the verifier to examine the card for errors. A successfully verified card is given a small semicircular punch at its right margin.

□ CARD PUNCHES

Of the three principal unit record devices, card punches are the only ones that *may* be absent in a full-scale computer organization. It is *possible* to read in data and program cards and store their contents on magnetic devices only. However, there are so many uses for a card punch that most installations have them. Among the uses are:

Punchout of program decks (binary cards)
Preparation of duplicate records for preservation purposes
Prepunching information on punched card bills and checks

These devices look very much like card readers and, in fact, are often mistaken for them. Their actions are identical except that the card is punched out by punches instead of being read in. Blank cards are generally placed in the hopper, and the punched cards are held in one or more stackers. Some punches have stations where the information just punched can be read back for validity checking and for verification.

Card reading can be done "on the fly," but the moving cards must halt momentarily to be punched. Consequently, card punches operate at much slower speeds than card readers do—generally one-third to one-half the speed.

CARD READ PUNCHES
Yes—it is possible to economize by combining the two similar devices in a single unit. Such units are called *card read punches* and are available for most computers. They have two hoppers—one for blank cards to be punched and one for punched cards to be read—and five stackers. There is also a less expensive one-hopper device which carries cards from one hopper to one stacker, and either reads or punches. It provides a good

solution for the problems of the low-budget installation which needs only small amounts of card punching.

□ PRINTING THE OUTPUT

You have probably already received a number of computer printouts from insurance companies, banks, the Internal Revenue Service, etc. The printout

LINE PRINTER.

is normally the termination point in computing—it gives the ultimate reader a printed account of the result of the processing. A computer printout is often referred to as hardcopy.

Virtually all printers operate like this:

1   Full-width paper, which has perforated strips attached at the sides to align and guide the paper, is threaded through the machine by the printer's *pin-feed* mechanism, which guides the paper by means of the

perforations (comparable to movie film threaded through a projector). The paper comes in *fanfold form* and feeds smoothly. Since paper rates may reach 75 inches per second, rapid movement with accurate registration is required. Where multiple copies are required, the fanfold paper is purchased with a full carbon paper filler already inserted for each copy needed.

2   The printing is invariably carried out *one line at a time*. There is no horizontal movement—the paper advances (normally) one vertical space per line. Rates of 500 to 1,500 lines per minute are common.

3   Special controls—built into the program or handled by a special *carriage control paper tape*—make the printer skip one, two, or more lines, suppress line spacing, or eject (rapid vertical movement) many inches. These mechanisms control *page overflow* and leave proper margins at the bottom and top of each page.

THE PRINTED LINE—A UNIT RECORD

As you can see, the principal action is the second item above—the printing of one line. Lines are generally from 100 to 144 characters in width. The most common width is the 132-character line. This requires that a 132-character record be transmitted from main memory to the printer. The programming mechanism is similar to that for a read—an SIO command is given to the computer, naming channel, control unit and device. Channel Command Words are used to designate the main memory bytes to be transmitted to the printer. Corresponding to scatter-read, there is *gather-write*, which allows any number of characters to be obtained from various parts of memory. The printing of a line is generally caused by vendor-furnished utility programs in the form of system subroutines.

As with other unit records, the character set is important. If you wish to print numeric characters only, for example, you may use a printer which operates at 600 lines a minute with only 13 characters available. For 39 characters, the speed is 300 lines per minute; for 63 characters on the same device, the speed is 200 lines per minute. Even larger sets are available, with correspondingly slower speeds.

☐ HOW THE CHAIN PRINTER OPERATES

While there have been many mechanisms developed for line printers, the most successful to date has been the chain printer. It combines speed and flexibility with excellent alignment. The chain consists of an endless metal belt with 240 characters embossed on it. Driven by two gears, it moves at very high speed. A control mechanism causes a metal hammer to push the paper against a selected character. There is a precise calculation which determines when the desired character on the chain will be passing the desired print position. This calculation is carried out automatically by the printer. There are 132 hammers, one for each print position.

The speed with which a line can be completely printed depends upon the number of times the character set is repeated on the chain. Now you see why the speed of printing varies with the size of the character set.

It is possible to have printers equipped with different chains. The chain mechanism is enclosed in a cartridge that can be substituted for another in only a few minutes.

In case you are trying to visualize a fast-moving typewriter ribbon to ink the original copy, that is *not* how ink is provided. There is a ribbon whose width is equal to that of a page; it moves vertically, as the paper moves (though at a much slower rate).

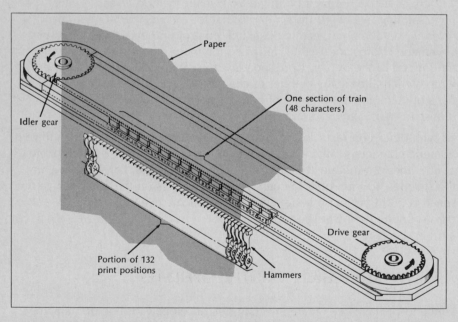

COMPLETE TRAIN COMPOSED OF 5 SECTIONS (80 TYPE SLUGS WITH 3 CHARACTERS PER SLUG).

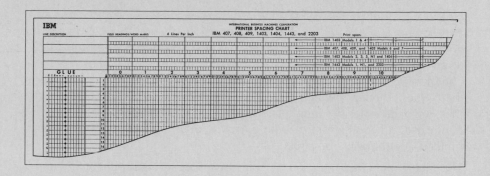

☐ FORM LAYOUT FOR PRINTING

Sooner or later, every computer user must lay out a printed output page. To help him, there is the Printer Spacing Chart. He first determines the width and length of the page and outlines it. Next he fills in titles and identifying information that will always be printed. Then he indicates the position of variable information with XXXX for letters and 000000 for numbers. Punctuation marks are supplied directly.

When the layout is complete, the programmer's task is reduced to developing the code on a line-by-line basis (since each unit record is one line). The user must also develop the controls for the interline spacing.

One topic covered here deals with special problems of blank spaces, zeros, dollar signs, and commas. If no special *editing* is performed, printouts might look like this:

```
CHARLES DAVIS          $00034543
DON JONES              $00000536
LESTER P. JONAS        $00198345
```

instead of the result of properly editing each line:

```
CHARLES DAVIS          $34,543
DON JONES                 $536
LESTER P. JONAS        $198,345
```

The three editing actions were (1) suppressing "leading zeros," (2) comma insertion, and (3) "floating" the dollar sign so it precedes the first nonzero (significant) character.

CARRIAGE CONTROL BY PAPER TAPE LOOP

As you can see, detailed attention to a single line is not enough to assure a good page layout. You must also control vertical skipping (one line at a time) and ejection. The most common way is by means of a short continuous paper tape loop that controls a special paper-positioning unit in the printer. The tape, which has 12 columns (channels), is made into a loop that is several times the length of the page whose vertical spacing is to be controlled. It is preperforated with a row of round holes in the center for pinfeed control of its movements.

The tape is punched with square holes by a special hand punch. Column 1 is used for top-of-the-page positioning and column 12 for bottom-of-the-page ejection. The vertical tape position corresponds to the point on the paper at which ejection takes place. The intermediate columns may be punched to indicate intermediate page positions. The paper tape is glued to form a loop; and whenever the desired page is printed, it is first threaded into the carriage control mechanism on the printer.

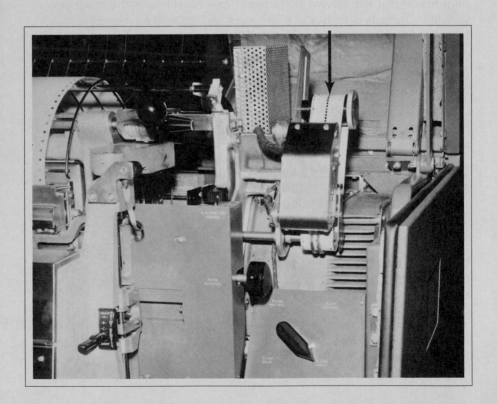

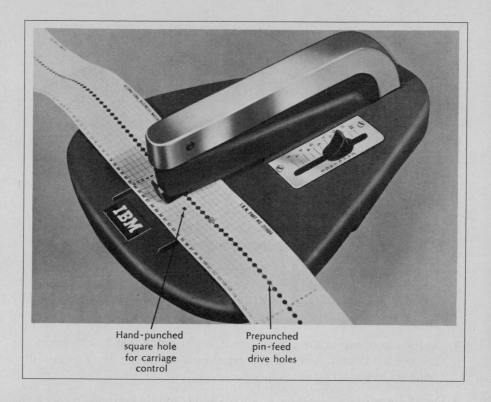

Hand-punched
square hole
for carriage
control

Prepunched
pin-feed
drive holes

In use, the programmer signals, for example, "skip to channel 5," to position the print line at the point where there is a square punch in column 5 of the paper tape.

In many printer systems, a special first character in the unit record is *not* printed. Instead, it acts as a skipping-control character and tells whether the printer should single-space or double-space after the line is printed. Incidentally, special attention must be paid to whether a skip takes place *before* or *after* the printing.

□ UNIT RECORD HANDLING

You should keep in mind that the programmer's responsibility includes not only his program, but all forms of unit records that bring information to and from his program. Card layout, printer control, etc., are detailed tasks that, while different from coding itself, require neatness and attention to detail.

Remember that cards must be punched by *people* and printouts read by *people*. Therefore it is up to the programmer to see that data are presented in easy-to-keypunch form, and that results are printed in clear layouts which are easy to read and understand.

☐ QUESTIONS

1 A defective card reader is unable to read holes punched in position number 11. How will it read the name "JOHN SMITH" from a punched card?

2 Get an unpunched card or make a sketch of one and mark it to represent your name and address with the appropriate punches.

3 Discuss the pros and cons of card verification. Does verifying guarantee error-free cards? Would double-verifying guarantee this? Can verifying increase the number of errors? Under what conditions would verifying be unjustified?

4 In the discussion of the printed line, the text stated that 13 characters are needed to print numeric characters only. What are the 3 needed in addition to the 10 decimal digits?

5 In all cases of card reading, card punching, and line printing devices, the higher-speed models are the more expensive. What considerations would lead a user to want the higher-priced models?

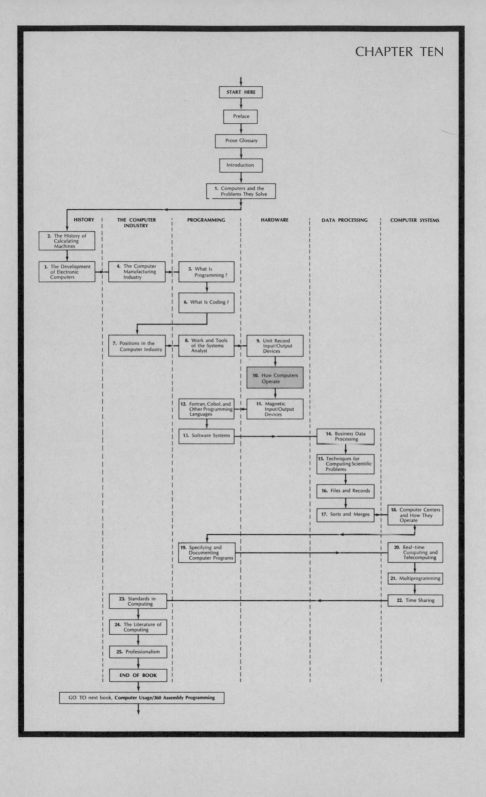

CHAPTER TEN

HOW COMPUTERS OPERATE

This chapter will give you your first explanation of how a computer is able to carry out its function. While it is not necessary for a programmer or a user to become involved with the actual equipment (often called the hardware), it is worthwhile to have some idea of the basic design principles and the methods by which these principles are converted to functioning electronic or magnetic devices. In this chapter we will cover the following subjects:

1   How the computer uses the binary system to represent numbers
2   How the binary number system works
3   How main memory uses magnetic cores for storage
4   How main-memory addresses activate the specified magnetic cores
5   How instructions are decoded and carried out
6   How computer circuits are fabricated
7   How numbers are added using electronic circuits
8   How negative numbers are represented and manipulated

The material covered in items 1, 2, and 8, although descriptive of the hardware, is *essential* to your learning to program. Items 3 through 7, while not as vital for programmers and users, are *important* for understanding general concepts of cost, size, etc.

The descriptions that follow are general and apply to a number of today's computers, including the IBM System/360.

□ THE DECIMAL SYSTEM

The familiar numbers we use—0, 1, 2, 3, 4, 5, 6, 7, 8, 9—are what we call the *decimal* system, because it uses *ten* different numbers. Do not confuse the decimal system with the "decimal point"—that's another story. But with the decimal system, we can represent any value, no matter how large, with only ten different numbers. We do this by using what is called "positional notation." That is, when we write a numerical value that has more than one digit in it, we automatically assign different values to the digits depending on their *position*.

What do we mean by this set of four digits?

1969

We do not mean $1 + 9 + 6 + 9 = 25$. Instead we mean one thousand plus nine hundred plus sixty-nine. (We even say it this way: "One thousand, nine hundred, and sixty-nine.")

$$
\begin{array}{cccc}
1 & 9 & 6 & 9 \\
\| & \| & \| & \| \\
1,000 + & 900 + & 60 + & 9
\end{array}
$$

In other words, we follow a convention that the rightmost digit is taken at its ordinary value, the next digit to the left is to be considered as multiplied by ten, the next digit to the left is to be considered as multiplied by one hundred, the next digit to the left is to be considered as multiplied by one thousand, and so on. As we move to the left in the row of digits, each one is taken to be multiplied by ten times the multiplier of the previous digit, and then the whole thing is added together.

This is a convenient scheme, but the decimal system is not by any means the only possible number system. There is actually an infinity of possible number systems using positional notation. The one we choose to employ in a particular case will sometimes be determined by tradition and sometimes by the ease with which we or our equipment can use it.

The different number systems are distinguished by the multipliers used to multiply the values written in the different positions. Thus the decimal system multiplied the rightmost digit by 1, the next digit to the left by 10, the next digit to the left by 10 times 10, the next digit to the left by 10 times 10 times 10, and so on. That is, the decimal system is based on the multiplier 10. It is said to be a number system to the base 10.

If we were to think of a number system to the base 2, we would use a positional notation in which the rightmost digit was taken at its face value, the next digit multiplied by 2, the next digit multiplied by 2 times 2, the next digit multiplied by 2 times 2 times 2, and so on. Such a number system is called the binary number system.

☐ THE BINARY SYSTEM

The decimal system is fine for pencil-and-paper arithmetic and for mechanical calculators. But it's difficult and wastefully expensive to construct an electronic computer using purely decimal devices. Mechanical desk-top calculators use slow-speed components that can easily switch to ten different states, but such calculators can never match the speed of all-electronic computers.

High-speed computers rely on electronic devices, such as the transistor and the magnetic core. No electronic device can reliably assume ten different states, such as *off, a little on, a little more on, slightly more on,* up to *fully on.* It's much better to use *fully off* and *fully on,* as with a switch or an electric light.

A lamp has two states, off and on. With one lamp, the *off* and *on* states can be used to represent *zero* and *one.* With two lamps, there are four states: both off, one off and one on, the other off and the first one on, and both on. Thus two lamps can represent 0, 1, 2, and 3.

Using 0 to indicate a lamp off and 1 to indicate a lamp on, these four states of two lamps are:

00
01
10
11

With three lamps, 8 states are possible:

LAMP			
A	B	C	COUNT
0	0	0	0
0	0	1	1
0	1	0	2
0	1	1	3
1	0	0	4
1	0	1	5
1	1	0	6
1	1	1	7

On   Off   On

THREE LAMPS REPRESENTING THE NUMBER 5.

If you apply the rules given for the binary system to the entries in the above lamp table, you will see that the decimal numbers listed in the column headed "Count" are represented in binary notation in the entries in the columns headed "Lamp." Look at the line with the count of 5. The binary number entry is 101. We take the rightmost digit at its face value, 1, add it to the next digit, 0, multiplied by 2, and add that to the next digit, 1, multiplied by 2 times 2. This gives us a total of 5.

Put in other terms, in the lamp example, lamp C has (when lit) a value of 1, lamp B has (when lit) a value of 2, and lamp A has (when lit) a value of 2 times 2, or 4. Any lamp has a value of 0 when it is not lit.

Here is the same table rewritten with the multipliers expressed at the tops of the columns.

LAMP			
A	B	C	COUNT
×4	×2	×1	
0	0	0	0
0	0	1	1
0	1	0	2
0	1	1	3
1	0	0	4
1	0	1	5
1	1	0	6
1	1	1	7

Examine the table and check all the values to make sure you understand how the binary system works.

As binary numbers get larger it is necessary to use multipliers, such as 2 times 2 times 2 times 2 times 2, and so on at great length. Mathematicians have a shorthand notation for such expressions. The shorthand involves the use of exponents: smaller numbers written above and to the right of the base number. Thus 2 times 2 is written as 2^2, and 2 times 2 times 2 times 2 is written as 2^4. 2^2 is pronounced "two to the power two" or "two squared." 2^3 is pronounced "two to the power three" or "two cubed." 2^4 is pronounced "two to the power four" or "two to the fourth power." "Two to the power one," 2^1, is just 2 itself, and for reasons of consistency in certain rules relating to powers and exponents, "two to the power zero," 2^0, is 1. [In fact, any number raised to the power 0 is 1, and any number raised to the power 1 is the number itself. That is, $(5,607,899)^0 = 1$ and $(5,607,899)^1 = 5,607,899$.]

To express all this in a table, we write:

$$2^0 \qquad\qquad\qquad\qquad\qquad\qquad\qquad\qquad\qquad = \quad 1$$
$$2^1 = 2 \qquad\qquad\qquad\qquad\qquad\qquad\qquad\qquad = \quad 2$$
$$2^2 = 2 \times 2 \qquad\qquad\qquad\qquad\qquad\qquad\qquad = \quad 4$$
$$2^3 = 2 \times 2 \times 2 \qquad\qquad\qquad\qquad\qquad\qquad = \quad 8$$
$$2^4 = 2 \times 2 \times 2 \times 2 \qquad\qquad\qquad\qquad\qquad = \quad 16$$
$$2^5 = 2 \times 2 \times 2 \times 2 \times 2 \qquad\qquad\qquad\qquad = \quad 32$$
$$2^6 = 2 \times 2 \times 2 \times 2 \times 2 \times 2 \qquad\qquad\qquad = \quad 64$$
$$2^7 = 2 \times 2 \times 2 \times 2 \times 2 \times 2 \times 2 \qquad\qquad = \quad 128$$
$$2^8 = 2 \times 2 \times 2 \times 2 \times 2 \times 2 \times 2 \times 2 \qquad = \quad 256$$
$$2^9 = 2 \times 2 \times 2 \times 2 \times 2 \times 2 \times 2 \times 2 \times 2 \quad = \quad 512$$
$$2^{10} = 2 \times 2 \times 2 \times 2 \times 2 \times 2 \times 2 \times 2 \times 2 \times 2 = 1024$$

Now that we understand exponents and powers, we can express our notions about binary notation more compactly. The rightmost digit in a binary number is taken to be multiplied by 2 to the power 0, and the digit in each successive position to the left is taken to be multiplied by 2 to successively higher powers.

Now consider a longer binary number: 11110110001.

$$
\begin{aligned}
10000000000 &= 1 \times 2^{10} = 1 \times 1024 = \quad 1024 \\
01000000000 &= 1 \times 2^9 \ = 1 \times \ \ 512 = \quad 512 \\
00100000000 &= 1 \times 2^8 \ = 1 \times \ \ 256 = \quad 256 \\
00010000000 &= 1 \times 2^7 \ = 1 \times \ \ 128 = \quad 128 \\
00000000000 &= 0 \times 2^6 \ = 0 \times \ \ \ \ 64 = \quad \ \ \ 0 \\
00000100000 &= 1 \times 2^5 \ = 1 \times \ \ \ \ 32 = \quad \ \ 32 \\
00000010000 &= 1 \times 2^4 \ = 1 \times \ \ \ \ 16 = \quad \ \ 16 \\
00000000000 &= 0 \times 2^3 \ = 0 \times \ \ \ \ \ \ 8 = \quad \ \ \ 0 \\
00000000000 &= 0 \times 2^2 \ = 0 \times \ \ \ \ \ \ 4 = \quad \ \ \ 0 \\
00000000000 &= 0 \times 2^1 \ = 0 \times \ \ \ \ \ \ 2 = \quad \ \ \ 0 \\
-00000000001 &= 1 \times 2^0 \ = 1 \times \ \ \ \ \ \ 1 = + \ \ \ 1 \\
\hline
11110110001 &= \qquad\qquad\qquad\qquad\qquad\qquad 1969
\end{aligned}
$$

Or, more simply, sum the powers of 2 that correspond to ones and ignore those that correspond to zeros:

1024	512	256	128	64	32	16	8	4	2	1
1	1	1	1	0	1	1	0	0	0	1

$$1024 + 512 + 256 + 128 + \ 32 + 16 \ + \ \ 1 = 1969$$

☐ HOW MAGNETIC-CORE MEMORIES WORK

Computer memories consisting of hundreds of thousands of magnetic cores provide the best way, at present, of storing a great many bits in very little space, and with a minimum *access time*. In a core memory, any bit may be accessed in 1 to 4 millionths of a second (called *microseconds*). The cores used in modern computer memories are no bigger than the head of a pin; over 2,000 of them will fit in a cubic inch, along with all the wires necessary to put information into the cores and to take it out.

The cores are strung on wires to form *core planes,* which are stacked up to form a *core stack*.

Ordinary iron becomes temporarily magnetized while subjected to a magnetic field, and loses all but a tiny amount of the magnetization when

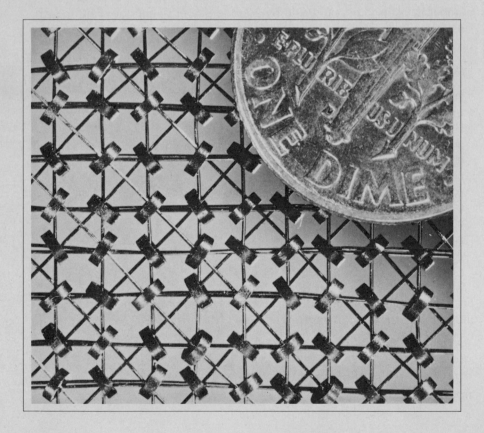

the field is removed. Memory cores, molded from special metallic powders, are designed to retain the maximum magnetization, so that even if the computer is turned off, the core memory will still keep its pattern of zeros and ones.

Just as an iron bar can be magnetized in one of two directions, north-south or south-north, a memory core can be magnetized in a clockwise or a counterclockwise direction, depending on the direction of the magnetizing current. Either direction can be called a zero or a one, depending on the designer's choice. The magnetic core is inherently stable; that is, once magnetized in one direction, it will retain its magnetism indefinitely, unless deliberately changed.

MACHINE ADDRESSES

You learned in Chapter 6 that, as a programmer, you give symbolic names to main-memory addresses. The assembly program converts these symbolic addresses to *machine address*. With the instruction ST 6,DATA, for example, you place the contents of register 6 into main-memory location DATA. The assembler will assign to DATA a machine address: for example, 01110101011010. That machine address will determine where in main memory are the 32 cores that will be magnetized in one direction or the other upon receiving the contents of register 6.

The computer separates the machine address into three parts. One part determines which core "stack" will be used for storage. The other two parts determine which vertical string of 8 cores in that stack will be addressed. (For simplicity's sake, we will discuss only 8 of the 32 cores involved; that is, 1 byte of the 4 bytes in the full word.) The figure on page 170 shows cores representing three different bytes.

Assume the computer has *four* stacks of cores, each of which can hold 4,096 eight-bit bytes. Only two bits are required to determine which stack is to be addressed, because there are four ways of arranging two bits: 00, 01, 10 and 11. So 10 could be used for the address of the third stack.

Now that the proper stack is located, 8 cores must be located out of the 4,096 strings of 8 cores in the stack. Consider only the top layer or plane in the stack, remembering that there are 8 planes altogether. Any core in this top plane is the first core in the string of 8 that are in a row beneath it, down through all the planes.

Each plane of cores in the stack contains 4,096 cores: 64 in what is called the X direction, 64 in the Y direction. The top core of the desired core string is at the intersection of one of the 64 X columns and one of the 64 Y rows.

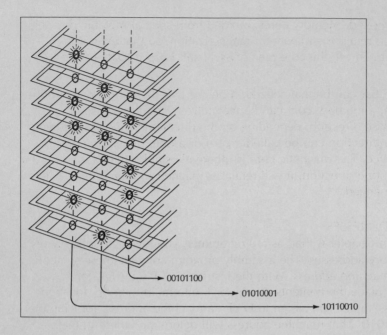

THE SELECTION MATRIX

To select one of either the 64 rows or 64 columns, we use a *selection matrix*. This is an electronic circuit that contains a waffle-like grid of 64 locations, 8 by 8, that determine which of the 64 lines to the memory plane is to be activated. For the X direction, just which of the 64 lines is to be activated is determined by which of the 8 X selectors and which of the 8 Y drivers are activated. To select one of the 8 X or Y selectors or drivers takes three bits, because there are 8 possible combinations of three bits (as shown in the lamp example).

Look again at the main-memory machine address, 01110101011010. The first two bits (01) determined which stack will be addressed. The remaining 12 bits will be used in groups of three (110-101-011-010) to activate X and Y drivers and selectors. The first three bits activate line 7 in the Y selector; the second three activate line 6 in the Y driver. This combination activates line 42 in the Y selection matrix. The third group of these bits activates line 4 in the X driver circuit; the fourth group activates line 3 in the X selector.

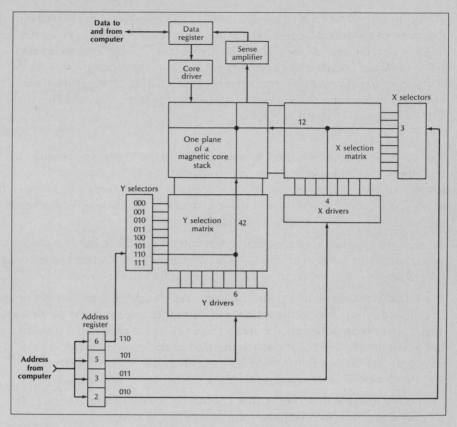

HOW 110 101 011 010 SELECTS ONE MAGNETIC CORE IN A PLANE.

This combination activates line 12 in the X selection matrix. Then X-line 12 and Y-line 42 determine just one of the 4,096 cores in the memory plane.

STORING DATA
Now that the desired core string has been located, the next step is to load it with data. Assume, for the examples to follow, that the clockwise magnetization is 1. The data to be entered into main memory are stored momentarily in an 8-bit data register. When the data are to be stored in the core stack, the X and Y lines send to the 8 cores the current required to magnetize all 8 in the 1 direction (clockwise).

The X lines send half the required current, the Y lines send the other half, so that only the 8 selected cores, where the X and Y lines cross, receive the full magnetizing current. At the same time, the 8 core drivers send an inhibit pulse (a strong counterclockwise current) to those cores that must remain a 0, in order to prevent them from assuming the clockwise magnetization. Thus, the 8 cores are magnetized in the desired pattern of 1s and 0s.

FETCHING DATA

The same basic system is used to read data from the cores. The 8 sense amplifiers, used only for readout, are connected to all the cores in their respective planes. But because of the selection matrices, only one string of 8 cores has its contents read out of main memory. Each sense amplifier reads the contents of only one core in its plane.

To read information from magnetic-core memory, use is made of a *sense wire* that passes through *all* the cores in one plane. Information is then read by pulsing the selected 8 cores with a counterclockwise current.

If a 1 had been stored in a particular core, the change of direction of current in that core, from 1 to 0, causes a small current to appear in the sense wire. This current is amplified by the sense amplifier. If the core had a 0 in it to begin with (meaning that it was magnetized in the counterclockwise direction), no current flow would be induced in the sense wire by a counterclockwise readout current.

Obviously, pulsing the cores with a counterclockwise current results in their all containing 0s, destroying the information that was stored in them. Therefore, to *retain* a given bit of information in core memory, other circuits must be used to read the information back into the cores. This "read in after read out" is performed automatically by main memory.

☐ INSTRUCTION DECODING

When you instruct System/360 to store, you simply use an instruction such as ST, as described in Chapter 6. What happens to that instruction inside the computer, however, is not so simple, although it is entirely automatic.

First, the instruction is translated into binary code. The ST instruction's code is 01010000. All System/360 instructions can be represented by an eight-bit code. There are 256 combinations of eight bits, more than enough for the 141 instructions available in System/360.

An instruction register decodes the instruction into binary code, and sends out electronic signals to activate the various parts of the computer that are involved in that particular instruction. The ST 6,DATA instruction permits the contents of general register 6 to be read out, sent to main memory, and stored in location DATA—the symbolic address that the assembly program has converted to machine address 01110101011010, in the example earlier.

The binary codes for instructions are called operation codes. Here are the operation codes for the other instructions dealt with in Chapter 6. All the 141 operation codes in System/360 are carefully constructed and arranged in groups that have similar characteristics.

LR	00011000
AR	00011010
SR	00011011
A	01011010
S	01011011

Look at these binary operation codes. The first two bits tell you the basic format: 00 for the RR (register-to-register) format; 01 for RX (register-to-main memory) format. The second two bits, 01 in all these examples, tell you that these are full-word instructions. The third pair of bits, 10, indicates that an arithmetic-type operation is involved. The last pair of bits tells, in these five examples, what operation it is: 00 for load, 10 for add, 11 for subtract. (01 for compare is used in other instructions.)

The ST code is 01010000. The first two bits indicate that this is an RX format, the second two that it is a full-word instruction. In the RX format, all operation codes ending in 0000 are "store" instructions.

☐ COMPUTER CIRCUITS

In Chapter 2 you learned that the first computers were electromechanical. They used relays about the size of your hand, and stepping switches about twice the size of your fist. They were not much faster than modern desk calculators and took up quite a lot of space.

Then came the vacuum tube, tried and tested in radio circuits for several decades previously. Although the vacuum tubes were smaller than relays (about the size of your thumb in the latter stages of development), they still took up a lot of space and they gave off a lot of heat. Nearly all vacuum tube computers, with their thousands of tubes, required special, expensive air conditioning to carry off the immense amount of heat generated.

Then came the transistor, which gave off no heat and was the size of a couple of aspirin tablets, permitting the central processing units of computers to be made as small as a file drawer.

In System/360 circuits, the transistors are very small, only 28/1,000 inch square. These transistors are mounted on ceramic modules about ¾ inch square. The circuit pattern has been printed on the modules with metallic inks, to provide resistors and certain other components as well as interconnecting wiring. An automatic assembly line puts these circuits together and tests them.

A protective coating of plastic is then placed around each completed module, which is mounted with other modules on a small plastic board. Hundreds of these module boards are mounted in racks and wired together to form registers, arithmetic circuits, logic circuits, and all the many other subsystems which make up System/360. The circuit boards are the basic "building blocks" of System/360, each consisting of a dozen or so microelectronic circuit modules known as Solid Logic Technology (SLT) modules.

THE FLIP-FLOP (THE BASIC TWO-STATE DEVICE)
Magnetic cores for main memory cost a few cents each. The SLT modules used for general purpose registers cost several dollars each. As was stated in Chapter 6, register storage is much more expensive than main-memory storage. This is why computer designers allow for relatively few registers.

The basic circuit for general purpose registers, and for any registers in a

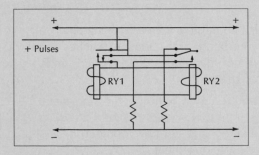

RELAY FLIP-FLOP.

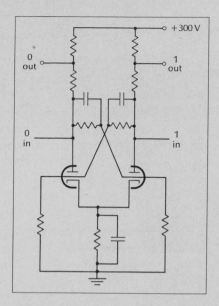

VACUUM-TUBE FLIP-FLOP.

computer, is a two-state device usually known as a *flip-flop*. As the name indicates, it is either on or off. The flip-flop stays on or off until it is made to change to the other state, in which it stays until again made to change. The basic flip-flop is constructed of two transistors (or two vacuum tubes in the previous generation of computers), along with resistors, capacitors, and diodes that form the flip-flop circuit.

Those who understand electronics will realize that the pair of relays are connected as a counter circuit, which changes state with every input pulse: on-off-on-off, etc. The vacuum-tube and transistor circuits are both set-reset flip-flops, as used in shift registers. Each requires a 1 pulse at the "1 IN" input to turn it on and another 1 pulse (perhaps from another source) at the "0 IN" input to turn it off. If the 1 IN and 0 IN inputs are connected, the circuit becomes a counter, with one input pulse turning the counter on, the next turning it off, then on, etc.

ELECTRONIC REGISTERS

In a simple register, flip-flops are connected in series, as many flip-flops as there are bits in the word to be stored in the register. The register can be

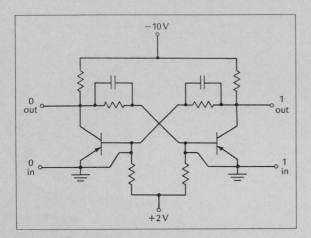

TRANSISTOR FLIP-FLOP

loaded in two ways: in serial or in parallel, and unloaded in serial or in parallel. (As constructed, they usually are loaded in serial and unloaded in parallel, or vice versa; registers are seldom built with all four capabilities.)

In serial loading, the data to be stored passes into the register "in single file," bit by bit, until the register is loaded. It can then be read out the same way, bit by bit, or the bits can all be unloaded at one time, in parallel. The bits could also have been all loaded at one time, in parallel. Whether loading and unloading is done in serial or parallel depends upon the nature of the circuit or device from or to which the information is being transmitted.

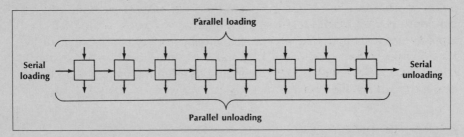

FLIP-FLOP SHIFT REGISTER.

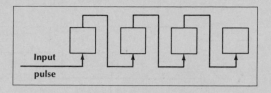

COUNTER.

COUNTERS AND ADDERS

Flip-flops can also be connected together to form a *counter* adding a 1 every time the counter receives a 1 in the form of an electronic pulse. And they can be used to provide input for an *adder*, which adds together long strings of binary bits. There are both serial and parallel adders, depending on whether the bits of the two data words are to be added together pair by pair, or all pairs together at once.

An adder would be a simple device if there were no such thing as a carry. A carry results when the capacity of a counter is exceeded. When 1110 is added to 0011, the sum is 10001. The counter then contains 0001 and there is a 1 carry.

Because of the carry, all sorts of problems arise. For instance, if a counter contains a long string of 1s and a 1 is added, every single flip-flop will change from 1 to 0, right down the line like a row of dominos falling, each one knocking down the next. The time required for this "ripple-through" can be excessive when the counter is a long one and high speed essential.

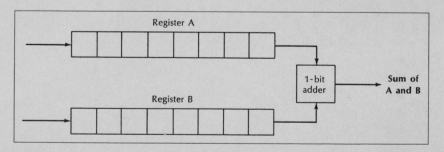

SERIAL ADDER.

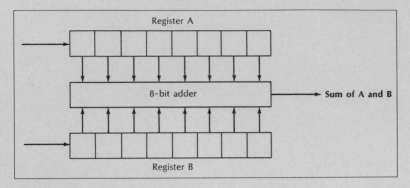

PARALLEL ADDER.

Modern computers contain counters so designed as to avoid the problem of ripple-through, when 1 is added and the counters go

from 0111111111111111111111111
to 1000000000000000000000000.

The arithmetic required to operate an adder is simple: $0+1=1$; $1+1=10$. If that second addition seems odd, think of it in decimal: $1+1=2$. A decimal 2 is equal to a binary 10.

Eight different input situations can occur in an adder, depending on whether the "A" input is a 0 or 1, whether the "B" input is a 0 or 1, and whether the carry from the previous "column" is a 0 or 1. Here is a table of all eight, calling the carry from the previous flip-flop a "carry in" (CI) and a carry to the next higher flip-flop a "carry out" (CO):

A	B	CI	CO	SUM
0	0	0	0	0
0	0	1	0	1
0	1	0	0	1
0	1	1	1	0
1	0	0	0	1
1	0	1	1	0
1	1	0	1	0
1	1	1	1	1

Although this may seem complicated, it's all based on the two simple rules for binary addition, and the fact that $A+B+CI=CO+Sum$. For instance, the last case says that 1+1+1=11. In decimal counting, 1+1+1=3. Three in binary is 11. Think of that addition as 1+1=10; 10+1=11.

☐ COMPLEMENT ARITHMETIC

You've learned how computers perform addition. Subtraction is performed by most computers, including System/360, by *complement* addition. The complement of a one-digit number is found by subtracting that number from ten. The "tens complement" of "true number" 3 is 7. Also, the complement of 7 is 3. Extending this principle to larger numbers, the tens complement of 45 is 55 (100—45), and the tens complement of 465 is 535 (1000—465).

To subtract one number from another, find its complement, add it to the other, and discard the carry from the highest order.

To subtract decimal 456 from 847, you do it this way:

$$
\begin{array}{r}
847 \\
-456 \\
\hline
391
\end{array}
$$

A decimal computer would do it this way:

$$
\begin{array}{r}
847 \\
+544 \quad \text{(complement of 456)} \\
\end{array}
$$

discard ①   391

Binary subtraction works the same way. Simplified, the rule is: *invert each binary digit* (inverting a 1 gives 0; inverting a 0 gives 1) *and add 1.* Thus, the complement of 110 is 010 (inverting 110 gives 001, adding 1 gives 010). To subtract 0110 from 1011, complement the 0110 to 1010 and proceed·

$$
\begin{array}{r}
1011 \\
+1010 \\
\end{array}
$$

discard ①   0101

Note that the process of inverting each binary digit and the adding 1 gives the same result as if you subtracted the number from 10000:

0110	invert	1001	10000
		+ 1	− 0110
		1010	1010

This is the "twos complement," which is the binary equivalent of the decimal "tens complement."

□ QUESTIONS

1   What are the decimal equivalents of the following binary numbers: 11001, 11111, 00011111, 10101010, 10000001?

2   To convert decimal numbers to binary, you divide by 2 repeatedly and use the *remainder* resulting from each division (it will always be 1 or 0) to build up the binary number from the right.

Convert the decimal number 161 to binary:

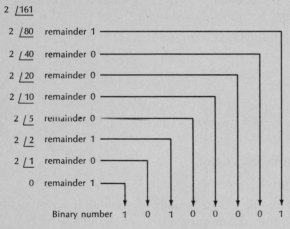

```
2 /161
  2 /80    remainder 1
  2 /40    remainder 0
  2 /20    remainder 0
  2 /10    remainder 0
   2 /5    remainder 0
   2 /2    remainder 1
   2 /1    remainder 0
     0     remainder 1

Binary number   1   0   1   0   0   0   0   1
```

Now check this by converting it back to decimal:

$$1 \quad 0 \quad 1 \quad 0 \quad 0 \quad 0 \quad 0 \quad 1$$
$$128 + 0 + 32 + 0 + 0 + 0 + 0 + 1 = 161$$

Using this technique, convert the following decimal numbers to binary: 20, 444, 1489, 1111, 2047.

3   What is the tens complement of 1969, 1000, 89, 9, 0?

4   What is the tens complement of each of these complements?

5   What is the twos complement of the following binary numbers: 10011, 11111, 10000, 101110111101?

6   What is the twos complement of each of these complements?

7   Convert all the decimal numbers and complements of question 3 to binary. Is there any obvious relationship between the binary number that represents a decimal number and the binary number that represents its complement?

8   Convert all the binary numbers and complements of question 5 to decimal. Any relationship?

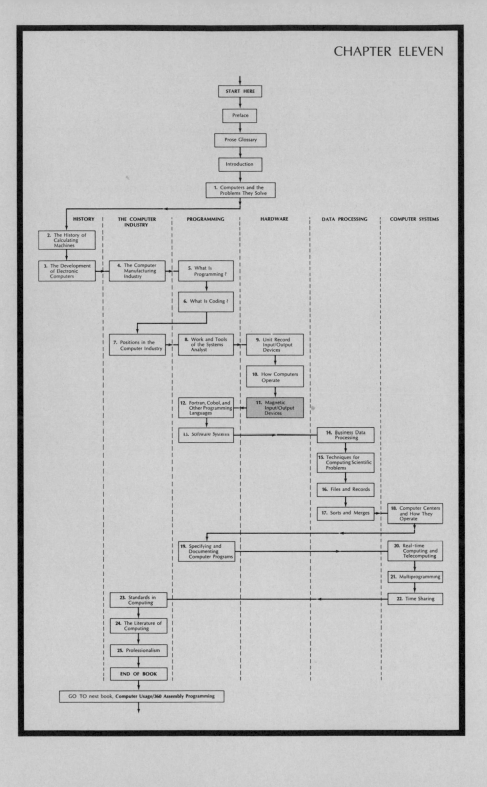

START HERE

Preface

Prose Glossary

Introduction

1. Computers and the Problems They Solve

HISTORY | THE COMPUTER INDUSTRY | PROGRAMMING | HARDWARE | DATA PROCESSING | COMPUTER SYSTEMS

2. The History of Calculating Machines

3. The Development of Electronic Computers

4. The Computer Manufacturing Industry

5. What Is Programming?

6. What Is Coding?

7. Positions in the Computer Industry

8. Work and Tools of the Systems Analyst

9. Unit Record Input/Output Devices

10. How Computers Operate

11. Magnetic Input/Output Devices

12. Fortran, Cobol, and Other Programming Languages

13. Software Systems

14. Business Data Processing

15. Techniques for Computing Scientific Problems

16. Files and Records

17. Sorts and Merges

18. Computer Centers and How They Operate

19. Specifying and Documenting Computer Programs

20. Real-time Computing and Telecomputing

21. Multiprogramming

23. Standards in Computing

22. Time Sharing

24. The Literature of Computing

25. Professionalism

END OF BOOK

GO TO next book, **Computer Usage/360 Assembly Programming**

MAGNETIC
INPUT/OUTPUT
DEVICES

Memory requirements of the computer are largely responsible for the use of binary rather than decimal arithmetic. As explained in Chapter 10, the circuits designed to perform arithmetic operations using binary numbers are simpler than those which would be required for decimal arithmetic because only two conditions, rather than ten, are represented. Likewise, the storage of binary numbers is simpler because any on-off device can be held in either one of its two stable states to indicate the 1 or 0 condition of the bit represented.

Of the many proposed types of storage devices that have undergone extensive study for use in the memory section of computers in recent years, few have emerged as being practical. The most commonly used storage devices over the years have been magnetic cores, electrostatic tubes, magnetic drums, magnetic tapes, acoustic delay lines, magnetic discs, magnetic cards, and thin films. We will be concerned here with all but electrostatic tubes and acoustic delay lines, which are no longer used.

A short review of the principle involved in representing on-off conditions using magnetic devices may be of value here. Let the magnetized condition of the material (or any small portion of it) represent the 1 condition, and the nonmagnetized or demagnetized portions represent the 0 condition. In the case of magnetic cores, each core is small and the entire core is magnetized in one direction to represent a 1 state and in the opposite direction to represent the 0 state. Magnetic drums and tapes (as well as magnetic discs, cards, and thin films) represent data as small magnetized or nonmagnetized areas indicating 1s and 0s; or areas of one polarity for 1s and of the opposite polarity for 0s on the surface of the device. Review Chapter 10 for further details.

□ ACCESS TIME AND CAPACITY

Three terms are commonly used to describe any storage device. These are *access time* (how fast data can be extracted from the storage device), *capacity* (the amount of data that can be stored), and *transfer rate* (how fast data can be read from one place and stored in another place). The *form* of the stored data can be considered as a fourth factor involved in the description.

In magnetic storage devices associated with digital computers, magnetic fields are used to represent binary 1s and 0s, with pulses of electric current being translated into static magnetic states and vice versa, so that data can be transferred between the storage device and the computer.

Access time is determined by the nature of the device. In certain devices, such as magnetic cores, equal amounts of time are required to read out any group of stored bits. A core storage system is thus a device with random access. Any core can be selected at random, and the desired location made available, in about 1 to 2 microseconds. (A microsecond is a millionth of a second.)

When magnetic tapes, drums, discs, and strips are used, a fixed amount of time is required to read or write on the surface. However, there is a second and variable amount of time required to position the desired material under the read-write head. A saying among computer engineers goes: "You always know where your desired data is—it has just passed under the head." This means you have to wait for the next complete cycle of surface travel (say, for a drum to make a full turn) in order for the desired data to return to the reading position under the head.

Surface storage devices (tapes, drums, discs, and strips) are non-random access devices. That is, the access time for a piece of data depends on where it is located on the surface. The access times given for these devices are average access times and are often equal to half of the maximum possible access time. For example, if a magnetic drum is driven at 12,000 rpm (revolutions per minute), any particular spot on the drum will come under the read-write head once every $1/_{200}$ second, or every 5 milliseconds. This is the *maximum* access time, occurring when the desired data have just passed under the head. *Minimum* access time, which is nearly zero, occurs when the desired data are just in the right position, approaching the head. The average access time, then, is 2.5 milliseconds. The same considerations apply to magnetic discs, tapes, and strips.

The access time for a magnetic-core memory, if taken as 1.5 microseconds, is 5,000 times faster than the average access time for a small disc or drum, which is 3 times faster than for a large (greater than 50 million bits) disc file, which in turn is more than 600 times faster than for magnetic tape.

☐ MAGNETIC CORES

Most magnetic cores used in computers are called "ferrite" cores. They are made by molding finely ground ferrite (a ceramic iron oxide possessing magnetic properties), into a toroidal (doughnut-shaped) form. The ferrite particles are then heat-fused or "sintered" by the application of heat and pressure.

A representative magnetic core has an outside diameter of $1/_{20}$ inch, which is 0.050 inch; an inside diameter of 0.030 inch; and a thickness of 0.015 inch. The ferrite core is magnetized by the field produced by an electric current flowing in a wire threaded through the core. (See Chapter 10.) A representative core is switched from one state to the other in about 1.5 microseconds.

☐ TERMINOLOGY

Magnetic cores provide high-speed random access *nonvolatile* storage. A storage component is considered nonvolatile if it retains its binary state when all power is removed from the equipment. The term *high-speed memory* is defined relative to the time required to gain access to data in memory when other types of storage elements such as magnetic drums or tapes are used. It may be defined in terms of the shortest access time of two or more systems that use the same type of storage element. In all cases, the term "high-speed" is relative.

☐ THIN FILMS

The essential requirement of a material for a random access magnetic memory is a magnetic characteristic that allows a single element of a large array of elements of the material to be stably magnetized in either of two directions. Certain thin metallic films also have this characteristic.

Thin-film computer memory consists of a series of metal dots, a few millionths of an inch thick, made by depositing vapors of iron, nickel, cobalt, or other ferromagnetic metals or their alloys on a suitable base, such as a thin glass plate. Many types of thin-film memories have been devised, including flat films and films deposited on wires or glass rods. Some film memories are in service and many more will be used in the future.

☐ MAGNETIC DRUMS

Magnetic drums provide a relatively inexpensive method of storing large amounts of data. A magnetic drum can be made by using either a hollow cylinder (thus the name "drum") or a solid cylinder. Most drums are made by spraying on a thin layer of iron oxide. The surface is covered with a thin coat of lacquer and is then buffed.

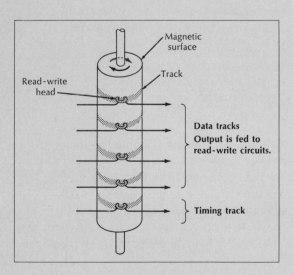

A representative drum has a diameter of 5 to 20 inches. The surface of the drum is divided into tracks or channels which encircle the drum. A number of read-write heads are used for recording and reading. Usually there is a head for every track, and the heads are fixed in position. In some devices there are several fixed heads aligned with a single track, and in some devices several tracks share a single head which is automatically moved from one track to the other. The drum is rotated so that the heads are near— but not touching—the drum surface at all times.

Large drums are driven more slowly than smaller ones. Driving speeds range between 120 and 20,000 rpm. Some drums weigh about 50 pounds, while others weigh well over 500 pounds. The access time decreases as the speed of the drum increases.

READ-WRITE HEADS

The read-write heads are placed about 0.002 inch from the surface of the drum. This spacing is critical; much more so than for the magnetic heads used for sound recording.

Spacing changes, such as those caused by drum wobble, cause variations in the strength of magnetic field recorded or read. This can produce faulty data and lead to a variety of complications. To avoid this, the space between the drum and the read-write heads must be kept constant. Thus, the drum must be perfectly balanced and the bearings must permit very little wobble. Computer installations using magnetic drums are usually air-conditioned, so that temperature changes will not cause the drum to expand and make contact with the read-write heads. Contact will groove the drum and ruin it.

During the write process, current pulses through wires wound around the pole piece in the read-write head induce small magnetic fields on the drum surface within the associated track. Each of these magnetized areas is called a "cell" and is capable of storing either a 1 or 0 state. The direction of current in the drive coil determines the polarity of the induced magnetic field. The current pulses are always the same size, so the magnetic fields are always the same size.

Each read-write head is connected in a separate circuit, so that read or write operations can take place on any or all tracks simultaneously. The data that appear under all heads at the same time form a "slot."

In some machines, the magnetized spots may represent 1s and the unmagnetized spots 0s. In other machines, 1s and 0s are represented as

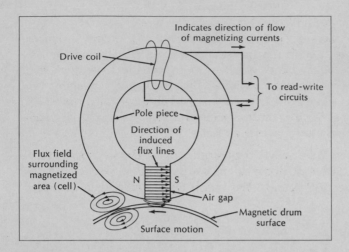

magnetized spots of opposite polarity. The convention chosen is set by machine design and is always the same for any given computer type.

ADDRESSING

A timing track on the drum contains a series of permanently recorded timing signals used to locate any drum slot. The timing tracks are used for synchronization, and are sometimes called control or clock tracks. Some drums have two or even three timing tracks.

In older magnetic drum memories, data locations are addressed individually by track and by location on that track. For instance, a drum address might be 0134. This would activate the read head for track 01, and when bit 34 on the timing track came under the timing head, the data in location 34 on track 01 would be read out.

Because of the problem of long access time with such a system, ways were sought to reduce access time. One way is to place separate read-write heads at intervals around each track. In such cases, a writing head records data on the drum, and a fraction of a revolution later, when the data move in under the reading head, the data are read and returned to the previous writing head. This combination of a writing head, a short space on the drum, and a reading head connected back to the writing head, makes a "revolver loop." All data in the loop are read continuously as the drum revolves and can be sent off for processing if desired. Some drums have several revolver loops to

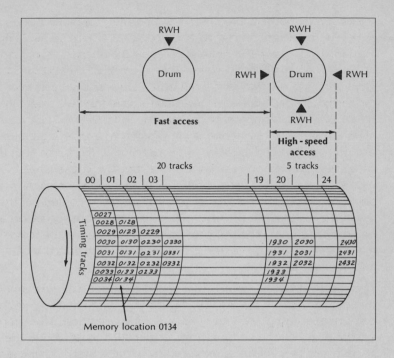

Memory location 0134

shorten the access time, for data on a few tracks, to a small fraction of the maximum access time.

☐ MAGNETIC TAPES

A third type of storage device is magnetic tape (similar to the tape used with commercial tape recorders). Magnetic tape is used mainly for bulk storage; that is, it is used for storing reference data and to provide large-capacity demountable storage.

The magnetic surface of tapes usually consists of a thin coating of red or black iron oxide in a lacquer-like binder on a metal or plastic backing. Tapes are about 0.0022 inch thick and range in length up to 2,400 feet. Most computer tapes use channels or "tracks" along the length of the tape. A separate read-write head is used for each track, so that a number of bits can be written or read simultaneously. Standard System/360 tape has nine tracks and is thus capable of reading or writing nine bits at one time: eight data bits (making up one byte) and one parity bit (to be explained shortly). The nine bits across the width of the tape are referred to as one "column" of data. A space is provided between columns to prevent interference. Tape travels across the read-write heads at speeds ranging from 25 to 200 inches per second. If it is assumed that a tape travels across the heads at a speed of 75 inches per second, data can be transferred at a rate of 60,000 bytes per second. (As mentioned in Chapter 6, a byte is a group of eight bits that are handled together.) This means that $^{60,000}/_{75}$, or 800, bytes of data are contained on each inch of the nine-track tape (speed 75 inches per second) and that 100 bytes (or 800 bits) are written on each inch of a particular track. The number of bits that can be recorded per inch of tape is referred to as the "bit density." Of course, there are spaces on a tape where no data are stored. These spaces are used to separate the words of one record from another. A single record of data is separated by an interrecord gap before and after it.

The spaces between records correspond to about twice the amount of tape that passes under the read-write head while the tape drive mechanism is coming to a stop at the end of each writing operation. This space is allowed so that there will be no danger of accidentally coasting into the next record at each stop. End-of-file is indicated by a "tape mark" character. The physical end-of-tape mark is usually a reflective material on the tape, such as aluminum foil, ranging from ⅜ to 3¾ inches long. The beginning of the tape, or "load point," is similarly indicated by reflective foil, but on the opposite edge of the tape.

In the IBM tape drives, a lamp projects a beam of light on the magnetic tape. When the load point reflective foil passes, light is reflected to a photocell,

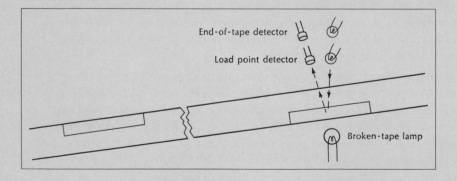

and a signal is given to indicate that the read or write operations can begin. Another lamp and photocell combination detects the end-of-tape reflector, beyond which no read or write operations are to be performed. The two sets of lamps and photocells are embedded in plastic so that there is no interaction between the two detectors. If the tape should break, light from a lamp beneath the tape would shine on both photocells, producing a broken tape signal to alert the operator.

When writing, the computer tests the tape for the end-of-file reflector so as not to write too far. When reading, the computer checks the tape for "tape mark" characters in order to know when the end-of-file is reached. To prevent a tape from being written on when it already contains important data, nearly all tape drives require that a special plastic protective ring, about 5 inches in diameter and ¼ inch thick, be placed in the circular slot at the rear of the tape reel if the tape is to be written upon. Without this ring, no writing can be done on the tape. When used, the ring pushes in a small pin just above the hub on which the reel is placed, and a signal is sent to the computer which permits it to write on this reel of tape.

A 2,400-foot reel of nine-track tape, at a density of 200 bits per inch, can store all the information contained on 20,000 eighty-column punched cards. Newer tapes have bit densities up to 1,600 bits per inch and thus have larger capacities. For the many operations that do not require a full 2,400-foot reel (10½ inches in diameter), there are smaller reels containing less tape:

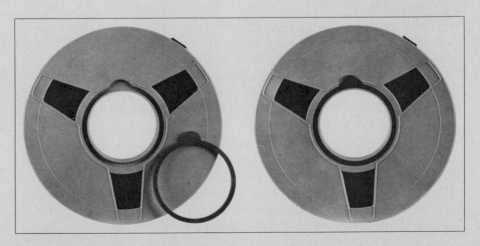

TAPE REELS AND RINGS.

1,200 feet (8½ inches), 600 feet (7 inches), and 250 feet (6 inches in diameter). The 250-foot reel is called "minitape" and costs about $5, whereas the 2,400-foot reel costs about $30 when purchased in quantity. At a speed of 75 inches per second it takes about 6½ minutes to get from one end of a 2,400-foot reel of tape to the other.

The magnetic tape units provided for System/360 read or write nine tracks on half-inch Mylar standard or heavy-duty tape. There are several types and models of tape drives having different characteristics of tape speed and bit density. There are two standard bit densities, 800 and 1,600 bits per inch (on each of the nine tracks), and five standard tape speeds of 18.75, 37.5, 75, 112.5 and 200 inches per second, giving transfer rates ranging from 15,000 to 320,000 bytes per second. (On tape each byte consists of a group of nine bits lying across the tape. The function of the ninth bit will be explained shortly.)

Each tape unit will drive at only one speed, but units can be obtained that will handle both bit densities. In some cases 2, 4, or 6 tape drives are housed in a single cabinet. All tape units are programmed the same.

TAPE DRIVING MECHANISM

There are many models of tape drive mechanisms. They all consist of an assembly of motors, magnetic clutches, linkages, and tape driving capstans (rubber rollers with metal hubs). These components are used together with electrical control circuits to stop, start, rewind, and drive the tape past the read-write head assembly.

Two reels are used. The file reel holds the tape, and the machine reel pulls in the tape after it has been written upon or read. This arrangement is similar to the one used with rolls of film on a motion-picture projector. Tape motion is produced by pressing the tape against a motor-driven capstan. By using solenoid-operated mechanical linkages, it is possible to press the tape against the forward-driving capstan, the reverse-driving capstan, or a nonrotating stopping capstan.

The mechanical inertia of the reels imposes limitations on the starting and stopping of the tape. To solve this difficulty, a large loop of tape is used on both sides of the read-write head assembly. These loops act as buffers or overflow banks to minimize stresses on the tape. When the tape is started, tape can be drawn out of one bank by the drive capstan, fed through the read-write head assembly, and added to the loop on the other side.

Meanwhile, the reels can be accelerating up to full speed in order to wind out more tape from one bank and to take up slack from the other bank. In this manner, tape passes the read-write head assembly at the correct speed during the time that the tape reels are accelerating or decelerating.

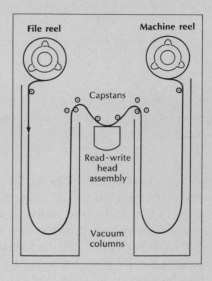

Vacuum columns hold the loops of tape that are used as banks, to keep the tape taut so it does not buckle at the read-write head during the starting or stopping of the tape reels. The vacuum columns are vertical containers with rectangular cross sections. Air is pumped out of the bottom of each column. As a result, the pressure of the air on the inside surface of the loop keeps tape taut and reduces air friction. The position of the tape loop in each vacuum column is detected by the air pressure differences above and below the loop, and the reel drives are operated to keep the loop position correct.

TAPE CODE AND ERROR DETECTION
The nine-channel tape code is shown. Because the code is used to represent both alphabetic characters and numerals, it is called an "eight-bit alphanumeric" code, the ninth bit used for parity check.

```
    0123456789  ABCDEFGHIJKLMNOPQRS TUVWXYZ   ! "#$%&' ( )*+
4
6
0
1
2
P
3
7
5
```

The nine channels or tracks are referred to as 0, 1, 2, 3, 4, 5, 6, 7, P. The nine-bit code is popular mainly because it is on a narrow (½-inch) tape, yet it can be handled easily.

PARITY ERROR DETECTION

The eight channels 0, 1, 2, 3, 4, 5, 6, 7, contain data bits. If a single bit were to be accidentally added or dropped from one of these channels, the character represented by the byte would be changed. The ninth channel, P, is the parity channel. This is to guard against errors due to lost or gained bits. As can be seen, the P (parity) bit for any column is 1 whenever the total number of 1s in the other eight tracks for that column is odd. If any vertical column contains an odd number of 1s (including the P bit), an error will be indicated. The P bit is called a "parity" bit, used for the vertical "parity check, "which could just as well be an odd parity check, instead of the even parity check described. Whether odd or even parity is used depends on the particular type of computer involved. All IBM System/360 computers use even parity.

As each record is written, the number of 1 bits in each of the nine lengthwise channels is recorded. At the end of each record, a parity bit is added to each track that contains an odd number of 1 bits. When reading the tape, an odd number of bits in any one of the tracks of any record indicates an error. Thus checks are made across both vertical and horizontal dimensions of the tape to ensure accuracy. Similar parity checks are also made in other memory devices.

Each of the tracks on a tape has a separate head positioned over it. Some tape systems use a single combination read-write head for each track. Others use a separate read head and a separate write head for each track. Tape units that use a single combination read-write head cannot detect errors during a continuous recording process. A reading of the tape after recording will reveal the presence of errors if, in fact, errors exist. Tape units that use separate read and write heads can perform a read operation (for error detection) as the data are being recorded. Data recorded on the tape at the write head are read (or checked) an instant later at the read head. The use of separate read and write heads is therefore faster, since errors are almost immediately detected and may be corrected before the total recording process is completed. Similar accuracy or validity checks are made each time the tape is read.

TAPE TERMS

Users of magnetic tapes have developed a large vocabulary of terms to refer to various concepts. Here are some of the more common of these terms:

1 *Multifile* refers to storing several files on a single tape. In one multifile application, a tape may contain personnel files, payroll information, and accounts payable. However, multifile tapes are tending to disappear now that minireels have become widely available.
2 In a *multireel* application, several reels of tapes are required to hold a single file. (There are files of over 1,000 reels. Insurance company files, for example, may take from 5 to 30 reels.)
3 *Blocking* involves writing many short records together on a tape, so as not to waste tape space with interrecord gaps and also to avoid excessive start and stop time. All the records in one block are read into core memory all at once. From then on, they can be processed as individual records.
4 *Error handling* deals with detecting parity errors and making corrections. To correct a parity error on a read instruction, the tape is backspaced and read again, up to a fixed number of rereadings. This usually corrects most single-track errors, but nothing can correct errors due to actual physical damage to the tape or flaking off of the tape's magnetic surface.
5 A *label* is *not* a piece of paper on the reel telling what the reel contains or what number it is in a sequence. Because all tapes look alike, the programs must have some way of telling them apart. So the user writes a (magnetic) label as a record at the beginning of the tape, indicating the date when the data was recorded, its identity, etc. Business data operations are especially concerned with labels, because so many reels

are used that it becomes vitally important to process only the correct reel.

6 *Copying* is frequently performed in some installations. This computer operation reads one tape and writes a copy of it on another tape. One reason for copying is that a master tape may be getting worn, and data may be lost if a new copy is not made. Or perhaps the data is too valuable to have it on only one reel (or group of reels), so a copy is made and stored in a vault.

7 *Label checking* is a programming check to make sure the tape reel has the correct label. The computer reads the label and checks that the tape is the correct one for the program and that it is the correctly numbered reel in a multifile operation. If not, a message is typed out to the console operator telling him that a mistake has been made, and what corrective action should be taken.

8 In a multireel operation, *automatic tape swapping* means that the system will automatically switch, after detecting the end-of-file mark on one tape, to the beginning of the next reel on another tape drive. After the system has switched from the end of reel 17 to the beginning of reel 18, the operator must replace reel 17 with reel 19. (The computer will type out a message telling him to do so and requiring a keyboard reply from him after he has done so.) When the system switches back to reel 19, the operator replaces reel 18 with reel 20 on the second tape drive, and so on. Thus, the program can continue while a completed tape is rewinding.

☐ DIRECT ACCESS DEVICES

Let us now take a look at what have come to be known as direct access devices, including magnetic drums, discs, disc packs, and data cells. In older computers, each of these is treated as a separate type of device, with each type addressed separately and specifically. In most System/360 applications, the programmer merely specifies direct access memory, and the system does the rest, assigning whatever direct access device is available and most suited to the requirement. The programmer does not know which device will be used, nor does he need to know. The supervisory program assigns the device and records which device has been assigned which material so that, if ever required, the exact device used for any particular operation can be determined. This "unified" treatment of direct

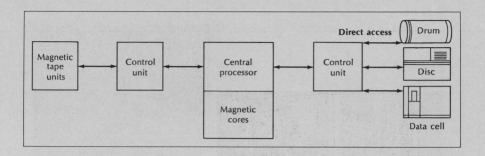

access devices, called "device independence," frees the programmer from continually having to assign such memory devices. It also allows the operator to assign the best device which can be assigned at the moment of execution.

MAGNETIC DISC MEMORIES

Magnetic disc memories use a number of iron-oxide-coated discs (which resemble phonograph records) arranged in much the same way as a record stack in a modern jukebox. All the discs are continuously revolving and are spaced apart so that a read-write head, driven by an access mechanism, can be positioned over the data tracks between the discs. Older magnetic disc systems use a single read-write head, which must travel up and down as well as in and out. Others use a read-write head for each disc, and still others use several for each disc. The more heads per disc, the faster the access time, but the greater the cost of the device.

Data are recorded at a certain address on a specified disc. When read-out of a particular bit of data is desired, the read-write head is automatically positioned over the proper track, and the data are read serially from the surface of the selected disc. Air ejected from the read-write head onto the disc creates an upward draft which maintains a given spacing of the head from the disc.

The main advantage of magnetic disc storage is its high storage capacity obtainable from a bank arrangement containing several discs. Access time for a magnetic disc memory bank is generally more than for magnetic drums; that is, it takes longer to get data in and out. Some magnetic disc systems can store up to 5 million coded digits.

The IBM 2302 disc memory used with the System/360 contains 25 discs.

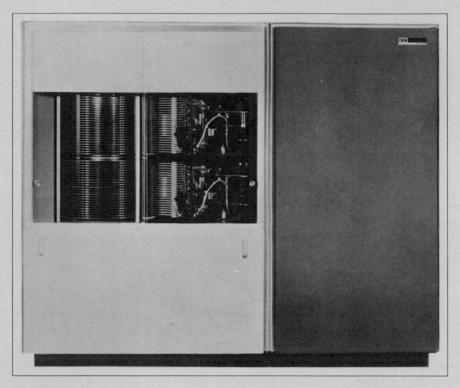

IBM 2302 FIXED DISC UNIT.

Each of the 50 disc surfaces is divided into 500 tracks. Each disc memory module has two access mechanisms and a capacity of 112.14 million bytes. The transfer rate between this memory and the processing unit is 156 thousand bytes per second.

MAGNETIC DISC PACKS

Although magnetic disc memories provide a large amount of storage, there are a number of occasions when a memory with removable magnetic discs is more economical when all things are considered. Therefore, IBM developed the Model 2311 disc pack, a 10-pound assembly of six 14-inch discs, mounted half an inch apart on a vertical shaft. The inside ten disc surfaces are used for recording data; the two outermost surfaces are protective plates.

IBM 2311 SINGLE REMOVABLE DISC STORAGE DRIVE.

A disc pack can be removed from the disc storage drive and replaced with another pack in less than a minute to provide unlimited storage capacity. Each disc pack contains 7.25 million bytes.

A faster, higher-capacity disc pack memory, the Model 2314, consists of eight independently operating drives housed in one long cabinet, with a ninth drive available as a spare for immediate use if one of the eight needs servicing. The 14-pound 2314 disc packs contain 11 discs, 14 inches in diameter, with 18 surfaces used for recording data. More than 7,000 bytes (twice the 2311's capacity) are stored on each 2314 disc track, for a total of

IBM 2314 MULTIPLE REMOVABLE DISC STORAGE DRIVE.

more than 25 million bytes per disc pack, and a grand total of just over 207 million bytes for the eight-pack 2314.

☐ MOVABLE MAGNETIC STRIPS

Magnetic strips provide an economic method of extending on-line random access storage capabilities to a volume of data beyond that of other storage devices. The plastic strips coated with a magnetic material can store large amounts of data in a relatively small space, at the expense of a longer access time. Each strip must be individually selected and brought to the read-write heads by mechanical means.

The IBM Data Cell Drive permits storage of 400 million bytes of on-line data. Each data cell drive contains one to ten data cells, each having a capacity of 40 million bytes. The data cells are interchangeable, permitting the establishment of libraries of data cells.

The storage medium is a magnetic strip 2¼ inches wide by 13 inches long. Each data cell contains 200 of these strips. A rotary positioning system aligns the selected cell beneath the access station, much like the revolving chamber of a six-shooter. Access time to a strip varies from 175 to 600

IBM 2321 MAGNETIC STRIP DATA CELL DRIVE.

milliseconds, depending on the addressed strip and the particular data
arrangements on the cards.

DATA ACCESS METHODS

In data access operations, a programmer must consider the way data
are arranged within memory, and whether input and output requirements
may be anticipated in advance or whether input and output will occur as

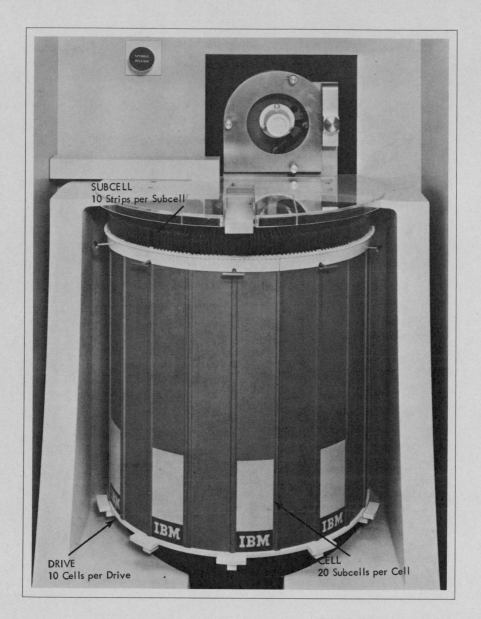

CLOSE-UP OF DATA CELL DRIVE.

the immediate result of an instruction. The combination of these factors defines the access method. Each of the following seven access methods has its own particular advantages, from which the programmer can select those suitable to the application.

1 *BSAM (Basic Sequential Access Method).* In BSAM the organization is "tape-like," even when storage is on a direct access device. The data are organized sequentially, but as physical blocks of data rather than logical records, as in QSAM. The user must specify when the data are required, and program execution is suspended until the retrieval is completed.

2 *QSAM (Queued Sequential Access Method).* This access method anticipates the need for logical records based on their sequential order. Normally it will have the desired record in storage, ready for use, before the fetch instruction is issued.

3 *BPAM (Basic Partitioned Access Method).* This method is designed for efficient storage and retrieval of sequences of data (members) stored on a direct access device. Each member has a simple name. Included in the data is a directory that relates the member name to the track address where the sequence starts.

4 *BISAM and QISAM (Basic and Queued Indexed Sequential Access Method).* With the indexed sequential organization, data records on direct access storage devices are arranged in logical sequence on a *data key.* When a record is stored, the data key is placed in a hardware-defined key field associated with the record. The data also contain indexes relating the data keys of records to physical addresses. To retrieve records in sequential fashion, QISAM retrieves logical records sequentially, using successive fetch instructions. Selective reading is performed by BISAM, using a read instruction, and specifying the key of the logical record to be retrieved.

5 *BDAM (Basic Direct Access Method).* This access method allows records within a certain collection of data to be organized for direct access in any manner chosen by the programmer. When a request to store or retrieve a record is made, an address either relative to the beginning of the data or an actual address (that is, device, cylinder, track, or record position) must be furnished. This address can be specified as being the address of the desired record or as a starting point within the data, where the search for the record begins. When a record search is specified, the programmer must also furnish the data key (for example, part number or customer name) that is associated with the desired record.

6   *BTAM (Basic Telecommunications Access Method)*. Telecommunications devices have some characteristics that are significantly different from local input/output devices. Remote terminals are not under positive control of the central processing unit, particularly when the data source is a keyboard. In some applications, messages of unpredictable length must be handled. And the number of remote terminals may be very large compared with the number of local input/output units such as tapes and discs.

Although the control of communications devices is considerably different from the control of local input/output equipment, the transmittal of data records between buffers and the user's program is much the same in both cases. This similarity allows the programmer to design processing programs for BTAM in much the same way as he would for BSAM, despite differences between telecommunications and local input/output devices. The result is that the programmer does not deal at all with remote terminals; he deals instead with locally available blocks of data records from which he may receive input, and to which he may add output.

Many other message-related functions can be performed automatically by the BTAM programs. Terminals sharing the same transmission line can be addressed and polled, to permit bidding for line use on a controlled basis. Message headers can be analyzed to determine where messages are to be routed.

7   *QTAM (Queued Telecommunications Access Method)*. The same polling and line-control functions of BTAM are provided in QTAM. Both input and output records are spaced on queues specified by the programmer. The determination of which queue a record should be placed on may be influenced, for example, by the priority of the message, by the receiving or transmitting terminal, and by the identification of the processing routine. The sequence of records in each queue is based on their time of entry into the queue; the earliest record on an input queue is provided when data are requested from the queue by a fetch instruction.

☐ CONTROL UNITS AND MULTIPLE MEMORIES

More than one of each of these memory devices can be connected to a System/360. All of them require a control unit, which can control only a limited number of memory units. For instance, one tape control can control as many as eight tape drives. Several tape control units can be connected to one System/360 computer, the exact number depending on the number and types of data channels available. There is a limit to the variety of memory devices that can be connected to a System/360 computer. All the memory units described here could be attached to a single System/360 computer. In practice, however, this would probably not be done, as there are few if any computer installations requiring such a wide mixture of memory devices.

☐ QUESTIONS

1 Why was the average access time of a drum figured to be half the maximum? If the *minimum* access time of a drum is 4 milliseconds and the maximum is 8 milliseconds, what will the average be? Why?

2 If data are stored along the full length of a 2,400/foot tape and are being read from this tape at random, what will the average access time be? (Assume a 75-inch-per-second tape drive.)

3 Compare the advantages and disadvantages of storage on the magnetic input/output devices described, considering access time and capacity. Distinguish between the situation for extremely large files and very small files. How would the activity of the file influence a decision on which to use? (In an active file, almost all the items are frequently referred to; in an inactive, most of the items are seldom referred to.)

4 Check the data codes shown in the figure on page 194. Do they all have even parity?

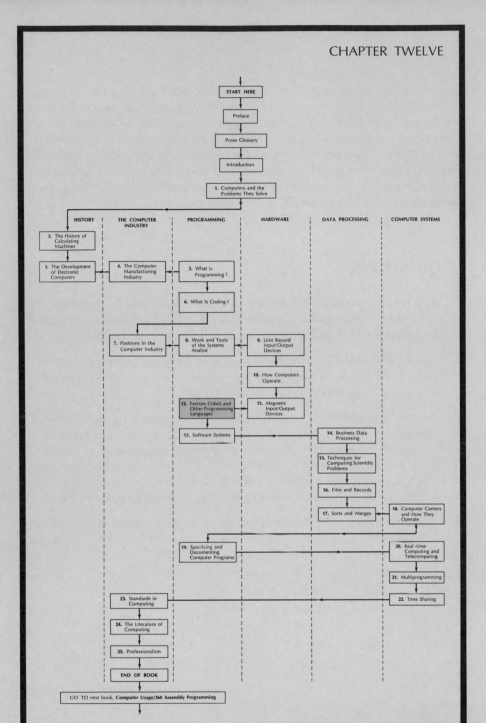

FORTRAN, COBOL, AND OTHER PROGRAMMING LANGUAGES

There are two basically different ways to program a computer. In the *assembly language* method you address yourself directly to the computer. You use the specific commands that the computer was wired to receive, and you refer to the computer memory locations using the code numbers that the computer builder assigned to these locations. You are dealing with the computer on the computer's own terms. Chapter 6 gave you a taste of this method. Another book in this series, *Computer Usage/360 Assembly Programming,* will teach you how to program the IBM System/360 using assembly language.

In the *programming language* method you describe what you wish to compute in a "high-level" programming language. Assembly language is "machine" oriented while a programming language is "problem" oriented. The major programming languages are *machine-independent* and can be processed on UNIVAC 1108, Honeywell H-1800, Burroughs 5500, CDC 6600, and others, as well as on IBM System/360.

Thus your attention will shift from specific computer details to *language* details—punctuation, vocabulary, grammar, etc.

☐ THE DEVELOPMENT OF PROGRAMMING LANGUAGES

Originally, all computers were programmed only in machine and assembly languages. In the early 1950s, a number of computer pioneers speculated on the possibility that computers could prepare programs themselves—*given a statement of the processing required.*

While not the first developed, Fortran was the first really successful language. It has remained popular for more than ten years. Later other languages were developed, the most popular of which are:

Cobol—For business computation
Algol —For scientific computation
PL/I   —For both business and scientific computation.

There have been over a hundred other languages developed—some primitive, some sophisticated. Many of these are special purpose languages used in applications or research areas.

The four major languages—Fortran, Algol, Cobol, and PL/I—are now undergoing some process of national and international standardization. This will ensure their machine independence.

☐ THE PROS AND CONS OF PROGRAMMING LANGUAGE USAGE

The question whether a programming language like Fortran or assembly language is better cannot be answered completely, since it depends on some specific circumstances. Here is a list of the general advantages and disadvantages of Fortran—as a typical programming language.

Advantages:

1   Fortran is easy to learn. After a relatively short study of Fortran, a scientist or engineer can usually state his problem so that it will run on a computer. He does not need to pursue a detailed study of the computer he is going to use.

2   Fortran programs can be written and debugged quickly. The same scientific problem coded in Fortran would usually require a program five to ten times as long in assembly language. In general, the less you need write, the less likely you are to make mistakes. Fortran error detecting capability is also very useful.

3 Since Fortran is available on all new computers, the lifetime of programs written in Fortran is greater than those in the assembly language of an obsolete computer. (It is not unusual for engineers to define a computer as "a machine that understands Fortran.")

4 Over the years, a vast library of easily obtained Fortran programs has accumulated, thus preventing needless duplication of effort. In fact, when presented with a new problem, the first step a Fortran programmer often takes is to look through the library of programs to see if there is already a Fortran program which solves that problem.

Disadvantages:

1 A Fortran program is usually inefficient. Compared with a program written in assembly language, the program produced by the Fortran compiler is slow-running and wasteful of computer memory. This is the major disadvantage of Fortran and precludes its use for certain applications. For instance, in a real time application, Fortran might not allow the computer to respond with the required speed. If the computer's memory is small, there may not be room for a bulky Fortran object program. Also, if a program is to be in production and run continually, its slowness would in the long run waste a significant amount of computer time. However, with most scientific work, where usually only a few sets of data are run with a program, the inefficiency of Fortran does not make a difference. Minutes of computer time are never worth more than hours of a programmer's time.

2 Many Fortran compilers—the special software which converts programming language programs to machine language programs—are very slow. In some cases, an installation may spend 50 percent to 70 percent of its machine time *compiling* programs instead of executing them. This is especially true since each Fortran program must be compiled several times for testing and correcting (debugging) during its development.

□ WHY FORTRAN AND COBOL?

In planning this series of books, careful attention was given to the selection of the programming languages to be presented.

Fortran and Cobol were selected over Algol and PL/I. Fortran and Cobol are widely used, standardized, and generally accepted. Excellent Fortran compilers and good Cobol compilers are available for IBM System/360 and other computers. Cobol is more difficult to learn but, because of its steadily growing usage, it was considered an essential part of your study course.

Algol, widely used internationally, was not chosen because of its limited acceptance in the United States.

PL/I was not chosen because it is too new, neither standardized nor accepted by non-IBM computers, not yet in general use, quite difficult to learn, and lacking in good compiler availability.

☐ MORE ABOUT FORTRAN

Fortran was developed in 1955 jointly by IBM and some of its customers. Its purpose was to allow scientific and mathematical problems to be programmed quickly and easily. Although it is oriented to mathematical formulas—the name FORTRAN is derived from "FORmula TRANslator"—it is also useful for solving many other types of problems.

Fortran was the first widely accepted programming language. The term "language" is used in the sense of a means of communication between the problem solver and the computer (or between the problem solver and other people).

Fortran is—as it was intended to be—quite similar to the language of mathematics, although it is used in many nonmathematical applications. There are, however, subtle but important differences between Fortran's use of certain operations and terms and algebra's use of the same things.

There is no "Fortran computer"—that is, there is no computer available which directly executes Fortran statements. Instead, a program written in the language of Fortran is input as data to a special program called a *compiler*. There is a different Fortran compiler for each computer. The compiler program translates the Fortran program into an assembly language or a machine language program that can then be fed to the particular computer. Although there is a different Fortran compiler for each computer, the Fortran language is generally standard. Except for certain details, a Fortran program will be accepted and translated correctly by any Fortran compiler.

HOW A FORTRAN PROGRAM IS COMPILED AND EXECUTED
The basic concept of Fortran can be made clearer if at this point we go into

some detail about the mechanism of compiling and running a Fortran program. The diagram illustrates the stages in processing a Fortran program.

The program is first written on Fortran coding sheets. These sheets go to a keypunch operator, who converts each line on the sheet into a keypunched card. The deck of these cards constitutes the "source program" which will be used during the compiler phase.

In the compiling phase, the Fortran compiler program is read into the computer (from tape or disc). The computer, now operating under control of the compiler program, reads the keypunched source program and translates it into an object program in machine language. During compilation, a listing of the source program is printed out for reference. The compiler is able to recognize certain errors in a program, and it will

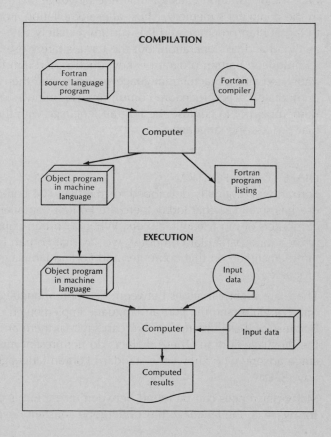

indicate those it finds on the listing. The error messages are generally called "diagnostics."

The final step is to execute the object program. The object program, now in machine language, is read into the computer and, when execution starts, controls the computer. It may read in some data, do its calculations, and then print out answers in whatever form was prescribed. In regular practice, if the program is to be "put into production"—that is, rerun many times with different sets of data—then a copy of the corrected program in machine language is saved on tape or disc or in a punched card deck to avoid future compiler runs.

This is meant only as a general description of the steps a Fortran program may go through. Depending on the computer and on the compiler used at a particular installation, there can be variations of this procedure. For any of the input or output steps, other media (cards, paper tape, etc.) may be used. One major variation calls for machine language program output to remain in the computer's memory. Thus, after compilation, control is passed directly to the Fortran program, and it is run immediately with data. This was known as "load-and-go" operation, but the term is rarely used now. With this technique, a Fortran program is keypunched, fed into the computer, translated into a machine language program, and then executed immediately. The procedure commonly uses minutes of computer time. Remember not to confuse the Fortran *language* with the Fortran *compilers* that process the language.

DIALECTS OF FORTRAN

Fortran was originally developed for the IBM 704 computer. Since then, its use has spread so that today there are Fortran compilers available for most computers of most manufacturers. When a Fortran compiler has been written for a particular computer, we say that Fortran has been "implemented" on that computer and Fortran language programs may be processed.

There are slight variations between the Fortran language implemented on one computer and the Fortran language implemented on another computer. Because of these differences, we can say that there are various "dialects" of the language Fortran. These dialects do not present much of a problem, since anyone who knows the standard Fortran language can easily handle any dialect.

Many differences can be found between recent forms of Fortran and older forms, since the language has undergone constant development and improvement. The specific version of Fortran described in another book in this series is known as Basic Fortran IV. It is one of the Fortran language versions that have been implemented on the IBM System/360.

There is a nationally accepted Fortran. It is defined in two booklets put out by the USA Standards Institute, a nongovernmental voluntary industrial association. One booklet describes the full Fortran language and is called USA Standard X3.9-1966 FORTRAN. The other describes a somewhat limited Fortran language and is called USA Standard X3.10-1966 Basic FORTRAN. Basic Fortran is a subset of the full Fortran. That is, everything in Basic Fortran is also in full Fortran, but there are some things in full Fortran that are not in Basic Fortran. To put the subset idea in other terms, a program written according to the rules of Basic Fortran would be correctly compiled by a Basic Fortran compiler *or* by a full Fortran compiler; a program written according to the rules of full Fortran would be correctly compiled by a full Fortran compiler but *would not* be correctly compiled by a Basic Fortran compiler if the program included things that are allowable in full Fortran but not in Basic Fortran.

Basic Fortran IV, as implemented on the IBM System/360 and as described in *Computer Usage/360 Fortran Programming,* another book in this series, is identical with the USA Standard Basic FORTRAN.

☐ MORE ABOUT OTHER PROGRAMMING LANGUAGES

Not only has Fortran improved over the years, but other computer languages have appeared. The best known is COBOL (COmmon Business Oriented Language) designed specifically for business applications.[1] It is described in detail in another book in this series, *Computer Usage/360 Cobol Programming.* ALGOL (ALGOrithmic Language) is a scientific language more powerful but also more simple in some ways than Fortran. It is widely used in Europe. Other scientific languages are LISP (LISt Processing) and JOVIAL, whose name, due to amusing circumstances that are too lengthy to recount, stands for "Jules' Own Version of International Algebraic Language." The latest major language is PL/I (Programming Language I, pronounced "Pea Ell One") which was devised for both business and scientific applications.

Besides these established languages, practically every month an article is published describing a new language developed around an unusual new

---

[1] The nationally accepted version is defined in USA Standard X3.23–1968 COBOL.

```
CHKPDATE.
    IF PRIOR-DATE = '        ' GO TO CHKLDATE.
    IF PRIOR-DATE IS NOT NUMERIC MOVE 'PRIOR DATE' TO P-ERROR
    GO TO BAD-CARD.
    IF PR-MO < 01 OR  PR-MO > 12 MOVE 'PRIOR DATE' TO P-ERROR
    GO TO BAD-CARD.
    IF PR-DA < 01 OR  PR-DA > 31 MOVE 'PRIOR DATE' TO P-ERROR
    GO TO BAD-CARD.
CHKLDATE.
    IF LAST-DATE = '        ' GO TO CHKPMD.
    IF LAST-DATE  IS NOT NUMERIC MOVE 'LAST DATE ' TO P-ERROR
    GO TO BAD-CARD.
    IF LA-MO < 01 OR LA-MO > 12 MOVE 'LAST DATE ' TO P-ERROR
    GO TO BAD-CARD.
    IF LA-DA < 01 OR LA-DA > 31 MOVE 'LAST DATE ' TO P-ERROR
    GO TO BAD-CARD.
CHKPMD.
    IF PROF-MEM-DATE = '       ' GO TO CHKBD.
    IF PROF-MEM-DATE IS NOT NUMERIC MOVE 'P-MEM-DATE' TO P-ERROR
    GO TO BAD-CARD.
    IF PR-MEM-MO < 01 OR PR-MEM-MO > 12 MOVE 'P-MEM-DATE' TO
    P-ERROR GO TO BAD-CARD.
CHKBD.
    IF BIRTH-DATE = '        ' GO TO SETUP.
    IF BIRTH-DATE IS NOT NUMERIC MOVE 'BIRTH DATE' TO P-ERROR
    GO TO BAD-CARD.
    IF BI-MO < 01 OR BI-MO > 12 MOVE 'BIRTH DATE' TO P-ERROR
    GO TO BAD-CARD.
    IF BI-DA < 01 OR BI-DA > 31 MOVE 'BIRTH DATE' TO P-ERROR
    GO TO BAD-CARD.
```

A PORTION OF A COBOL PROGRAM.

```
real procedure loggamma (x);
    value x;  real x;
comment  This procedure evaluates the natural logarithm of
    gamma(x) for all x > 0, accurate to 10 decimal places. Stirling's
    formula is used for the central polynomial part of the procedure.;
begin
    real f, z;
    if x < 7.0 then
    begin f := 1.0;  z := x − 1.0;
        for z := z + 1.0 while z < 7.0 do
        begin x := z;  f := f × z
        end;
        x := x + 1.0;  f := − ln(f)
    end
    else f := 0;
    z := 1.0/x ↑ 2;
    loggamma := f + (x−0.5) × ln(x) − x + .91893 85332 04673 +
        (((− .00059 52380 95238×z+.00079 36507 93651) × z − .00277
        77777 77778)×z+.08333 33333 33333)/x
end loggamma
```

AN ALGOL PROGRAM.

```
  1           OUTPUT :PROCEDURE OPTIONS(MAIN);

  2                   DCL   A FIXED,
                            B FLOAT,
                            C FLOAT COMPLEX,
                            D BIT(10),
                            E CHAR(10),
                            ARRAY(2,2) ;

  3                         A,B=12345;
  4                         C=A+123451;
  5                         D='1100111'B;
  6                         E='ABC''DEFG';

  7                         DO I=1 TO 2; DO J=1 TO 2;
  9                         ARRAY(I,J)=I+J;
 10                         END; END;

 12                         PUT PAGE LIST('EXAMPLES OF LIST/DATA/EDIT OUTPUT');

 13           LIST:         PUT SKIP(2) LIST('LIST DIRECTED EXAMPLES:');

 14                         PUT SKIP(1) LIST(A,B,C,D,E);

 15           DATA:         PUT SKIP(2) LIST('DATA DIRECTED EXAMPLES:');

 16                         PUT SKIP(1) DATA(A,B,C,D,E);
 17                         PUT SKIP DATA(ARRAY);

 18           EDIT:         PUT SKIP(2) LIST('EDIT DIRECTED EXAMPLES:');

 19                         PUT SKIP(1) EDIT(A,B,C,D,E)
                                (F(10,2),E(10,0,5),C(E(10,0,5)),X(5),2A);
 20                   END;
```

A PL/I PROGRAM.

principle. These languages serve a purpose, since experimental languages help in exploring the capabilities of computers and point the way to future language and computer design. It is quite possible that the next generation of computers will not operate in the step-by-step machine language you are using today, but will directly execute one of the higher-level languages.

Programmers themselves are split, often vehemently so, as to whether it is better to write in a higher-level language or in assembly language. A professional computer user should be acquainted with Fortran, Cobol, and IBM System/360 Assembly Language, all of which are covered in other books in this series.

☐ QUESTION

1 Discuss the pros and cons of a computer installation, adopting each of the following policies toward programming languages:

a   Each programmer may use whatever language he judges to be most
    suitable for the job at hand.
b   All programming must be done in System/360 Assembly Language.
    No other language may be used.
c   All programming must be done in Fortran. No other language may
    be used.
d   All programming must be done in Cobol. No other language may
    be used.

In addition to the obvious considerations, take account of future changes
of personnel, changes in computers, running efficiencies, programming
efficiencies, costs of training, and costs of compiling. Would these
policies be viewed differently if the computer installation were part of a
university than if it were a commercial installation? Why?

START HERE

Preface

Prose Glossary

Introduction

1. Computers and the Problems They Solve

HISTORY	THE COMPUTER INDUSTRY	PROGRAMMING	HARDWARE	DATA PROCESSING	COMPUTER SYSTEMS

2. The History of Calculating Machines

3. The Development of Electronic Computers

4. The Computer Manufacturing Industry

5. What Is Programming?

6. What Is Coding?

7. Positions in the Computer Industry

8. Work and Tools of the Systems Analyst

9. Unit Record Input/Output Devices

10. How Computers Operate

12. Fortran, Cobol, and Other Programming Languages

11. Magnetic Input/Output Devices

13. Software Systems

14. Business Data Processing

15. Techniques for Computing Scientific Problems

16. Files and Records

17. Sorts and Merges

18. Computer Centers and How They Operate

19. Specifying and Documenting Computer Programs

20. Real-time Computing and Telecomputing

21. Multiprogramming

23. Standards in Computing

22. Time Sharing

24. The Literature of Computing

25. Professionalism

END OF BOOK

GO TO next book, **Computer Usage/360 Assembly Programming**

When the computer manufacturer ships a computer, he actually sends two major items known as the *hardware* and the *software*. The hardware comprises all the physical components that you can see and touch. This is the computing system you have studied thus far. The software cannot be seen nor touched—it consists of a collection of programs that make the computer easier to use and more effective. This collection of programs, supplied by the manufacturer for extending the capability of the equipment, should be clearly distinguished from *application programs* written by the *user* of the equipment to get his computational tasks performed. Sometimes the term software is mistakenly used for all aspects of programming.

Generally speaking, programming to produce software is a complex task requiring considerable specialized training, and there is a large area for the employment of specialists in this field.

In this chapter, you will be introduced to the major software components and to a typical software system; other chapters cover miscellaneous aspects of software in connection with other topics.

☐ THE IMPORTANCE OF SOFTWARE

Do you recall the phrase "without a program, the computer is a dead machine, waiting to be brought to life?" If the word "program" is used to include only application programs, the machine will still not come to life—but modifying this phrase to say "without software and an application program, the . . . , " will now make it quite correct.

The first generation of computers used very little software. The second generation required substantial amounts. It is the third-generation computers like the IBM System/360 that require enormous quantities of software. In fact, the cost of System/360 software development exceeds the cost of System/360 hardware development.

Software and hardware items cooperate to produce a single powerful computing system. Since the manufacturer's objective is to supply the best computer at a competitive price, he can rightly decide on which facilities to build into the computer and which facilities to program into the software. Third-generation computers can be ordered in various configurations with a wide choice of auxiliary equipment, so that their manufacturers have chosen to *standardize the hardware* and allow for *variability in the software*.

To carry out this software-dominated plan, the machine language instruction set of System/360 contains a group of *privileged* instructions which are used by the *software only*, and not by any applications program. If an applications program uses one of these instructions—for example, SSK (set storage key)—and attempts to execute it, the program will be immediately halted and rejected.

The relation between application programs and the software may be emphasized in the following manner:

Hardware
Software   } Supplied and maintained by the manufacturer

Application programs } Written and maintained by the users' programmers

☐ PRINCIPAL SOFTWARE COMPONENTS

Software systems generally include four classes of components: (1) control programs, (2) input/output systems, (3) language processors, and (4) utility programs. Some manufacturers distribute a single integrated system, whereas others distribute most parts as individual "stand-alone" systems. Since all systems are large, they cannot fit into core storage (main memory) and therefore *reside* on magnetic tape, magnetic drum, or magnetic disc. But whether a system is integrated or consists of stand-alone elements, its principal components are:

1   The control program (also called supervisor or monitor), which sequences and controls all other programs.
2   The input/output system, which is closely tied into the control program.
3   Language processors, which convert programs from assembly language or from a programming language like Fortran to actual machine language. (Fortran compilers are in this class.)
4   Utility programs, which consist of several dozen very useful miscellaneous programs not otherwise classified.

☐ THE CONTROL PROGRAM—AS THE USER SEES IT

A feature of computer software systems is nonstop operation. In this generally accepted way of operating computers, a long sequence of computational jobs is stacked together to make up a two- to perhaps a six-hour nonstop run. This stack may consist of routine production runs, Fortran compilations, assemblers, Cobol compilations, test trials, data edits, etc.

One of the main functions of the control program is to regulate the "stacked job" processing. The control program (through one of its many subordinate components) handles the initiation and termination of each job. It checks for valid setup, records the amount of time used and the department to be charged, changes assignments of I/O units, resets certain indicators, etc. While running, the control program detects abnormal operation (via the computer's *interrupt* system) and takes appropriate action. At the same time, the control program is communicating with the operator. It sends him messages at the console typewriter—either progress messages (JOB 6 COMPLETED; JOB 7 STARTING and FORTRAN COMPILATION TERMINATED—17 ERRORS) or messages requesting information (DESIGNATE RESTART TAPE, which calls for him to type in the symbol C7 if that is to be assigned as the restart tape).

AN EXAMPLE OF STACKED JOB PROCESSING
Following through an example of stacked job processing should clarify the

various steps involved. Here is the stack to be processed, consisting of four jobs:

1   A Fortran compilation
2   An assembly
3   A routine run of a program named PAY3
4   A Cobol compilation

During the processing, the control program will:

1   Record the elapsed time actually used for each job.

2   Give messages to the operator noting whether the compilations and the assembly were successfully completed or whether there were too many serious errors diagnosed.

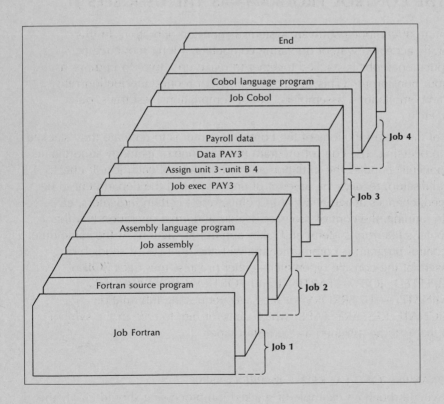

3   Halt execution of program PAY3 should any of a series of mishaps occur, including those of:
    a   Machine trouble
    b   A privileged instruction given by the application program
    c   The occurrence of certain invalid data conditions

    At this abnormal termination, dump of memory and registers will be made to enable the programmer to pinpoint the trouble. A message about the termination is also sent to the operator.

4   Before loading program PAY3, one of the tape units will be given a reassignment as needed by this program.

BEYOND STACKED JOB PROCESSING
Actually, stacked job processing was fairly well perfected for second-generation computers. It was described as a basis for covering third-generation computer control programs.

One objective of modern computer systems is to get the greatest *throughput* (computation per unit time) while, at the same time, shortening the *turnaround time* (hours between submitting a job and receiving the computed result). In stacked job processing, long stacks increase throughput, *and* short stacks decrease turnaround time. The following solutions to the problem have been made:

1   Multitasking
2   Dynamic scheduling
3   Multiprogramming
4   Simultaneous Peripheral Operation Off-Line (SPOOL-ing)

In multitasking, a single program is broken into tasks that could be performed in parallel. Then, when facilities are available, multiple tasks are performed at once. For example, the task of computing result 3 can continue while printing result 2, punching result 2, rewinding a tape, and positioning a magnetic disc head. In this way, programs run at maximum speed, thereby increasing throughput.

Dynamic scheduling allows continuous manipulation of the job stack awaiting execution. New jobs can be added, deletions made, sequence altered, and a priority system used to select the next job to be run. This allows high-priority jobs to have a shorter turnaround time than lower-priority jobs.

Multiprogramming (see Chapter 21) allows more than one job to be run at

Job 1 to disc				
Job 2 to disc	Job 1 to computer			
Job 3 to disc	Job 2 to computer	Job 1 computing		
Job 4 to disc	Job 3 to computer	Job 2 computing	Job 1 results to disc	
Job 5 to disc	Job 4 to computer	Job 3 computing	Job 2 results to disc	Job 1 printing
Job 6 to disc	Job 5 to computer	Job 4 computing	Job 3 results to disc	Job 2 printing

the same time by one computer. Although certain computers were built to aid this, any third-generation computer can be made to do multiprogramming with its control program. Often, processing several jobs at once will increase throughput and reduce turnaround time.

Spooling is a special form of multiprogramming. It permits card-to-tape (disc, drum) and tape (disc, drum)-to-printer (punch) to proceed continuously while computations are in progress. Properly organized and used with the three other techniques, it converts the third-generation computer into an effective processing machine which handles enormous throughput and gives short turnaround time.

If each job and each operation took exactly the same length of time, the description above would lead to regular printing of results starting with the fourth job down the stack. Actually, neither assumption is true, but the effect is the same: a continuous stream of cards enters the computer, and, with some delay, the results from job after job are printed out.

☐ INPUT/OUTPUT SYSTEMS

A comprehensive description of input/output systems is well beyond the scope of this book. This section is designed to cover the *software* aspects.

Perhaps the simplest way to follow this is to span the gap between the instructions for IBM System/360 that perform I/O—and the manner in which you'll actually call for input or output to be performed.

System/360 has four I/O instructions:

SIO   Start I/O
HIO   Halt I/O
TIO   Test I/O
TCH   Test Channel

These are *privileged* instructions reserved for use by the software and not available to the applications programmer.

In application programming, if you write in a programming language like Fortran or Cobol, the processors will compile the proper code to communicate to the I/O system. If you write in assembly language, you'll probably use only the following five macro instructions:

DTF   Define a file
OPEN   Prepare the file for use
GET   Get one record from an input file
PUT   Put one record into an output file
CLOSE   Complete the file operations

In practice, the first is used only to *inform* the I/O software of the structure of your files and records. The other four are converted to SVC (Supervisor Call) instructions which cause appropriate branching to the control program that calls upon the I/O system to carry out the requested function.

PHYSICAL AND LOGICAL INPUT/OUTPUT SYSTEMS

The difference between usage of the five macro instructions and the issuance of the four privileged instructions is the difference between *logical* and *physical* I/O systems.

The user sees only *logical* files and records. Generally, he does not know the details of exactly how and in what form his data is stored. The hardware, on the other hand, is concerned only with *physical* entities—channels, units, bytes, and bits written and read.

There are in most software systems two related I/O systems. The logical system is concerned primarily with records, files, and labels, whereas the physical system is actually an integral part of the control program. It is concerned with keeping all the I/O equipment as fully loaded as possible and handling any I/O errors detected.

Such systems attempt to be *device-independent*. This means that the user does not need to think too much in specific physical terms—his files will be

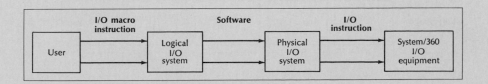

written on magnetic drum now, or magnetic disc later, or if he chooses, on magnetic tape. He may also currently write a tape for later printing, and tomorrow he may print directly. No changes in program are required. The I/O assignment may be made at run time either by an operator or by using a special assignment control card.

☐ LANGUAGE PROCESSORS

Although languages and processors were discussed in Chapter 12, they were not covered from the viewpoint of a complete software system. All that need be said here is that:

1   Language processors are part of the software system.
2   The processors look like any other user program as far as the control program is concerned.
3   Object program execution is under the supervision of the control program.
4   The whole job—compilation of one or more programs followed by execution—(if there were not too many diagnostics) is directed by means of *control cards* read in by the supervisor (the control program).

The relation to the whole is seen here:

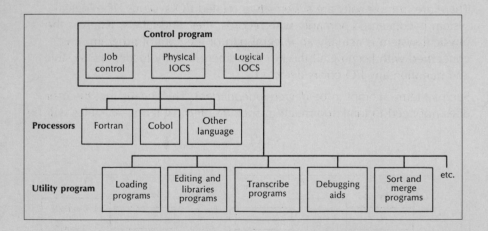

☐ UTILITY PROGRAMS—LOADING AND CATALOGING

Modern software systems go beyond older systems in which each programmer kept his own program decks in his desk drawer. To avoid loss and misunderstanding and to simplify program maintenance and execution, program libraries are part of the software. Programs are cataloged into a library by special librarian programs. There are several types of libraries— source programs, partially assembled or compiled programs, and machine language libraries. The libraries include all commonly needed functions and subroutines. In fact, much of the software system itself (like processors and utility programs) may be in the libraries.

When an application program is *processed* by an assembler or compiler, the results may be (1) loaded for immediate execution, (2) cataloged into a library for repeated use or merely for temporary storage, or (3) cataloged *and* loaded for execution. Of course, a fourth situation is allowed— a previously cataloged program may be simply called from the library to be loaded and executed.

OTHER UTILITY PROGRAMS
Some of the other utility programs are covered in Chapter 17 on sort and merge programs. Besides these, there are many individually useful programs, which include:

1   Card-to-tape, tape-to-card, tape-to-printer.
2   Initialize magnetic disc or drum.
3   Punch out disc, drum, or tape.
4   List disc, drum, or tape.
5   Copy tape, disc, or drum to a similar unit.
6   Debugging.

☐ IBM SOFTWARE FOR SYSTEM/360

For the main-line System/360 models (25-30-40-44-50-65-67-75-85-91), IBM offers five different software systems. These have major differences in the facilities they provide, depending on the installation's main-memory size and auxiliary equipment. A simplified chart is shown on the following page.

	BPS: Basic programming support	BOS: Basic operating system	TOS: Tape operating system	DOS: Disc operating system	OS: Operating system
Minimum main-memory size	8K	8K	16K	16K	32K
System residence	Cards or magnetic tape	Magnetic disc	Magnetic tape	Magnetic disc	Magnetic disc or drum
Programming languages	Fortran	Assembly Language	Fortran, Cobol, PL/I	Fortran, Cobol, PL/I	Fortran, Cobol, PL/I
Mode of operation	Single jobs	Stacked jobs	Stacked jobs	Stacked jobs, Some multiprogramming, Some spooling	Dynamic scheduling, Multitasking, Multiprogramming, Spooling

☐ QUESTIONS

1 Almost all computer operations, beyond the very basic ones, can be implemented in the hardware or in the software. It is almost always more expensive to implement operations in the hardware, but the software implementation makes each program run longer. Also, the software occupies more storage space which would otherwise be available for computing use. Discuss the pros and cons of the hardware-software balance from the point of view of the computer vendor (who also furnishes the software) and the computer user (who pays the bills).

2 The current arrangement is that the cost of the computer covers the cost of the vendor-furnished software. Some firms which sell software only and do not sell hardware have proposed that hardware vendors offer their computers at a reduced price if the user does not want their software. Discuss the implications of such a separate pricing scheme to the vendors, the users, and the independent software houses. The software is said to cost as much as the *design* of a modern computer, but software has no manufacturing costs beyond the cost of its initial creation, while hardware has a manufacturing cost which is probably 80 to 90 percent of its total cost.

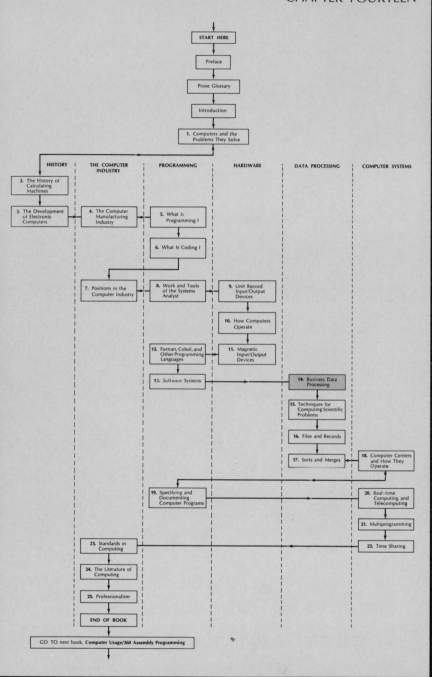

START HERE

Preface

Prose Glossary

Introduction

1. Computers and the Problems They Solve

HISTORY | THE COMPUTER INDUSTRY | PROGRAMMING | HARDWARE | DATA PROCESSING | COMPUTER SYSTEMS

2. The History of Calculating Machines

3. The Development of Electronic Computers

4. The Computer Manufacturing Industry

5. What Is Programming?

6. What Is Coding?

7. Positions in the Computer Industry

8. Work and Tools of the Systems Analyst

9. Unit Record Input/Output Devices

10. How Computers Operate

12. Fortran, Cobol, and Other Programming Languages

11. Magnetic Input/Output Devices

13. Software Systems

14. Business Data Processing

15. Techniques for Computing Scientific Problems

16. Files and Records

17. Sorts and Merges

18. Computer Centers and How They Operate

19. Specifying and Documenting Computer Programs

20. Real-time Computing and Telecomputing

21. Multiprogramming

23. Standards in Computing

22. Time Sharing

24. The Literature of Computing

25. Professionalism

END OF BOOK

GO TO next book, **Computer Usage/360 Assembly Programming**

BUSINESS
DATA
PROCESSING

Business data processing (BDP) is the manipulation of information that affects the operations of a business. Management is concerned with this information because the nature of the data and the way in which they are handled can frequently determine the success or failure of a commercial enterprise.

In this chapter the concept of business data processing, as opposed to any other form of electronic data processing, is of interest. The word *concept* was chosen deliberately, for in differentiating various areas of EDP it is almost impossible to give precise limits.

In the computer field there is much overlapping from area to area; this has been mentioned in earlier chapters. It is especially important to know the basic differences between scientific computing and business data processing. One of the major differences involves input/output. In BDP there is relatively little computing for each specific item. Instead the process involves feeding data into the computer (input) and having them processed and printed out in a previously determined form (output). In *scientific data processing* (SDP), computing usually takes precedence over I/O. The results of mathematical equations are one of the primary concerns in scientific data processing; in work of this nature the printout form is sometimes of less importance than the computation.

But the basic difference between business and scientific data processing is that business data processing is concerned with files and file manipulation, while scientific data processing is dominated by complex mathematical calculations. Thus file manipulation at a scientific laboratory would use the techniques of BDP, and a complex operations research calculation done by a business firm on its accounting computer would use the techniques of SDP.

☐ SCIENTIFIC PROGRAMMING TECHNIQUES

The mathematical demands of scientific programming have already been mentioned. Formulas, symbols, and numerical expressions are the tools of the scientific programmer. His programs often use *floating point arithmetic,* covered in Chapter 15.

As you learned in Chapter 12, *Fortran* is a widely used programming language for scientific processing. It was designed for problems that can be expressed best in algebraic notation. It is a very popular programming language. Most computers have Fortran compilers as part of the software.

In this chapter, scientific programming has only been mentioned as one more type of programming. Chapter 15 will deal exclusively with the various techniques of scientific computing and all the many facets that these techniques entail.

☐ BUSINESS PROGRAMMING TECHNIQUES

When programming a business application, the basic problem is translated into block diagrams by a systems analyst (see Chapter 8). From these diagrams, which are coded for processing, the programmers develop the individual programs that will form the business data processing application. Among the techniques employed are the use of Cobol, the handling of files, the protection of money, the protection of long runs, etc.

In addition to programming the problem from the flowchart, the programmer must concern himself with the problems unique to business data processing. Among these special problems are file labeling, file sequence control, audit control, error detection procedures, and many more. Some of these points are taken up in detail in Chapters 16 and 17.

USING COBOL

Until recently, nearly all business programs were written in assembly language, but programming languages are now being used more and more frequently. The most widely used programming language in business data processing is COBOL, which stands for "COmmon Business Oriented Language." Designed to facilitate programming business applications, it uses terms quite similar to ordinary business English. Cobol is covered in detail in another book in this series, *Computer Usage/360 Cobol Programming*. When Cobol was introduced in 1959, its announced purposes were:

1   To standardize a language for all present and future computers
2   To simplify the writing of BDP programs so that management could program directly, just as physicists use Fortran
3   To be self-documenting

The work of the developers of Cobol was that of preparing a Common Business Oriented Language. The word "common" indicates that the source program language would be compatible among a number of computers. Although machine differences make *total* compatibility impossible, the designers of Cobol were aiming for maximum compatibility.

It was felt that four important descriptive elements existed in a data processing problem:

1   Procedures specifying how data is to be manipulated
2   Description of data involved
3   Information pertaining to the specific computer on which the program will be run
4   Information identifying the program

As a result, Cobol was designed to include four major divisions:

Procedure division
Data division
Environment division
Identification division

Interestingly enough, Cobol was not as great a success in the business areas as Fortran was in the scientific areas (an indication that BDP is possibly not as easy as one might think). One difficulty was that the ease of using Cobol was oversold, so that too much was expected of it. People had many illusions about Cobol which were not valid. The disillusionment that followed caused many users to discard Cobol.

```
      IF SEQUENCE-U IS NOT NUMERIC MOVE 'SEQUENCE #' TO P-ERROR
      GO TO BAD-CARD.
      IF SEQUENCE-U = 01 GO TO PROC-U-01.
      IF SEQUENCE-U = 02 GO TO PROC-U-02.
      IF SEQUENCE-U = 03 GO TO PROC-U-03.
      MOVE 'SEQUENCE #' TO P-ERROR.
      GO TO BAD-CARD.
  PROC-U-01.
      IF NO-ENTRY = ALL ' ' MOVE 'NO ENTRY ' TO P-ERROR
      GO TO BAD-CARD.
      IF MAIL-PREF = ' ' GO TO CHKSTCD.
      IF MAIL-PREF < '1' OR MAIL-PREF > '2' MOVE 'MAIL PREF ' TO
      P-ERROR GO TO BAD-CARD.
  CHKSTCD.
      IF STATE-CODE = '  ' GO TO CHKFLAG.
      IF STATE-CODE IS NOT NUMERIC MOVE 'STATE CODE' TO P-ERROR
      GO TO BAD-CARD.
      IF STATE-CODE > 56 MOVE 'STATE CODE' TO P-ERROR
      GO TO BAD-CARD.
  CHKFLAG.
      IF FLAG = ' ' GO TO SETUP.
      IF FLAG < 'A' OR FLAG > 'C' MOVE 'FLAG      ' TO P-ERROR
      GO TO BAD-CARD.
      GO TO SETUP.
  PROC-U-02.
      IF NO-ENTRY = ALL ' ' MOVE 'NO ENTRY ' TO P-ERROR
      GO TO BAD-CARD.
      IF COMP-CODE = '  ' GO TO CHKUCA.
      IF COMP-CODE IS NOT NUMERIC MOVE 'COMP CODE ' TO P-ERROR
      GO TO BAD-CARD.
  CHKUCA.
      IF UNRES-CRED-AMT = '      ' GO TO SETUP.
      IF UNRES-CRED-AMT IS NOT NUMERIC MOVE 'UN-CRD-AMT' TO P-ERROR
      GO TO BAD-CARD.
      GO TO SETUP.
  PROC-U-03.
      IF NO-ENTRY = ALL ' ' MOVE 'NO ENTRY ' TO P-ERROR
      GO TO BAD-CARD.
      IF EXP-DATE = '    ' GO TO CHKDUES.
      IF EXP-DATE IS NOT NUMERIC MOVE 'EXPIR DATE' TO P-ERROR
      GO TO BAD-CARD.
      IF EXP-MO < 01 OR EXP-MO > 12 MOVE 'EXPIR DATE' TO P-ERROR
      GO TO BAD-CARD.
  CHKDUES.
      IF DUES-AMT = '    ' GO TO CHKPDATE.
```

A PORTION OF A COBOL PROGRAM.

Recently, Cobol has gained wider acceptance in BDP because of a more realistic attitude toward the language and its capabilities, and also because of the development of more efficient compilers than were available in the early 1960s. As mentioned in Chapter 12, Cobol is now standardized. Today Cobol is a tool for systems analysts and business programmers, but its limitations are recognized. No programming language ever saved one minute of systems analysis. A good language saves time only after the systems analysis has been completed.

☐ MONEY AND BUSINESS DATA PROCESSING

One of the most important differences between BDP and all other forms of electronic data processing has been money. Business requires the safe and accurate handling of actual dollar amounts involved in a computer application. The security of the cash handled directly is of extreme importance. Where money is involved, *no mistakes* may be made. Systems analysts build *financial controls* into their business systems. These may include various *validity checks* at key points in the operation and predetermined *audit trails* for the auditors handling or checking the company records. An audit trail is a process whereby the data path can be followed by reference to the documentation for the program. Proper provisions can eliminate the need for considerable clerical effort in referring to input documents, checking and printing all intermediate files, and checking all intermediate and final results. It is absolutely essential that lucidity be built into the system for the sake of control.

A final note, though not a pleasant one, is the necessity of taking precautionary measures to guard against people who have access to elements of the computer system using this access to divert money into their own pockets. Business systems which handle money must have some method of control built in, to protect the system from tampering of this nature.

FILES
Computer-readable files are essential to any BDP application. For example, consider a computerized bank. No banking system could exist without an extremely efficient file system that can be constantly updated, corrected, protected, and purged without destroying the useful information already on file. These same requirements exist for all business data processing applications, whether the system is for banking, for inventory control, or for a payroll application. Files which were once kept on paper or cards are now most often maintained on magnetic tape, but the use of magnetic discs and drums for file storage is increasing. Chapter 16 on *files and records* will pursue this subject further.

FILE LABELING

File labeling is a technique by which an identification of a file—that is, a label—is recorded on the magnetic medium on which the file is also recorded. This is a particularly necessary safeguard to ensure the use of the current and correct file and to prevent the use of an old file or an inapplicable one.

At the beginning of each file, the initial record is used to identify the file found on that tape. This is the file label. The file is identified in some of the following ways:

1   File name
2   Reel number (if a multireel magnetic tape file)
3   Date on which the file was generated
4   Current status of the file
5   Retention period of the particular file (date on which it will be obsolete)

Before processing a file, the computer is instructed to read the label of each input file into memory and check it. All Cobol programs, for example, read the labels of every input tape. The Cobol verb is OPEN . . . . An example of this instruction is OPEN MASTER. Once the name of an input file is given, the computer reads the label and checks that it is the correct file. For an output file, a label is generated and written on the new tape or disc.

Reading the file label is necessary when updating or purging a file. Once it has been established that the tape is the correct one for the operation, the cycle and the retention period are checked. *Each processing is equivalent to one cycle, and the retention period denotes the cycle number before it*

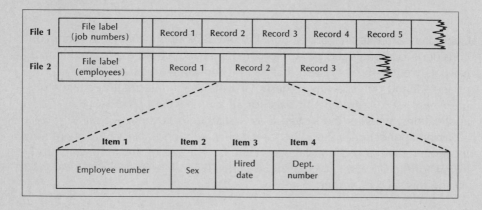

can be retired. Most tapes are retained for *three cycles* and are sometimes referred to as the son-father-grandfather. Such retention allows re-creation of the most recent (son) file from the previous version (father), or even the one before that (grandfather), in the event that the "son" file is lost or is found to be erroneous.

MONDAY	TUESDAY	WEDNESDAY
Grandfather	Father	Son

This is a diagram of a savings bank application. Note how each tape, new on one day, is the old file the next day. On Wednesday, the old master of Monday is grandfather, the old master of Tuesday is father, and the old master of Wednesday is son.

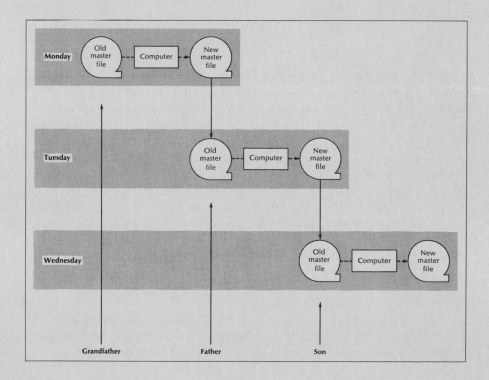

FILE SEQUENCE CONTROL

In business data processing files, each record in the file contains a *key,* consisting of numbers and letters which is used for the identification and sequencing of each record. Examples of this type of identification are a social security number, a charge-plate number, an employee number, etc. In addition to the key, each record contains the file information of the record, the taxes paid, the amounts of purchases, the amounts deposited, etc.

Files are generally sequential—meaning that the file is arranged in ascending (or descending) sequence of the key; for example, in alphabetic order by name, in numeric order by payroll number, etc. All references to such a file—reading, searching, changing, etc.—are carried out by reference to the key. For example, in typical file management operations, the BDP programmer instructs:

```
Delete. . . .Record 36-4913
Display. . .Record 29-1468
Replace. . .Record 18-6321
                    with
                    31-1968
```

SORTING AND MERGING

Sorting and merging are techniques that are a part of file sequencing. When records are to be changed to a new sequence, they are put in the new sequential order by a process called *sorting. Merging* is the process of combining two or more files already in an identical sequence into a single file in the same sequence. For example, a magnetic tape file contains records of employees with their departments listed. The file is in employee number sequence, but the application requires the file to be in department number sequence. The programmer requests that a computer sort (a program provided by the computer manufacturer) be used on the file, and he specifies the new sequence. Or the programmer might wish to combine the files for employees in two different plants. For this he uses a merge program. (Incidentally, Chapter 17 deals with this subject.)

OUTPUT ON PREPRINTED FORMS

Another feature that is sometimes of great importance is unique to BDP: the preprinted form. Bank checks or bills are among these forms. They create their own programming problem because printing by the computer on special forms must be done in such a way that it is accurate, is positioned in the correct spot, and looks good. It is the responsibility of the programmer to develop a program that can fulfill these requirements.

ERROR DETECTION PROCEDURES

In BDP a program *must* be run (even though there are errors in the data), but errors must be corrected for the balancing of books, etc. A successful business system must have its own error detection procedures built into it for commercial protection and expediency.

One important procedure involves the *exception file*. This file contains a printed record of all the errors detected by the computer in a particular run. When the run is completed, the exception file is submitted to an analyst whose job it is to correct all errors noted on the exception file. He then resubmits the corrected record for processing.

For example, a certain employee's weekly paycheck should have been for the amount of one hundred dollars ($100). Instead, the check was made out for ten thousand dollars ($10,000)—obviously a gross error. This error, however, has been detected by the computer, and the erroneous record written on the exception file. The exception file is turned over to the analyst; the mistake is found and corrected; and in the next run, the paycheck is issued. The mistake is also corrected on the active payroll file.

Obviously, the correction of the error is of great importance; but insofar as the business data processing programmer is concerned, *detection* is the program's responsibility; *correcting* the error is the human function.

CHECKPOINT RESTARTS

Checkpoint restarts are another error correction technique. They are particularly useful on long runs lasting 15 minutes to several hours. When a computer becomes incapable of functioning because of electrical or mechanical difficulties, processing cannot be continued. Once the computer is ready to resume, the processing is *restarted* from the closest *checkpoint*.

At each checkpoint, the contents of main memory, all registers, and the status of all input/output equipment are recorded on a specific checkpoint file. In addition, any partially calculated results on intermediate files are preserved.

Checkpoints are generally taken either every *n* records (100 or 1,000) or every five minutes. One of the most popular methods of taking checkpoints is at the end of each output reel and/or input reel. It is extremely important to designate the frequency of the checkpoint, for in business data processing most files and programs are so long that they cannot be processed in a short period of time. If other programs take precedence over the schedule, a checkpoint can also be taken in order to stop the one program and do the scheduled run. The original program is then continued later at the predetermined checkpoint, and the run is restarted.

□ CANNED PROGRAMS

One final note concerning business programming is the problem of the canned program. This is a master program, designed for a general type of application, which can be successfully used for similar applications in many locations. In scientific processing, canned programs are common because scientific problems are formulated in precise and standard terms.

In business processing, however, this does not apply. A payroll program, for example, is a typical business application. It seems probable that one payroll program could be designed for use throughout many companies. However, such is not the case. Each company has its individual problems and will even have variances from branch to branch. Payroll applications may differ owing to bonus systems, salaries based on sales percentages, tax differences from state to state and from city to city, union agreements, and company traditions.

Employees working on the railroads and traveling through several states on a job must be taxed on the wages earned in each state according to the tax law of the particular state. Piecework payment also presents many difficulties. Complications of this nature make canned programs inapplicable or inefficient in many BDP applications.

□ THE EXTENT OF BDP

It is interesting to note that at least half, if not more, of the computers running are used for business data processing. It should not then be surprising that about 55 percent of the people in the computer field are also connected with business data processing. Of the remainder, about 15 percent are involved in scientific processing, and the rest are doing real time computing, software production, etc.

☐ ATTITUDE OF THE BUSINESS PROGRAMMER

It is extremely important to realize that a scientific programmer is often looking for a single answer. He develops a program that enables the computer to find that answer; the program may not be run again. The business programmer, however, is interested in the repetitive handling of specific data that will regularly process selected information at given intervals.

In the interest of time and expense, the systems analyst is interested in speed, cost, flexibility, and maintenance. The business programmer is interested in saving microseconds, since millions of repeats add up to seconds and minutes. Minutes are a rather expensive commodity in electronic data processing. If a company is to compete commercially, then it must carefully assess and conserve every dollar.

☐ BUSINESS DATA PROCESSING IN THIS BOOK

A number of chapters in this book are particularly concerned with BDP. For purposes of future reference and review, it is important to be aware that these chapters are closely allied with BDP:

Systems Analysis (Chapter 8)
Unit Records (Chapter 9)
Magnetic Devices (Chapter 11)
Business Data Processing (Chapter 14)
Files and Records (Chapter 16)
Sorts and Merges (Chapter 17).

Another book in this series, *Computer Usage/Applications,* deals with typical computer applications, many of them in the BDP field, while *Computer Usage/360 Cobol Programming* teaches the standard BDP computer language.

☐ QUESTION

1 Reconsider the pros and cons of the language selection policies of the problem given at the end of Chapter 12. How would these policies affect a computer installation almost entirely devoted to business data processing?

START HERE

Preface

Prose Glossary

Introduction

1. Computers and the Problems They Solve

| HISTORY | THE COMPUTER INDUSTRY | PROGRAMMING | HARDWARE | DATA PROCESSING | COMPUTER SYSTEMS |

2. The History of Calculating Machines

3. The Development of Electronic Computers

4. The Computer Manufacturing Industry

5. What Is Programming ?

6. What Is Coding ?

7. Positions in the Computer Industry

8. Work and Tools of the Systems Analyst

9. Unit Record Input/Output Devices

10. How Computers Operate

12. Fortran, Cobol, and Other Programming Languages

11. Magnetic Input/Output Devices

13. Software Systems

14. Business Data Processing

15. Techniques for Computing Scientific Problems

16. Files and Records

17. Sorts and Merges

18. Computer Centers and How They Operate

19. Specifying and Documenting Computer Programs

20. Real-time Computing and Telecomputing

21. Multiprogramming

22. Time Sharing

23. Standards in Computing

24. The Literature of Computing

25. Professionalism

END OF BOOK

GO TO next book, **Computer Usage/360 Assembly Programming**

TECHNIQUES FOR COMPUTING SCIENTIFIC PROBLEMS

Isaac Newton, far from relying on a flash of inspiration, actually had to develop a new mathematical tool—differential calculus—in order to work out his discoveries. Scientists today, are relying on electronic computers to help them work out and test their theories. Computers provide a means of gaining control over the vast amounts of information that must go into scientific thinking, and are not a substitute for such thinking.

It has been said, "If mathematics is the handmaiden of science, then electronic computing is the handmaiden of mathematics." To the mathematician, computers are not only interesting machines in and of themselves, they also help collect information, analyze it, and perform huge amounts of arithmetic in a short space of time. The scientist and engineer derive aid from computers in designing electronic circuits, in planning the many complicated parts needed for our modern technology, in building bridges and space vehicles, as well as in providing some better understanding of the nature of our world and of the universe around us.

□ WHAT ROLE DOES MATHEMATICS PLAY IN THE SCIENCES?

No one can deny that the physical sciences have played a major part in molding our modern civilization. Mathematics has materially influenced our age through its connection with the physical sciences, and indeed with all fields of scientific investigation—including psychology, medicine, anthropology, law, and even politics. Mathematics is useful to the sciences, for it supplies a language, methods, and conclusions for scientific reasoning. It thereby enables scientists to predict results; furnishes scientists with ideas for describing phenomena, such as the motion of charged particles in the earth's magnetic field; and prepares the minds of researchers for new ways of reasoning.

It is not surprising, therefore, that in our time science has become more mathematical. When we look into the techniques being used in many sciences, we find that physical concepts are often being replaced by concepts which are mathematical in nature; that sciences have adopted the use of abstract concepts and postulates to explain phenomena; and finally, that our sciences have become more mathematical by making greater use of the deductive method of reasoning.

Immanuel Kant, the philosopher, once remarked that the degree of development of science depends upon the extent to which it has become mathematized. By this criterion our modern sciences are advancing toward a high degree of development. Even in some of those fields in which mathematics is little employed at present, there are many experts who believe that when mathematical ideas and methods are used more extensively, progress will be more rapid.

In the sciences, the mathematical method is an approach to problems which may be employed in all fields of inquiry. It is not the mere use of formulas and conclusions. Its core consists of the mathematical evaluation of assumptions used, hypotheses tested, and conclusions reached. Used in conjunction with the scientific method—strict objective inquiry—the mathematical method is an analytical tool of scientific judgment concerning adequacy and accuracy of theories. Some questions that are asked in proceeding with the investigation of a scientific problem by the mathematical method are much the same as the questions a computer programmer must ask before writing a program. They include:

How is the problem designed—purpose, scope, procedure, method?
How is the problem defined, delimited, analyzed?

What are the component parts of the problem? The objectives of each?
What is the state of art on the subject? What is known about the
problem? By what authority?
What assumptions are made? How reasonable is each one?
What hypotheses are used—projection or causation—and are they
plausible?
What conclusions are reached? Are they supported by adequate facts?
What are we attempting to show or prove? What has been shown or
proved?

From the point of view of the scientific programmer, problem solutions are
characterized by a minimum of input, a maximum of computing, and a
maximum of repetition of groups of computer instructions (looping).

The mathematical techniques involved in scientific computing require
special technical training, and our discussion of them here is for the sole
purpose of understanding how some of them expedite the solution of
scientific problems. One does not become a violinist merely by learning
about music and listening to records, or a chemist by learning how
chemistry provides better things for better living, or a novelist by reading
novels. To become a scientific programmer one must study and practice
techniques, as well as understand the ideas and their significance.

☐ HOW TO CHANGE NUMBERS FROM ORDINARY NOTATION TO FLOATING POINT NOTATION

One of the interesting developments of modern science is the use of larger
and larger numbers on the one hand, and smaller and smaller ones on the
other. Interplanetary distances and dimensions of galaxies, populations of
pathogenic bacteria, national incomes, and debts are among the many
quantities requiring very large numbers for their expression. The weight of
an electron, the diameter of an atom, the thickness of an oil film, the
wavelength of light—these quantities are expressed by very small numbers.
Such numbers are often so extreme that they cannot be calculated and
expressed efficiently by a computer, even one with a capacity of 45-bit
word lengths; and few computers have such a large capacity. For example,
how can we handle a problem in which the number of atoms in 1.008
grams of hydrogen is

606,000,000,000,000,000,000,000,000

Obviously there must be some way out of such a totally unacceptable situation. There is. Instead of writing zeros, we merely designate the location of the decimal point by employing exponents. (Exponents and powers were described in Chapter 10.) This is called *floating point notation*.

A number is said to be expressed in floating decimal when it is written as the product of an integral power of 10 and a number between 1 and 10. Thus 325 would be expressed as 3.25×10^2, 3.25 being the part between 1 and 10, and 10^2 being the integral power of 10. The number of atoms in 1.008 grams of hydrogen would be expressed as 6.06×10^{23}. The number 1.008 itself would be expressed in floating decimal as 1.008×10^0, recalling that any number to the power zero is 1.

To write very small numbers we use negative exponents, since raising a number to a negative power is the same as putting that number with the same positive power in the denominator of the fraction. That is, $10^{-2} = 1/10^2$. Therefore the floating decimal expression 3.25×10^{-2} is, in ordinary notation, the number .0325, since

$$3.25 \times 10^{-2} = 3.25 \times \frac{1}{10^2} = 3.25 \times \frac{1}{100} = .0325$$

A computer programmer needs to know how to change numbers from "fixed" decimal to floating decimal, and vice versa. This involves knowing how to multiply a number in fixed decimal by an integral power of ten.

To multiply a number by 10 we move the decimal point one place to the *right*, to multiply by 10^2 we move the point two places to the right, etc. Since $10^{-1} = 1/10$, to multiply by 10^{-1} means to multiply by 1/10, which is the same as dividing by 10. Therefore, to multiply by 10^{-1} we move the decimal point one place to the *left*. In like manner, since $10^{-2} = 1/10^2 = 1/100$, to multiply 10^{-2} we move the decimal point two places to the left, etc. Here are a few typical examples of conversions such as may be encountered in scientific computing:

Floating Decimal	Procedure	Fixed Decimal
6.87×10^4	Move decimal point four places to *right*.	68,700.
6.87×10^{-4}	Move decimal point four places to *left*.	.000687

Fixed Decimal	Procedure	Floating Decimal
286	Move decimal point two places to the left, yielding 2.86. This amounts to dividing by 100 or 10^2. To offset this, multiply 2.86 by 10^2.	2.86×10^2
.0286	Move decimal point two places to the right, yielding 2.86. This amounts to multiplying by 10^2. To offset this, divide by 10^2, or multiply by 10^{-2}, which is the same thing.	2.86×10^{-2}

Whenever the need exists to express very large or very small quantities, floating point notation is more concise than fixed point notation and more readily used by the computer; it is possible to multiply and divide with these quantities more conveniently.

☐ LIVE WITH ERRORS, AVOID MISTAKES, BE ALERT FOR MALFUNCTIONS

It is not an overstatement to say that consideration of any factor which may contribute to loss of precision in scientific computing, as well as general purpose data processing, should be uppermost in the minds of the programmer and everyone concerned with the operation of the computer. In the language of our specialty, essentially numerical *errors* occur in computational and mathematical methods; *mistakes* occur in programming, coding, data transcription, and operations; *malfunctions* occur in computer hardware. All three are contributing factors to loss of precision.

By definition, *error* refers to any deviation of a computed (computational) quantity or a measured (mathematical) quantity from the theoretically correct or true value. Programmers cannot do away completely with errors, since any number we write is necessarily in finite form, which is only an approximation of its infinite conception. There are a few exceptions—we may consider 0.500000000 to be an infinite decimal. Real numbers, with their infinite strings of digits, cannot be represented in the finite number of storage locations in a computer. They must be approximated by rational numbers. Consider the Greek letter pi, symbol of the familiar number that defines the ratio of the circumference of a circle to its diameter:

π is approximately equal to 3.1415926

A better approximation is 3.141592653589793. More precision would require more digits, but the computer can accommodate only a limited number. It is necessary to make an error and *truncate* the true number to fit it in. The errors cannot be avoided but, hopefully, their magnitudes can be estimated.

The inability to represent irrational numbers (π is an irrational number) is not the only source of error in scientific computing. Some others include:

Data Error—A deviation from accuracy in data that occurred prior to processing the data. For example: You are given a 4 and a 3 to multiply, but the correct data were 4 and 8.

Inherent Error—The error introduced by the inability to make exact measurements.

Overflow Error—A computer arithmetic operation resulting in a value that exceeds the capacity of the storage allowed for that word. This type of error occurs abruptly in a calculation, and when it does the result becomes nonsense. By contrast most of the errors discussed here are small and build up gradually.

Underflow Error—An operation producing a value that is diminished in a series of successive calculations until the internal floating point arithmetic requires more storage than was allowed for that word. It is similar in effect to an overflow error but less serious, since "zero" becomes a good approximation.

Rounding Error—An error resulting from rounding off a quantity by deleting the less significant digits and applying some rule of correction to the part retained. For example, 3.1561 can be rounded off to 3.16 with a rounding error of .0039. (Note contrast with truncation error.)

Truncation Error—This error occurs when a number is placed in a storage area which possesses too few digits to accommodate it. In the example above, if only three positions are allowed for 3.1561, the machine would cut off the least significant digits without rounding and store 3.15. Thus truncation error is more serious than rounding error. Truncation errors occur frequently in transferring input and output to the computer.

Propagated Error—An error, occurring in a previous operation, that spreads through and influences later operations and results which use the results of the erroneous operation.

☐ THE SIGNIFICANCE OF A NUMBER

The precision of a number is measured in terms of how many significant figures it contains. For example, 5600.0 has five significant digits, while 5600 probably has two significant digits. Significance depends upon the number of digits which are not for decimal point positioning only.

Any one of the digits 1, 2, 3, 4, 5, 6, 7, 8, 9 is a significant figure. 0 is not always a significant figure; a great deal depends on where it is located in a number. None of the three zeros in the number 0.00456 is significant because they are used simply to fix the decimal point. A zero that lies to the *left* of all other nonzero digits is not significant. But zeros that are positioned between nonzero digits are considered to be significant: for instance, 40056. Finally, there is the case in which the zero lies to the *right* of all other nonzero digits, as in 45600. It is not clear how many of the digits are significant. This must be determined from the context in which the number is written. If neither of the zeros is significant, we would write 456×10^2, while on the other hand, if the first zero were significant, we would adopt the writing convention 4560×10^1.

The number of significant digits is counted beginning with the one called the *most significant digit*, which contributes the greatest value, and ending with the *least significant digit*, the one which contributes least value. Consider the following numbers. Each has only four significant figures:

1,234   0.008739
9,702 $6,800 \times 10^2$
5,006   0.01205

In these examples the most significant figures are 1, 9, 5, 8, 6, and 1; the least significant figures are 4, 2, 6, 9, 0, and 5.

A number composed of n significant figures is said to be correct to n significant figures. (In this case n has the mathematical conventional shorthand meaning of "any number," for example, 6 or 9 or 5,280.) Writing the significant number 1.2392 implies that the true value represented by this number is less than or equal to 1.239249999, and greater than or equal to 1.23915. This can be indicated by writing 1.2392 ± 0.00005.

The process of reducing the number of significant figures has already been suggested in this discussion—it is *rounding off*. Less important or less significant digits are often dropped, and increased precision is obtained by adding the more significant digits that are retained. The rounding rule of adding 5 in the leftmost position to be dropped will change 3.4565 to 3.457

for rounding to three digits. The following numbers have been rounded to four significant figures:

Number	Rounded number
0.153956412	0.1540
58.775000	58.78
0.005218600	0.005219
286.3178	286.3

Programmers, who use approximate data in computations, make use of formulas which state limits within which the errors lie after each computation. A basic principle is this: *The result of a computation is not more reliable than the least precise item.*

MAINTAINING PROPER SIGNIFICANCE

Numerical computation performed by a computer reduces to the four arithmetic operations the problem of retaining significance. In many computing situations it is as bad to overestimate an error as it is to underestimate one.

In *adding* two positive numbers there is usually no loss of significant figures. In fact, the sum sometimes has one more significant figure than either of the operands. Suppose we compare the addition of two numbers in both their rounded and unrounded forms. In the first set we see, on comparison, that there is a gain of significance, because the rounding errors canceled out, and the added significant figure resulted from the carry. In the second set we see that the rounded result is off by 1 unit, since the errors in the least significant figures of the operands were maximum and were added together. In general, if we always include one more significant figure than is necessary, we will be more sure of having at least the required significance in our result.

I		II	
52,761	52,761.2	12,762	12,761.5
+71,437	+71,436.7	+11,437	+11,436.5
124,198	124,197.9	24,199	24,198.0
Rounded	Unrounded	Rounded	Unrounded

In *subtraction*, complete loss of significance is possible. Consider the following example. Although the subtrahend and minuend are correct to five significant figures, the difference has no significant figures—the 2 is way off.

```
  12,764    12,763.7
 −12,762   −12,762.3
  00,002    00,001.4
```
Rounded   Unrounded

When such a situation is encountered, use many more significant figures in the operands to begin with, and hope that enough significance will carry through to the result.

In *multiplication* (*and division*), up to two significant figures can be lost. In the following example we note that the multiplicand and multiplier are both correct to three significant figures, while the product is correct to only two:

```
   811      810.6
   112      112.4
  1622     32424
   811     16212
   811      8106
 90832     8106
           91111.44
```
Rounded Unrounded

Rounded to three figures, the third figure of the product—off by 3 units—is not significant.

□ NUMERICAL ANALYSIS

One of the biggest of the hurdles that face the novice programmer is the realization that digital computers cannot do anything more than the simplest arithmetical operations. Each of the common ones—addition, subtraction, multiplication, and division—is available with a single command from the program. The square root command is also available but, for the most part, digital circuits don't know a square root from an integral sign. All these more complex operations must be reduced to combinations of the fundamental arithmetic operations.

With the development of computer systems, it became desirable to revive an old mathematical tool, *numerical analysis*. This is the branch of mathematics that provides methods for transforming nonarithmetic problems into problems consisting of only simple arithmetic steps. It is possible—as we shall see—to integrate a function by adding the areas of infinitesimally narrow strips under the curve representing the function. It is rarely done this way by pencil-and-paper methods, because the operation is tedious and for most problems we have calculus to do it for us. But the computer knows no calculus, and cannot be taught. It does such problems the tedious way, but it does them so fast that the operation is quite practical.

We have already made use of some of the numerical analysis techniques—without labeling them as such—in our discussion of the arithmetic operations in relation to accuracy and error. Keeping the question of error in mind, we can now proceed to an elementary discussion of how a computer can be used to perform function evaluation, integration, or differentiation, or to solve ordinary and partial differential equations.

By definition, numerical analysis is concerned with the study of methods used to obtain useful quantitative solutions to problems that have been expressed mathematically.

A FREQUENTLY OCCURRING PROBLEM IN NUMERICAL COMPUTATION

The solution of simultaneous linear equations is a problem which arises frequently in all fields of scientific and engineering computing. Most people who have been exposed to algebra know that simultaneous equations are those in which the same unknown quantities have the same values, and they know a method of solving such systems of equations as:

$x + y = 12 \qquad x - y = 2$
Solution: $x = 7$, $y = 5$

Techniques for solving simultaneous linear equations include solving (1) *by determinants*, (2) *by elimination or reduction*, and (3) *by iterative operations*. From the standpoint of scientific computing, the *determinant* technique is not an effective method, as the number of arithmetic steps is often excessively large. Various *elimination* techniques are most often used. They operate to combine several equations containing unknown quantities, in order to deduce therefrom a smaller number of equations containing a smaller number of unknown quantities.

Iterative methods are used to obtain a solution or to improve the solution after an approximate result has been obtained by elimination. The iterative technique is a method for calculating a desired result by means of a repeated cycle of operations that comes closer and closer to the desired result.

As an example of one method used in scientific computing for simultaneous linear equations, consider a special set of equations:

$$a + s_{12}b + s_{13}c + s_{14}d = m$$
$$b + s_{23}c + s_{24}d = n$$
$$c + s_{34}d = o$$
$$d = p$$

These four equations can easily be solved for the four unknowns a, b, c, d, as $d = p$ is already given and it follows that

$$c = o - s_{34}d$$
$$b = n - s_{24}d - s_{23}c$$
$$a = m - s_{14}d - s_{13}c - s_{12}b$$

Thus, if we manipulate a series of n number equations so that the diagonal coefficients become 1 and the coefficients below the diagonal become zero, then the solutions can be readily obtained.

We can illustrate this with an actual set of four equations with four unknowns:

Equation No.	Equation
1	$3a + 9b + 6c - 12d = 9$
2	$2a + 8b + 12c - 2d = 2$
3	$3a + 12b + 21c - 9d = 15$
4	$-a - b + 8c + 8d = 5$

Dividing both sides of Equation 1 by 3, we get

5	$a + 3b + 2c - 4d = 3$

Now multiply this new equation by 2 and subtract from Equation 2, with the difference

6	$2b + 8c + 6d = -4$

Following the same process, we multiply Equation 5 by 3 and subtract from Equation 3, obtaining

7	$3b + 15c + 3d = 6$

Finally, we repeat the process by multiplying Equation 5 by -1 and subtracting from Equation 4, yielding

8	$2b + 10c + 4d = 8$

Continuing in the same manner, we repeat the entire process using Equations 6, 7, and 8. This gives us the new equations 9, 10, and 11.

9    $b + 4c + 3d = -2$
10    $3c - 6d = 12$
11    $2c - 2d = 12$

From 10 and 11 we obtain 12 and 13.

12    $c - 2d = 4$
13    $2d = 4$

This gives the value for d.

14    $d = 2$

The set of equations from which the solution is obtained is

5    $a + 3b + 2c - 4d = 3$
9    $b + 4c + 3d = -2$
12    $c - 2d = 4$
14    $d = 2$

From this we obtain the values

$d = 2$
$c = 4 + 2 \times 2 = 8$
$b = -2 - 3 \times 2 - 4 \times 8 = -40$
$a = 3 + 4 \times 2 - 2 \times 8 - 3 \times (-40) = 115$

The flowchart for solving simultaneous linear questions by this method is on page 225.

A POWERFUL TOOL FOR SUMMING

Whenever it becomes necessary to calculate some result that involves bringing together, or summing up, countless elements belonging to a continuous distribution of some sort—such as matter, or force—the process of integration is used. Use of integration provides the methods for computing the mass of a body of variable density, the total force of gravitational attraction between two bodies, the total force of attraction or repulsion between two electrically charged particles, and many other physical quantities.

A basic application of integration is the determination of the area under a

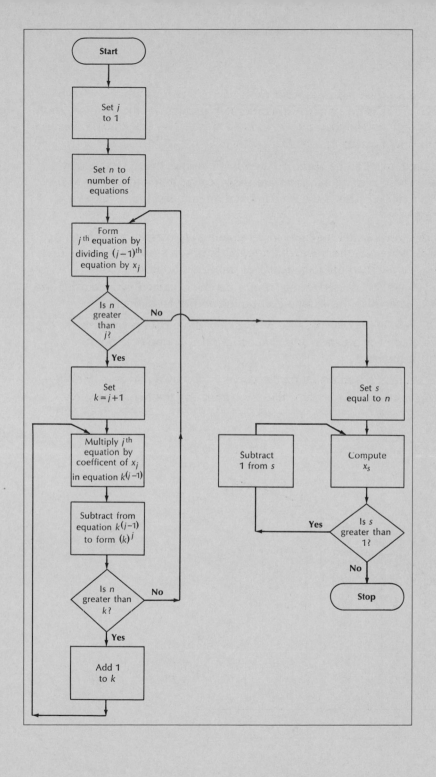

given curve represented as $f(x)$. For most curves, such as the one shown in the sketch, there is no simple, direct method to calculate the area (say, from $x = 0$ to $x = p$) as bounded by $y = f(x)$ and $y = 0$. This situation, however, is frequently encountered in scientific problems.

The required area can be approximated by covering it with rectangular segments. These rectangular areas are easily calculated and add up to the total area required. This is the fundamental technique used in *numerical integration*.

There are several better methods for evaluating an integral, including (1) analytical means, (2) the trapezoid rule, (3) Simpson's rule. Simpson's rule is more accurate than the rectangular or trapezoid approximations. Whichever method is used, better results can be obtained by increasing the number of intervals. This is time-consuming and often difficult.

Simpson's rule is popular because it considers three data points (intervals) at a time instead of two data points (trapezoid rule) or one data point (rectangular method).

Simpson's rule is based on fitting the curve $y = f(x)$ by a parabola and then integrating the parabola analytically. By comparing the two figures, one can

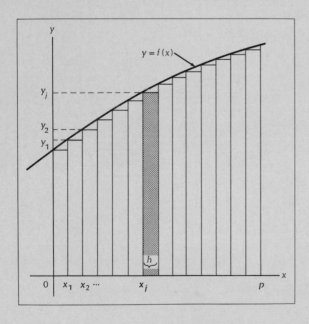

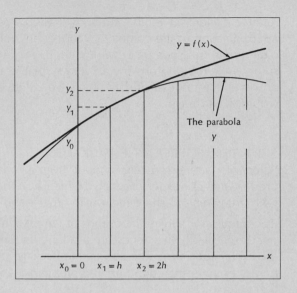

see that the parabolic approximation represents the area more accurately than the rectangular. If n points are used to represent the curve $y=f(x)$; the area given by Simpson's rule is

$$A = \frac{h}{3}(y_0 + 4y_1 + 2y_2 + 4y_3 + 2y_4 + 4y_5 + \ldots + 4y_{n-1} + y_n)$$

This formula is applied to many basic scientific problems. In physics, for example, we may be given a series of data points with each point assigned time and velocity values. If we integrate the velocity and time, we find out the distance traveled. In the graphic representations of such problems, velocities become the heights of the strips, and time becomes the width of the strips under the curve.

The accuracy of the integration is improved as we make the strips under the curve more narrow. In this kind of scientific computing, each program should be analyzed to determine how fine the interval we choose should be in relation to computer running time. This is a difficult problem, in which we must consider the capacity of the computer load, the number of calculations, the scale factor of the numbers involved, etc. In many cases the "happy medium" is based on a determination of the number of data points that can be carried in working the problem without increasing errors—such as rounding-off errors—to a degree where they will distort the results. This is a relative matter, since the solution will always be no more than an approximation of the completely correct answer. Where a large number of data points are given us to work with, it is relatively easy to select a sufficient number to provide an answer that is adequate. In practice, however, the number of data points we are given is usually fewer than we would like to have.

SCIENTIFIC SUBROUTINE PACKAGES
Scientific users also receive support from a collection of off-the-shelf predesigned computer programs, which have been prepared both by users who are willing to share them with others, and by hardware manufacturers.

Techniques for solving thousands of complex mathematical problems that occur repeatedly in science are available in these programs. For example, the System/360 Scientific Subroutine Package (SSP/360) is a ready-made library of more than two hundred problem-solving techniques that frees

SOME OF THE ROUTINES IN SSP/360

TALLY	Totals, means, standard deviations, minimums, and maximums	GTPRID	Transpose product of two general matrices
BOUND	Selection of observations within bounds	MADD	Add two matrices
SUBST	Subset selection from observation matrix	MSUB	Subtract two matrices
ABSNT	Detection of missing data	MPRD	Matrix product (row into column)
TAB1	Tabulation of data (1 variable)	MTRA	Transpose a matrix
TAB2	Tabulation of data (2 variables)	TPRD	Transpose product
SUBMX	Build subset matrix	MATA	Transpose product of matrix
MOMEN	First four moments	SADD	Add scalar to matrix
TTEST	Tests on population means	SSUB	Subtract scalar from a matrix
ORDER	Rearrangement of intercorrelations	SMPY	Matrix multiplied by a scalar
AVDAT	Data storage allocation	SDIV	Matrix divided by a scalar
TRACE	Cumulative percentage of eigenvalues	RADD	Add row of one matrix to row of another matrix
CHISQ	χ^2 test for a contingency table	CADD	Add column of one matrix to column of another matrix
UTEST	Mann-Whitney U-test	SRMA	Scalar multiply row and add to another row
TWOAV	Friedman two-way analysis of variance	SCMA	Scalar multiply column and add to another column
QTEST	Cochran Q-test	RINT	Interchange two rows
SRANK	Spearman rank correlation	CINT	Interchange two columns
KRANK	Kendall rank correlation	RSUM	Sum the rows of a matrix
WTEST	Kendall coefficient of concordance		

programmers from having to program computers to handle each individual problem. Essentially, the program provides the computer in advance with the means to solve a wide range of problems. The computer needs only data to provide answers.

The programs can be used separately or in combinations to provide answers to problems in medical research, orbital calculations, and thousands of other areas. They are written in Fortran language.

The user of this package (1) selects one or more of the programs from storage in tape, disc, or cards; (2) provides numerical values for the problem; (3) establishes limitations regarding scaling and other factors; and (4) instructs the computer what to do with the answer. The answer can be a numerical value for the next problem or can be printed out in matrix, graph, or other form.

Routines within this package deal with such techniques as:

Analysis of variance
Time series analysis
Simultaneous linear algebraic equations
Integration of given or tabulated functions
Finding real and complex roots of real polynomial equations
Polynomial evaluation, integration, differentiation, elliptic, exponential, sine, cosine function
Fourier analysis of given or tabulated functions
Multiple linear regression

□ QUESTIONS

1 Write the following floating decimal numbers in fixed decimal notation:

7.89×10^2 1.00×10^{-6}
9.876×10^0 3.46×10^4
0.00×10^8 -2.34×10^2
2.34×10^{-2}

2 Write the following fixed decimal numbers in floating decimal form:

1,000,000,000 .000000001
256 1675.45
000000.1 −2.34
−0.0000045 23.450008

3   Round these numbers to four significant figures:

.134526354	.000001564345
.111199999	0000011111.897
1000500000	1000499999
.9999000	.9999900
.999949	−.999949

4   What are the differences between scientific and business problems that make the listed error sources more significant for scientific problems? Which ones would occur frequently in business problems and which ones would occur infrequently? Under what conditions?

5   Follow the flowchart method given for solving simultaneous linear equations to solve this set:

$6a + 18b + 12c = 66$
$4a + 16b + 24c = 12$
$3a + 12b + 21c = 33$

START HERE

Preface

Prose Glossary

Introduction

1. Computers and the Problems They Solve

HISTORY	THE COMPUTER INDUSTRY	PROGRAMMING	HARDWARE	DATA PROCESSING	COMPUTER SYSTEMS

2. The History of Calculating Machines

3. The Development of Electronic Computers

4. The Computer Manufacturing Industry

5. What Is Programming ?

6. What Is Coding ?

7. Positions in the Computer Industry

8. Work and Tools of the Systems Analyst

9. Unit Record Input/Output Devices

10. How Computers Operate

12. Fortran, Cobol, and Other Programming Languages

11. Magnetic Input/Output Devices

13. Software Systems

14. Business Data Processing

15. Techniques for Computing Scientific Problems

16. Files and Records

17. Sorts and Merges

18. Computer Centers and How They Operate

19. Specifying and Documenting Computer Programs

20. Real-time Computing and Telecomputing

21. Multiprogramming

23. Standards in Computing

22. Time Sharing

24. The Literature of Computing

25. Professionalism

END OF BOOK

GO TO next book, **Computer Usage/360 Assembly Programming**

Ordinary business files contain records that are grouped according to some common characteristic. Records may be filed alphabetically, by part number or name, regionally, or in countless other ways. Files are used to hold information essential to a business, and must be maintained (i.e., kept up to date) if they are to retain their value.

Data processing commonly makes use of the computer's great speed to handle large files with high activity. Files that contain only a few hundred or thousand records need not be computer-run, and even larger files which have little activity may not benefit by computer use.

The computer is used to handle large files with low activity if the value of rapid file updating offsets computer costs. An example of this is an airlines reservation system, where up-to-the-minute information is necessary.

A file is usually structured for ease in location of particular records. An example is a telephone directory in which subscriber names are listed alphabetically. A different structure, such as the Yellow Pages, gives information differently. It has service and business classifications listed alphabetically, and then presents business names listed alphabetically (sometimes by neighborhood, too) under each classification.

Files may be accessed either sequentially or randomly (direct access). Sequential accessing involves reading a file until the desired record is found.

If the record happens to be the last in the file, all records before it must be passed over. Random access, as the name implies, permits direct record retrieval.

☐ TYPICAL FILES

A data file is basically a group of related records. How the records are related depends on the application involved. There are many types of files, and three of the most basic are illustrated as follows:

1 *Master File*—The master file for a particular application contains the most current records. Any reports that are needed are taken from the master file, and it is this file that is updated when new activity occurs for items within it.

2 *Transaction File*—This file contains all the new activity since the last updating of the master file. Activity records include sales, receipts, or new records to be added to the master file. When the transaction file is used to update a master, the file that results from combining the two is the "new" master, and the previously current master is now the "old" master.

3 *Auxiliary File*—Sometimes records in the master file cannot contain all the information that should be available. Information that is not regularly needed and requires infrequent updating is contained in an auxiliary file. For example, a master file record will contain an account number to identify it, but the actual account name and address may be in an auxiliary file. Much master file space is saved, and processing time decreased, by having less used information in a separate file.

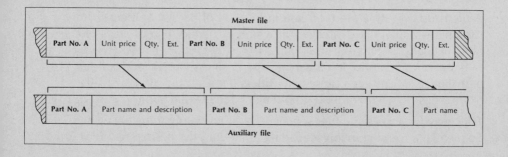

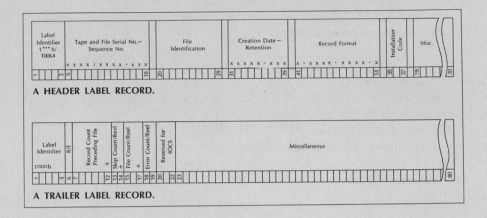

A HEADER LABEL RECORD.

A TRAILER LABEL RECORD.

☐ RECORDS

Files are composed of records. A record is a structured group of related data fields all related to a record key, which asserts the record's uniqueness. Some of the principal types of records are:

1   *Data Record*—This record contains pertinent information for a data processing task. It is the most common type of record.
2   *Trailer Record*—A trailer or overflow record contains information which could not be added to the master file record (also known as the "prime" record).
3   *Label Records*—Label records identify a file. The header label holds the file name, file number, and its creation date. Trailer labels signal the end of a file, or file sequence. They may also be used in keeping a count of the number of records or blocks in the file, and they may hold totals on the contents of a particular field in each record for checking purposes.

☐ PHYSICAL ORGANIZATION OF A FILE

Files may be organized either sequentially or randomly. Records on tape must be in sequence with respect to each other, while records on disc may have either sequential or random organization. As you will discover when you read the following paragraphs, there are benefits and drawbacks in the use of either system. Some of the reasons for choosing one, as opposed to the other, should become clearer.

SEQUENTIAL ACCESS
In a sequential file on either cards or magnetic tape, records are arranged in either ascending or descending order with respect to each control field or record key. To process a record in the middle of a file, all records before it must be read and passed over—a waste of computer time. The merits of using sequential accessing methods with magnetic tape will be discussed at the end of the following survey of direct access file device (DASD) organization (see page 269).

RANDOM ACCESS
Random access implies that a particular record can be reached directly, without a scan of other records which precede it in the file. This is true, though in most cases some indexing method which actually gives the record's location is used. Some files that are randomly accessed may be organized sequentially. Several types of random access files will now be outlined.

DIRECT ADDRESSING
In this system, the record control field actually equals the storage address. The upper and lower limits of record control field values must fit into the addressing range of the particular storage unit being used, and all

EXAMPLE OF DIRECT ADDRESSING STORAGE.

Record Key	DASD Address
21320	021320
21321	021321
	021322*
21323	021323
	021324*
	021325*
21326	021326
21327	021327
etc.	etc.

*Empty locations, since no records exist with matching keys.

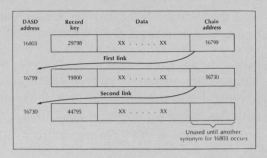

CHAINING.

intervening addresses must be reserved for the file. If the file organization is not compact when this system is used, much storage space is wasted.

RANDOM FILE
In this type of file the record control field (or record key) is applied to a predetermined formula to find the address where the record will be stored. The complexity of the formula is determined by the range of record control field values and available addresses of the storage unit.

When this method is used, it is possible that two records with different record control fields, after conversions, may have the same storage address.

The first record is stored at the proper address after formulation. The second record with that address (not record key address, but formulated address) is put into an overflow area if no adjacent area exists.

The first record has an area called a sequence link which is located after its data fields, and which provides the address of the next sequential record. This is called the chain address. The record that had the identical storage address and was put in the overflow area (called a *synonym record*) also has a sequence link field which contains the address of the next sequential record. The method of actually storing the address of the next sequential record in the record before it is known as *chaining*.

CONTROL SEQUENTIAL
In cases where random access is needed, but where processing is mainly sequential, the *control sequential* method is used.

The file is initially written in sequence, in the primary file area. As new records are added later, they are written into an overflow area. Each record in a control sequential file has a sequence linkage field which is used to keep the address of a next record which might be put in the overflow area. (Note that this is the same method used in the "random file.") The sequence linkage field of a record in the overflow area has the address of the next sequential record, which may be in the primary file area.

At certain intervals, the file is reorganized so that all records are sequentially arranged in the primary file area for more efficient sequential processing.

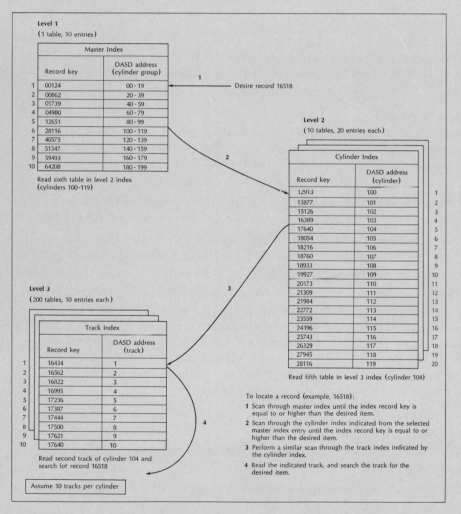

GENERALIZED INDEX SYSTEM FOR INDEX SEQUENTIAL.

When this file is randomly accessed, an index permits the direct reading of a record.

INDEX SEQUENTIAL

Initially, records are arranged in sequential order by their record key. When a record must be added, all records with higher record key values are moved down the track, to make space for the new record.

Records that are moved off the track go into an additions area within the file cylinder. Two indices are kept, and for extremely large files a third index is used. In this case, one index is used to locate the cylinder, another to find the correct track, and the third as a master index. This is illustrated on page 268.

☐ DIRECT ACCESS VERSUS SEQUENTIAL ACCESS

For an application in which only sequential accessing need be used (as in processing payrolls), a sequential medium like tape(s) is generally used to hold the file.

In cases where there is a large file and the response time to a query must be minimal, direct accessing is the preferred method. The cost of having a direct access system should be offset by the faster response time which it provides. In applications which can be either sequential or direct, the contrast between the cost factor and the benefits is important to consider.

Direct access devices that are set up and used primarily sequentially have many drawbacks. When additions are made to a file on magnetic tape, the outcome of the process is a new file with all records in sequence. When additions are made to a file on disc, the records are not physically in sequence, since overflow areas are used. Periodically, the disc must be reorganized so that its records are once again physically sequential. The great drawback of discs as sequential media is that very complicated formulas must be worked out so that additions do find room in overflow areas.

☐ RECORD DESIGN

There are several considerations involved in record design: the size of the record, blocking records, and other aspects such as how to condense record fields.

RECORD SIZE

Records may be either fixed or variable in length. Fixed-length records have fields whose lengths (relative to the same field in a different record) stay constant.

Variable-length records contain fields whose lengths change with the nature of the application. There are often three basic sections in a variable-length record:

The *fixed section* is primarily used to hold the record control field and other fixed-length fields.

The *variable section* includes a number of segments which are themselves groups of fields. An independent field is a single field, while an interdependent field consists of two or more related fields which are treated as a whole. Each of the segments in the variable section is of a fixed length.

The *control section,* when used, specifies whether certain segments in the variable section exist, and if they do, how long they are.

The fields in a record are arranged for ease of processing. Records may be either fixed or variable in length, but are usually not intermixed in the same file.

Example:

Fixed	Control Section				Variable Section		
Section	A	B	C	D	A	C	D

Segment B is missing in this record, but the control field for B is present. Normally, the control section follows the fixed section and is fixed in length.

RECORD BLOCKING

Two or more records which are read, written, or stored as one are considered *blocked.* When several records are moved as one, time is saved in the physical movement between I/O devices and storage. The greater the blocking factor (the number of records in a block), the more I/O time saved.

On tape, the space that separates records is known as an interrecord gap. Blocking reduces the number of gaps, thereby increasing usable space for data.

Each block is called a *physical record,* and each record of the block is a *logical record.* Though the records are in a block, actual processing is done on the individual logical records. The number of records composing a block is dependent mainly on the size of each record and the hardware involved.

It should be realized that blocking is an advantage only in sequential processing. Random direct accessing involves one record at a time, making blocking unnecessary.

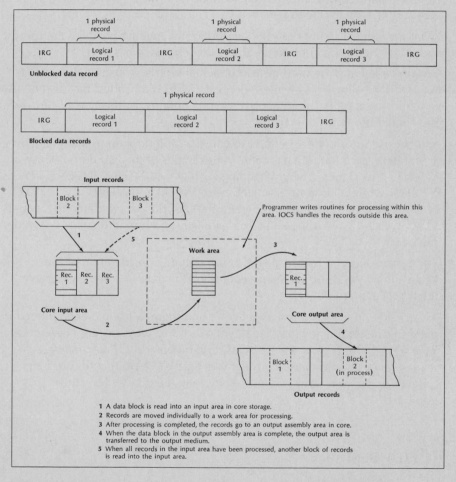

1 A data block is read into an input area in core storage.
2 Records are moved individually to a work area for processing.
3 After processing is completed, the records go to an output assembly area in core.
4 When the data block in the output assembly area is complete, the output area is transferred to the output medium.
5 When all records in the input area have been processed, another block of records is read into the input area.

FLOW OF DATA RECORDS FROM A BLOCKED DATA FILE THROUGH A PROGRAM CONTROLLED BY IOCS.

OTHER ASPECTS OF RECORD DESIGN

Space is one of the most important considerations in file design, and this section will give some examples of how record fields can be condensed.

A field that is used to denote quantities should be limited in size to the highest value that will be contained within it. The rare exception that might occur, where the value is too great for the field, can be handled as an overflow in processing that will not halt file operations.

Some items can be represented by a single bit. The *on* and *off* states (1 or 0) can have different meanings. If bit 1 equals 1, it might signify male, while a zero for bit 1 might mean female.

What the values signify must be tailored to the specific needs of the user, and if this method is used to the fullest, much space is saved.

Certain codes may be used instead of actual words. Thus the character 1 may indicate New York, while 7 denotes California. Codes may also be used to signify the type of information a record contains, or the type of processing that should be done to its fields.

Another use for a code would be to cause a table lookup to fetch lengthy information for a WRITE operation. An example of this would be to use a code of 11 to signify a report heading such as MONTHLY INVENTORY REPORT, while a code of 22 might mean WEEKLY INVENTORY REPORT. By using this method, the coded field, through proper programming, causes retrieval of the wanted heading from storage. Much record space is saved this way.

One other aspect of record design is important. Consideration of the hardware involved in specifying record lengths can, in some cases, save much processing time.

For example, if a record is very lengthy, and there is trouble encountered in reading it, several reads may be attempted. If I/O attempts are made on a short record, the time wasted is small; but repeated I/O attempts on a lengthy record could cause considerable delay. Where records are long, trailers can be used; and where files are long, auxiliary files can be employed.

☐ FILE DESIGN

A file design worksheet may be used to help specify the type of file organization and the storage medium that is necessary for a particular application.

| FILE DESIGN WORKSHEET | | | | | | | | | Date | Started _____ |
| | | | | | | | | | | Completed _____ |

File Name _____   Designer _____

Process Cycle		Record Characteristics			File Dynamics					File Media Requirements	
DA MO		Type:	Character Size	NO. REC.	YRLY %	YRLY%	5 YR %	TOT NO.	TYPE		AMOUNT
WK YR		Fixed	MIN MAX AV		ADD	DROP	GROWTH	REC			
		Var.		A	B	C	D	E			
							5(B−C)=D A+AD=E				

Information Required for Processing and Reporting	Type of Information Required	Field Size				Sequence			REMARKS
		TRIAL	TRIAL	TRIAL	FINAL	IN SOURCE DOC	IN RECORD	IN RELATED FILES	

First the rate of file processing (whether daily, weekly, etc.) is determined. Then the size, type, and quantity of records are calculated. With this information, the actual size of the file can now be figured. File design, however, involves planning for the future, and some estimate of yearly record additions and deletions must be made. Also, an approximation of the quantity of records expected after five years is needed.

With all this information, plus other variables, analysis can now be made of:

1   The size of the actual file
2   The structure of the file
3   The type of storage medium to be employed
4   Which accessing method is best
5   The future requirements of the system

FILE PLANNING
Because file space is valuable, care should be taken that only essential items be included in the main (master) file. Subsidiary information which is not often needed can be put on a companion to the master file, which is called an auxiliary file.

If there are several different files in an application, care should be taken to keep duplication of information to a minimum. Consolidation of many files into one or two may provide the needed information at a great saving of computer processing time and cost.

Though records are usually kept to a minimum size, if there is a possibility that an extra field may be needed in the near future, it should be included in the file design. This will save the expense of having the whole file modified at a later date.

Thought should be given not only to the number of records contained in a file, but to how often they will be updated and accessed.

Once a file is created, schedules must be worked out to provide an orderly method to use and update it. If a large file takes several hours to update—and this is done almost daily—there probably will be trouble in getting unscheduled access to that file. Therefore, schedules are necessary both to let the user know when he can get his information, and to keep the status of a file known at all times.

In the course of processing a file, it might be noted that a great number of records almost never have any activity. In using a tape system, much time is wasted if the whole file has to be run for a few records. The solution to this problem is that two masters should be made—one to hold the active records, the other the inactive ones.

Another type of timesaving technique is to use two masters at the same time. Transaction files follow the sequence of each master, and while one master is being processed, the other is being searched for an active item.

□ FILE ACCURACY AND CHECKING

When files are created, and every time they are updated, the chance exists that erroneous information might be supplied. Several methods are used to help minimize errors caused by both human and machine factors:

1   For the file itself, *label checking* is done. Before actual processing takes place, the serial number of the file, its identification number, and its creation date are checked. If any inconsistencies are found, no processing takes place.
2   *Record counts* can be made to ensure that the number of records before and after processing are the same. This guards against accidental loss of records.
3   A check can be made to see if certain fields contain (a) permissible

characters, (b) values within certain specified limits, (c) permissible numbers, and (d) self-checking numbers, whereby the sum of the numbers within a field should equal a certain control value.

The limit to error checking depends on the needs of the application and the programmer's ingenuity. When errors are detected, they may be listed on an exception file while processing is allowed to continue, or processing may be halted.

To safeguard a file, the most widely used method is the *son-father-grandfather* system which was covered in Chapter 14. It should be pointed out—and common sense dictates it—that for complete safety, the old master and the transaction files should be stored in a location remote from the current master tape library.

Files that are not updated should have copies made and kept at separate locations. Owing to the nature of magnetic tape, files that are left in tape libraries for a great length of time may become inaccurate because the tape has lost some of its magnetic properties. Stagnant files should be copied periodically.

☐ QUESTIONS

1 Refer to the figure that illustrates the generalized index system for index sequential and find the cylinder and track number for the following records. (Find as much as is possible for the records that are out of the range covered by the figure.)

16563, 17449, 21541, 14999, 12650, 55555, 00010

2 If the greater the blocking factor, the more I/O time saved, why shouldn't all records be grouped into enormous blocks? What considerations limit the blocking factor? Would the best blocking factor be dependent on whether the file processing applications usually worked on only one record in a block or on almost all of them?

3 What characteristics of a personnel file other than sex can be coded with a single bit? How many bits would have to be allowed for age in years? How many for hair color? If all employees are either active or retired, how many bits are needed to code this?

4 What common business data processing operations cannot be classified as operations with or on files?

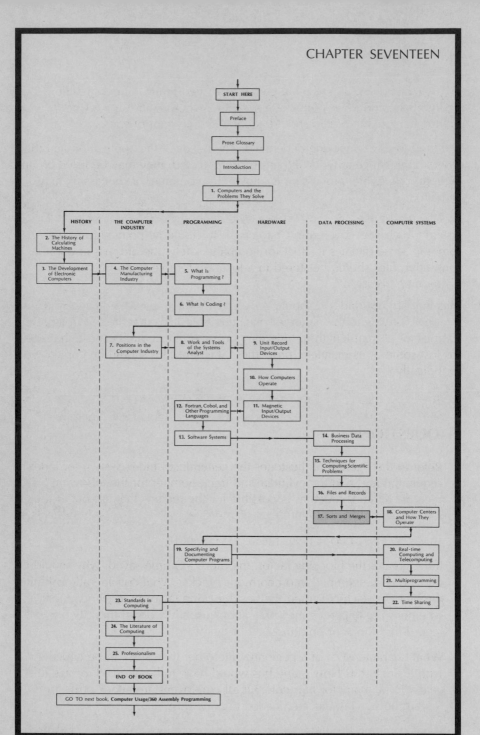

CHAPTER SEVENTEEN

In using computers to solve practical business, industrial, statistical, and scientific problems, data frequently need to be *sorted*. Sorting simply means arranging data into a specified sequence. It is obvious that information received by the computer in random order would need to be put into a meaningful, usable order for processing. On the other hand, data received in a specific sequence may be needed in a different sequence, or perhaps in several different sequences, in the course of solving a problem or retrieving information.

You will need to know more about how sorting is *used* than how it is *done*. Nevertheless, an understanding of some of the different types of sorting methods, without going into specific techniques, is necessary for an understanding of sorting in general.

Closely related to sorting, in fact a part of it, is *merging* data. Merging sets of data simply means combining these sets, which must be in the same *sort sequence*, to form a new set in that same sequence.

As you progress further in this lesson, it will become apparent that many sorts require merging as part of the process.

Before delving into a discussion of the types of sorts and methods of sorting, some of the uses of sorting in practical applications will be examined. In this way, you can see many different requirements for sorts and, from these, can determine the type of sorting needed to achieve the desired order.

☐ USING SORTS

Sorting is mainly used in two areas: first, in taking random input and organizing it into usable order; second, in rearranging stored information into the sequence required for reports.

Simple examples of this are to be found in every area in which computers are used. For example, business transactions may be fed to the computer in the order in which they occur, while a retailer, wholesaler, or manufacturer may want his transactions sorted *by item* and then filed, processed, and reported on by item order.

The sales office may want a monthly breakdown of these transactions sorted by *account number*—which would identify the consumer—and by item within each account number.

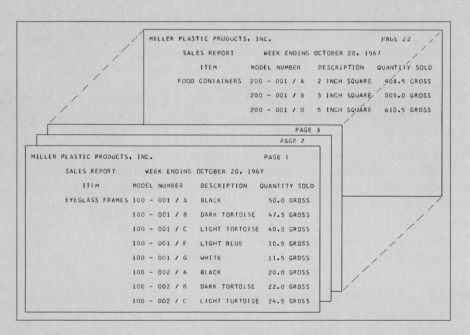

IN ORDER BY ITEM.

```
MILLER PLASTIC PRODUCTS, INC                              PAGE 1

   DISTRIBUTION REPORT   EYEGLASS FRAMES DIVISION   OCTOBER 1967

   ACCOUNT NO.  ACCOUNT NAME        CITY,STATE SALESMAN ITEM          QUANTITY

      1002    JAMES OPTICAL CO.    OLEAN,N.Y.   247    100 - 001 / A 2.00 DOZEN

                                                      100 - 001 / B  .50 DOZEN

                                                      100 - 002 / C 1.25 DOZEN

                                                      100 - 005 / G 1.00 DOZEN

      1004    SMITHE OPTICIANS     BETHESDA,MD. 629   100 - 001 / A 4.50 DOZEN

                                                      100 - 001 / B 3.00 DOZEN

                                                      100 - 002 / B 3.25 DOZEN

                                                      100 - 002 / D 3.75 DOZEN
```

IN ORDER BY ACCOUNT NUMBER.

The personnel office may want a report on the same transactions for the year, sorted by *salesman*.

It is obvious that the data have to be sorted three times in order to obtain the three reports. The field (or fields) which must be put in order is called the control data field, or the *key*. The order of rank of the numbers, letters, or characters in the key is called the collating sequence. The collating sequence of a numeric key is, naturally, in either ascending or descending numeric order. The collating sequence of a key containing all alphabetic characters is usually in alphabetic order. When the key contains a combination of alphabetic and numeric data, with or without additional special characters, the collating sequence must be specified. There are, however, certain standard collating sequences which are most frequently applied.

The key may contain any number of characters and any number of fields. In the case of the Miller Plastic Company's sales report, the transactions were sorted first by division (eyeglass frames or food containers), determined by a prefix of 100 or 200 in the model number. Within each division, the items were sorted by item number in ascending numeric order, determined by a three-digit number following the hyphen in the model number. Finally, for each item there is an alphabetic character which differentiates the items further by color, in the case of the eyeglass frames, and size, in the case of the food containers. Therefore, the data have a seven-character key (not including the blanks or hyphens, which were merely inserted in the report for readability) made up of three fields upon which they were sorted.

In order to obtain the second report, the same data need only be sorted on account number, since they were already ordered by item. It is possible to retain that order now when sorting on another independent key. If the report on consumers were required in alphabetic sequence, a sort would have to be made on the account name field instead of the account number field. For the third report, a third sort would be required using the salesman's number field as the key.

☐ USING MERGES

A merge is simply the process of putting together two or more files which are in the same sort sequence based on the same key. The result is a new file containing all the items from both of the original sets in the same sequence as the original sets.

If the two files to be merged are not in the same sequence, one of them must be sorted to match the other prior to the merge. If they are merged while in different order, it is obvious that the entire resulting data set will have to be sorted. This should certainly be avoided, since the *larger the body of data to be sorted, the more time the sort takes*.

Merging is most frequently used as an integral part of a sort. Nevertheless, merges are widely used by themselves. For instance, whenever new data are to be combined with existing records, merges are applicable. They are also useful in combining independently acquired sets of data.

A large university, with many thousands of students enrolled, may keep records about its students in computer files for computer maintenance. Each student's entire record would be kept in the tape file to be updated and printed at the end of each semester. At the start of each semester a file of new students is created. Both the New Student File and the Current Enrollment File are kept in alphabetic order of student's last names. A simple merge is all that is required to enter the new students into the Current Enrollment File. Although this is an oversimplification of the problem, the basic concept is what you are considering.

SOME EXAMPLES
Before considering sorting and merging techniques in more detail, examine a few other actual uses.

Statistical analysis depends heavily upon sorting and merging. Data must be separated and examined from many different points of view, each point of view implying a sort on a different key. The analysis of a census is a classic example. The population must be sorted by sex, by age, by age group, by occupation, by education, by family size, by family income, and by per capita income, to name just a few. Some examples of possible arrangements are:

1   All males, sorted by occupation
2   All males, sorted by income, then by family size
3   All males, sorted by family size, then by income
4   All heads of family, sorted by income, then by family size, then by sex
5   All heads of family, sorted by family size, then by income, then by sex, etc.

The possibilities are endless.

In a scientific application, the course of an object being tracked by radar may be determined by using the field containing the radar reading as the control field. During each circuit of the sweep line, a reading is produced at every sixteenth of a degree. The reading indicates the presence or absence of a blip (signifying an object reflecting the radar waves), the blips varying in intensity. Sorting on the reading can separate the blips from the nonblips. The position of the sweep line at successive blips indicates the history of the course of the object being tracked.

☐ SORT KEYS—MAJOR AND MINOR

The sort key, or control field, has been defined as the group of characters upon which a sort is made. In sorting, the keys and the items containing them are placed in the order of their chosen collating sequence. The key must be in the same position within every item to be sorted. In the abstract, an item may be of any size and possess any characteristics. It may be one character, a field, a word, a word string (a group of contiguous words), a record, many records, or some other configuration. In actuality, however, each sort program has its limitations—including the size of the items it can handle—as will be seen later in the discussion of sort packages.

If you look more closely at a sort key, you will see that it contains major and minor keys, unless it is a single character. As long as the key contains two or more characters there must be a determination of the rank of each in relation to the rest. In a simple numeric sort of two-digit numbers, the high-order digit (the first digit reading from left to right) is the major key and the low-order digit (second digit) is the minor key.

The low-order digit is sorted within the sort on the high-order digit. Although in practice a sort is not constructed this way, in effect the most significant character is examined and its position is determined by comparing it with all the other most significant characters in all the other keys. When two are found to be the same, the second-ranking characters are then compared and put in the order determined by their collating sequence. If these too are the same, then the third most significant characters are compared, and so on to the most minor character.

If the key characters are not contiguous and in left-to-right order of significance, each break creates an additional key field. The key fields must then be ranked. "Field" is used here to define any contiguous string of characters in left-to-right order of significance.

As was shown in the example of the Miller Plastic Company's sales report, the major key was the division (eyeglass frames or food containers) contained in the high-order three-character field of the model number. The second most significant field was the item number, and the most minor field was the description character in the low-order position of the model number.

Since all the key information is contained in the model number, with significance in left-to-right order, a single key, the model number, can be specified. The collating sequence can be specified as (0-9, A-Z, /, —). Since there is no conflict between the alphabetic characters, numeric characters, and special characters (they never appear in the same position), the groupings may be put in any order within the collating sequence. It is best, however, to put the characters which appear most frequently first. The preferred collating sequence for this sort is (/, —, 0-9, A-Z). If the / and the — are to be ignored, then three key fields must be specified, since the key information is no longer contiguous.

☐ TYPES OF SORTS

There are two categories of sorts: internal sorts and external sorts. If the data set to be sorted is small enough to fit into the main core memory of the central processing unit, an internal sort is desirable. Frequently, however, sorting must be performed on a great volume of items. If the data are contained on tapes, an external tape sort is required. If the data are on direct access secondary storage (such as a disc), then a disc sort is in order.

The most general category of sorts, and the most frequently used, is sorting of relatively small items which are stored on external devices and which cannot all be contained in core storage at one time. This requires a combination of internal and external sorts:

1 A block of items is read into internal memory.
2 An internal sort is performed, and then the string is written out again. This must be done for all the data. Then all the strings must be merged.
3 The collection of new strings must be merged repeatedly until the entire set of strings becomes one, in collating sequence, and equal in length to the sum of the lengths of the original strings.

A string is defined as a group of consecutive records, the keys of which are in collating sequence. When two strings are merged, the new string will be as long as the two original strings. When two sets of strings are merged, the result will be a set of half as many strings, each of which is as long as the sum of the length of the two of which it is comprised.

When the items to be sorted are large, it is possible for only the keys and certain information identifying the items to be sorted, the items themselves being untouched. This procedure is called a key sort. In this case, the items may be referenced in sorted order when they are being processed, although they are not physically in that order. This is particularly applicable when the items are on direct access storage. Alternatively, the items may be put into collating sequence at the conclusion of the sort on the keys. However, this may reduce or eliminate the advantage gained by sorting only the keys.

TIME REQUIRED FOR SORTING

Sorting is generally an extremely time-consuming process. If it can be avoided by either entering data in order or processing them as they exist, then the sort should be avoided. If sorting is essential, it should be kept to a minimum.

The length of time required to sort any given set of data depends upon the characteristics of the data and the characteristics of the hardware. Beyond this, available space is the variable limitation. When additional devices can be used (tapes, discs, etc.), sorting time will be lessened. When additional internal memory is provided, the time required will be further shortened by allowing more data to be held in main memory at one time and longer records to be processed. The factors in external sorting are *read time, write time, rewind time* (tapes), and *access time* (discs, drums).

INTERNAL SORTING

Three types of internal sorts will be described here, each totally different, to provide insight into three types of techniques. These will cover only one of many variations on each type of technique. There are many more types.

The most obvious type, and the least sophisticated, is sorting by *scan and move*. A scan of the key of each entry is made, in search of the highest-ranking value. When found, that entry is moved to the "top" of the "list" while all the rest are moved down to fill the gap. Then the second-highest is found and moved to the second position, and so on to the bottom. As you can see, for each entry moved up, a large body of entries must be moved down. This is very time-consuming. If a second area is provided, then the ordered values can be stacked in the second area, eliminating the time required for moving. As a variation, the entries may be inserted in collating sequence, one at a time, moving the rest to make room for the collated entry. However, faster and neater sorting techniques are available.

The *bubble sort* is, as its name implies, akin to bubbles rising in a bottle. It is a compare-and-switch method in which a finite number of passes over the data is required; that being one less than the number of entries. Each successive pass examines one less entry than the preceding pass, so that the last pass is a single comparison. The following illustration of the process of sorting four letters which are in reverse order will serve to clarify the description. To sort into alphabetic order:

$$\begin{bmatrix} D \\ C \\ B \\ A \end{bmatrix}$$

Starting at the bottom, adjoining entries are compared, two at a time. If the two entries are in the desired order (in collating sequence), then the second of the two entries is compared with the one "above" it. When two adjoining entries are not in the desired order, their positions are switched. Then the new second and the entry that follows it are compared, thus moving the largest entry to the top. The second pass will stop one entry short of the top, since it is known that that position contains the entry with the highest ranking key.

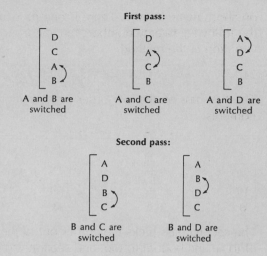

The result of the second pass is that the two highest-ranking entries are in position. The third pass will stop two entries short of the top, and so on until the final pass, when the last two entries at the bottom are compared, and switched if necessary.

The third method we shall mention is called *radix sorting*. It is identical to the way a card sorter operates. In essence, each position of the key is examined independently, and the value of the character (usually a digit) determines where the entry is to be positioned, regardless of its relationship to other entries. In effect, the entry is stacked in a hopper, where a hopper exists for every possible character in that position. Hoppers large enough to accommodate the maximum number of entries must be provided.

When all the entries have been stacked, the same procedure is followed for the next digit, preserving the resulting order of the first pass. The digits are processed from the low- to the high-order position. This method is best used on short, numeric keys. There is one pass for every position. Observe how the following twenty numbers ranging from 0 to 39 would be stacked in one variation of the method:

24, 37, 02, 32, 10, 26, 18, 15, 29, 07, 05, 16, 21, 33, 20, 36, 22, 23, 08, 12

The first pass on the low-order digit position yields the following hopper contents:

		12				36			
		22							
20		32	23		05	16	07	08	
10	21	02	33	24	15	26	37	18	29
0	1	2	3	4	5	6	7	8	9

The second pass picks the entries out of the hoppers from highest to lowest (9 to 0) and bottom to top, and separates on the next digit position yielding

		20	
		21	
	10	22	
02	12	23	32
05	15	24	33
07	16	26	36
08	18	29	37
0	1	2	3

Taking these out of their hoppers in the same way, highest to lowest, bottom to top, the result is

37, 36, 33, 32, 29, 26, 24, 23, 22, 21, 20, 18, 16, 15, 12, 10, 08, 07, 05, 02

which is in a decending numeric collating sequence.

EXTERNAL SORTS

The all-external sort, where the items are large and no internal sorting is required at all, can be treated in very much the same way as the all-internal sort. To start, there is a group of items, each containing a key, which must be put into collating sequence.

The first method to be described demonstrates the obvious advantage of using additional storage. It can be done with tapes, direct access devices, or even a combination. It is basically all *merging*. In the first pass, items are compared two at a time, that is, item 1 with item 2, then item 3 with item 4, etc. Each pair is put in collating sequence, and the output is in strings of two items each. In the second pass, the strings are merged two at a time, and output is in strings of four items each. Note that there are half as many strings now. The process of merging strings continues until there remain only two strings, each containing half of the items. The final merge yields the entire set of items in collating sequence. This process is the classical sort.

If four tapes are being used, the output strings can be written alternately onto two of them. Then, in the following pass, the strings can be read as they are being merged, one from each of the two tapes. If six tapes are available, it is possible to do a three-way merge (a merge of three strings), reducing the number of passes and thus speeding the process. More core memory allows for the additional blocks from additional tapes, or for larger blocks, which also serves to shorten processing time. This is called a balanced merge, since the number of input devices is equal to the number of output devices.

It is possible, but completely impractical, to do this sort using two tapes. It is more reasonable to do the sort on two discs (or other direct access devices), since alternate strings may be accessed directly from the same volume, although there is some time loss in the search.

□ SORT-MERGE TECHNIQUES

Most frequently, the items to be sorted are relatively small but voluminous and are stored on external devices. In this case, groups of them can be read and sorted internally. Finally, the sorted groups, now strings, are merged. For this, one of the sort-merge techniques is applied. These are the most general methods and therefore the most widely used. The sorting phase of a sort-merge is frequently referred to as a presort.

The most obvious method of merging the presorted strings is by a balanced two-way merge, using four tapes, similar to the one described above. The presort distributes the strings equally onto two of the tapes. At the first merge pass, the presorted strings are merged two at a time, one from each tape, distributing the new longer strings equally between two output tapes. This continues until the final pass, when one string exists on each tape and these two are merged. A string may be contained on several tape blocks and is not limited to the size of the core area reserved for one block. When possible, tapes are read both forward and backward to reduce rewind time.

The same technique may be used in a three-way merge or in an *n*-way merge, as long as there are $2 \times n$ tapes available. This is a balanced merge, since the number of input tapes is equal to the number of output tapes.

☐ UNBALANCED MERGE TECHNIQUES

More efficient merging techniques exist in the realm of unbalanced merges. One, the *cascade merge-sort*, will be described.

In the cascade—which again is more efficient if *backward reading* is available (the contents of tapes may also be read by moving the tape backward)—the presorted strings are distributed in a prescribed ratio onto all but one of the tapes. As an example, we will say that there are m tapes. The strings are now contained on $m - 1$ of the tapes, where m is any number, for example, $m = 4$. The first pass starts with an $(m - 1)$-way merge onto the mth tape until the tape with the least number of strings is depleted. Now the mth tape (containing output) waits while the $(m - 1)$st tape, the depleted one, is rewound and becomes the output of an $(m - 2)$-way merge of the rest of the tapes. This continues until there remains only the longest tape.

FOUR-TAPE CASCADE MERGE.

	Tape A	Tape B	Tape C	Tape D
Initial distribution of strings	14 strings	11	6	0 (ready for output)
After first pass				
After 3-way merge	8	5	0	6
After 2-way merge	3	0	5	
Copy	0	3		
After second pass				
After 3-way merge	3	0	2	3
After 2-way merge		2	0	1
Copy			1	0
After third pass				
After 3-way merge	2	1	0	1
After 2-way merge	1	0	1	
Copy	0	1		
After fourth pass				
After 3-way merge	1	0	0	0

THREE-TAPE MERGE.

Tape A	Tape B	Tape C
13	21	0
0	8	13
8	0	5
3	5	0
0	2	3
2	0	1
1	1	0
0	0	1

If there is to be backward reading, a final copy must be done so that all strings may be read backwards on the next pass. If there is no backward reading, the copy step is omitted; all tapes are rewound, and the remaining tape is positioned for reading the unprocessed portion. The process continues until all strings have been merged into one.

In the chart on page 288, you will see how the strings move in a four-tape cascade merge. (That is, $m = 4$.)

A cascade-like merge could be applied to three tapes by dividing the strings into two portions, putting one portion onto tape A and one portion onto tape B. The two are merged onto tape C until tape A, the shorter tape, is depleted. Then the longer, merged strings on tape C are again merged with those remaining on tape B onto tape A, until tape B is depleted. This continues back and forth until only one string results (see above table).

This is a special case of a sort-merge technique called the polyphase merge-sort. Again, the division of strings is in a prescribed ratio.

☐ DIRECT ACCESS SORTING

We have been discussing external sorting techniques primarily from the viewpoint of using tapes. There is a distinct advantage in using direct access devices instead of tapes since, on direct access, all strings are addressable and therefore equally accessible except for search time, which is minimal compared with tape movement time. The size of the data set is the major limitation. There must be storage available on the discs, drums, or data cells for all the items to be sorted.

Key sorting is particularly suitable to direct access storage except when the original records must be reordered at the end of the sort. In this case the entire list of items might as well be sorted in the first place. As long as only the keys and addresses of the items need to be in sequence, key sorting is preferred.

☐ CHOOSING AND USING SORT ROUTINE PACKAGES

Sorting routines are written for, and distributed with, almost every computer available today. For many computers there is a variety of sorts from which to choose. A sort package is a complete entity, a routine called for by the user. Some are designed to be subroutines called by a program; others are designed to be summoned by control cards or other methods external to a program.

The different packages for a given computer may use different sorting techniques, may be designed for different I/O hardware, and may contain different degrees of generalization. Most sort packages are generalized enough to encompass a wide range of parameters, such as hardware characteristics. Efficiency is always lower in a generalized routine than in a more specialized one. The level of performance must be compromised for generalization. Therefore, it is wise to choose the most specialized routine which covers all the requirements.

Sorting should be integrated with the overall processing of the data. There is an optimum point in the course of an application at which to sort the data being processed, and the phases of the sort may be inserted between segments of a program. Many sort packages allow exit points in the procedure at which time other processing of the data is possible. Other processing can and should be done in conjunction with sorting.

The specifications for each package will describe its characteristics as well as the method for using it and how to *parameterize* it.

Sort routines must be parameterized with such information as block size, item size, key size and position, collating sequence (if other than standard), and number of devices to be used, to name a few of the more usual parameters. Error routine entry points must also be specified, as well as the processing routines' entry points and final exit points. Such communication is accomplished with control cards or with subroutine calls as required by the system. In summary, a package must be chosen which can handle your data, making the optimum use of your equipment.

☐ QUESTIONS

1 If the file of all males were sorted by income and then by family size, where would the richest man with the largest family appear? If the same file were sorted first by family size and then by income, where would he appear? What is the difference between the results of these two orders of conducting the sorts? (Consider the relative positions of a rich bachelor in the two cases.)

2 Apply the radix sorting method to this series of numbers and illustrate the passage through the hoppers:

42, 73, 20, 23, 01, 62, 81, 51, 92, 11, 70, 50, 61, 12, 33, 02, 63, 22, 32, 80

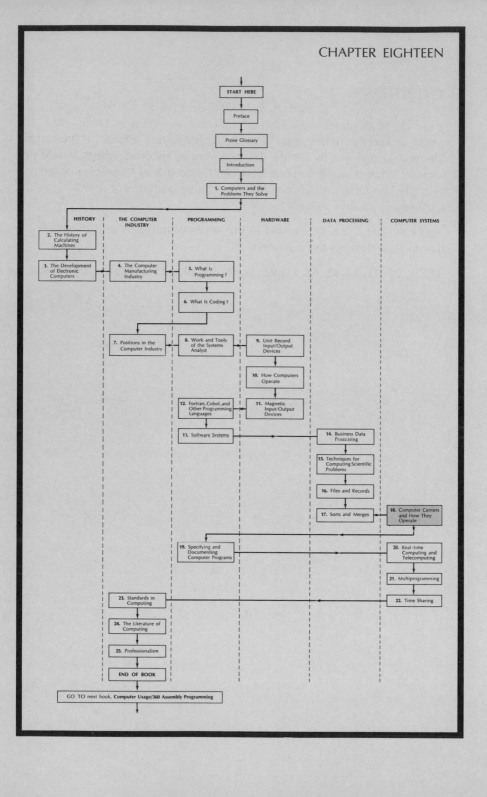

START HERE

Preface

Prose Glossary

Introduction

1. Computers and the Problems They Solve

HISTORY | **THE COMPUTER INDUSTRY** | **PROGRAMMING** | **HARDWARE** | **DATA PROCESSING** | **COMPUTER SYSTEMS**

2. The History of Calculating Machines

3. The Development of Electronic Computers

4. The Computer Manufacturing Industry

5. What Is Programming?

6. What Is Coding?

7. Positions in the Computer Industry

8. Work and Tools of the Systems Analyst

9. Unit Record Input/Output Devices

10. How Computers Operate

11. Magnetic Input/Output Devices

12. Fortran, Cobol, and Other Programming Languages

13. Software Systems

14. Business Data Processing

15. Techniques for Computing Scientific Problems

16. Files and Records

17. Sorts and Merges

18. Computer Centers and How They Operate

19. Specifying and Documenting Computer Programs

20. Real-time Computing and Telecomputing

21. Multiprogramming

22. Time Sharing

23. Standards in Computing

24. The Literature of Computing

25. Professionalism

END OF BOOK

GO TO next book, **Computer Usage/360 Assembly Programming**

The *computer center* consists of a computer, associated peripheral equipment, and a group of people trained to use the machines. When an organization gets a computer, it can't just "plug it in and let it sit somewhere." A department must be organized to handle the daily operation of the computer and shepherd the work through it.

A computer center is part of an organization which has the kind or amount of work that demands electronic data processing. These organizations may be industrial companies, banks, insurance companies, retail stores, colleges or universities, government agencies, states or cities, racetracks, or even independent computing centers organized to offer computing services to anyone. Independent service computing centers are organized like internal or captive computing centers, with the exception that processing and service costs plus a reasonable profit are billed directly to the outside user or customer. These charges are the counterparts of the interdepartmental charges issued by the internal or captive computing centers.

Before the selected equipment can even be delivered, a suitable room (or group of rooms) must be prepared for its demanding and temperamental new resident. The space and the organization are generally referred to as a computer center whether the center is part of a large business operation, is

an independent profit-making center, or both. Although small computers may not have their operations formally organized into a computer center, the principles of operation remain the same.

☐ SELECTION OF THE EQUIPMENT

As you know from having studied Chapter 4, there are a great many types and models of computers to choose from—not to mention the overwhelming variety of peripheral equipment. The proper choice depends on an economic evaluation of the work to be done and the funds and equipment available. In addition to selecting an appropriate central computer, the customer must decide what combination of peripheral equipment will be needed by his particular applications. His list may include any or all of the following:

1   Magnetic discs and drums
2   Other direct access devices
3   Magnetic tape units
4   High-speed line printers
5   Card readers and punchers
6   Paper tape readers and punchers
7   Special data reduction equipment

8   Special data display equipment
9   Special digital reading equipment

This is just a partial list of essential and possible things that may be needed to serve the users of a computer center.

☐ PRELIMINARY PHYSICAL PLANNING DECISIONS

Once final equipment selections are made, the space for the computer center must be prepared. In an "internal" center, some thought must be given to the placement of the center. Considerations should include:

1   Floor space required for computers and peripheral equipment
2   Accessibility of the center to the users
3   Space needed for keypunch operations and tape library
4   Possibilities for public exhibition of the equipment
5   Power system and electrical wiring of building

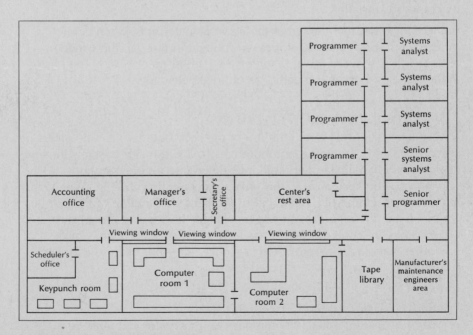

FLOOR PLAN OF A COMPUTER CENTER.

6   Air-conditioning requirements
7   Floor loading limitations
8   Exposure to damage and protection from fire
9   Office space for supporting personnel
10 Space for maintenance personnel

These and other considerations must fit the individual needs of the organization.

ONCE UPON A TIME
There is a classic tale from the dark ages of computer history (15 to 20 years ago) about an important company that decided to develop a computer center. In those long-ago days, the excitement of purchasing a computer was so wondrous that no one took the time to consider mere physical practicalities. The glorious day of delivery finally came (possibly a month or two later than anticipated) and the amazing machine arrived. But alas, there was a little problem; no one in that big company had thought to measure the computer and the entrances to the building. As you can surmise, there was only one solution—a wall was knocked down and the machine was installed. . . .

In the early days, half the fun of the new computer was watching the movers hoist it up 20 or 30 stories and bring it in through the window— enlarged for the occasion. In planning the earliest machines, no one had thought to find out the standard size of freight elevators.

COMPUTER INSTALLATION SPECIALISTS
Most dilemmas of this sort are things of the past, but there can be others if preparation and planning is not thorough. To avoid major mishaps in new centers and to facilitate their rapid integration into an organization, consultants who specialize in this area are frequently called in. They help management select, staff, plan, and understand the function of the computer center so that the organization will be capable of deriving the greatest benefit from the computer—with the fewest mishaps. Of course, most computer manufacturers provide this service free—but often to a limited extent.

PLANNING THE COMPUTER ENVIRONMENT
As we have already noted, the computer is a machine that must be pampered. In order to work well and allow the personnel in the center

comfortable working conditions, a special air-conditioning system must be installed. While the heat generated by the computer is no longer as great as it once was, thanks to solid logic circuitry, all the electric energy that is fed into the computer is converted to heat inside it. In spite of this heat, a reasonable temperature must be maintained in the computer room. The cooling problem involves furnishing the equipment both to cool the heated air and to distribute this air to the locations where it is needed. Air conditioning is always a problem in a new computer installation. The low humidity that results from cooling dry winter air often leads to electrostatic discharges which interfere with computer operations. This may require adding moisture to the air.

Another important consideration is the flooring for the computer room. Computers do not rest on one floor—but on two. On the subfloor lie the cumbersome electric cables that interconnect the parts of the computer; these cables would block movement in the computer room if they were not placed beneath the *pedestal floor*. This is a type of flooring designed specifically for computer rooms. Each individual square piece of flooring rests on pedestals at the four corners, or on a combination of pedestals and rails.

These floors are raised 6 to 12 inches from the subfloor in order to make an underfloor space to contain the cables. They must be strong enough to support the heavy static load of the computers and peripheral equipment, in addition to the moving weight of computer personnel. The floor sections must be removable so that cables can be repaired and equipment installed or moved. Suction cups are used to pick up the individual sections.

The space between this double flooring is often used as the distribution duct for the room-cooling air, holes in the floor under the machines letting the cool air into the room where it is needed.

☐ STAFFING THE COMPUTER CENTER

The number and nature of the staff of a computer center will depend on the size and purpose of the center. There are, however, certain personnel patterns and titles which are more or less standardized.

MANAGER

At the head of the computer center is the manager (and in a large center, probably one or more assistant managers). His responsibilities include

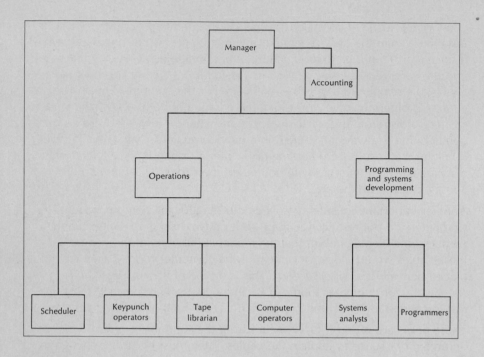

organization, personnel, and administrative duties related to electronic data processing. The manager must develop the budget and determine the expenses of the center; he may be assisted by the accounting staff. His budget is then reviewed, modified if necessary, and approved by corporate management. The manager will oversee contacts with the computer vendors and must be familiar enough with both hardware and software to best determine the requirements of the center. The manager decides what equipment is acquired and how it will subsequently be used. He is also involved in the selection of personnel and in the training of his new staff and must be prepared to submit performance statistics and financial reports to his superiors.

In computer circles, much has recently been discussed and written about the role of the computer center manager. There is a running debate about whether it is better to select a person with computer data processing capability and train him to be a manager, or to select an experienced manager and train him in the computer operations. So far neither solution has been clearly established as the best answer to an important question.

□ MACHINE OPERATIONS STAFF

There are a number of standard positions in the operations staff of a computer center. The titles may vary from center to center, but the functions will always be needed.

SCHEDULER
One of the most responsible jobs in the computer center is that of scheduling the actual computer operations. The scheduler has the overall responsibility for planning the hour-by-hour activity of the computer room,

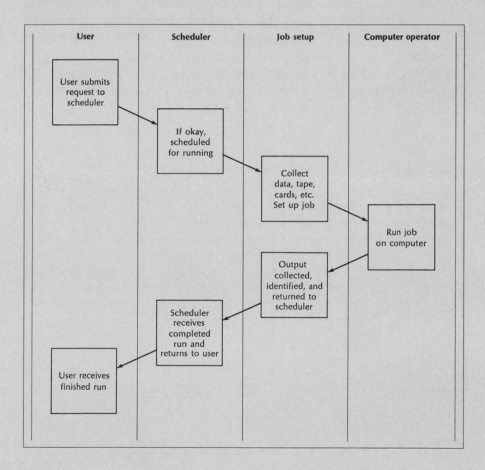

for logging in and logging out each job presented to the computer, and for keeping track of the status of each job at all times. In addition, the scheduler must check that all is in order on the request form; for example, he must see that the programmer is authorized to use the indicated priority and that his charge number corresponds to his department.

A considerable amount of skill is required to organize the sequence of jobs so that:

1 Maximum work is processed by the computer each day.
2 Operations proceed smoothly with a minimum of panic, confusion, and screaming.
3 The relative priority of jobs is accommodated.
4 Sequential operations are run in the proper order. (A particular job may have several programs that must be run one after another in a stated 1, 2, 3, order. The scheduler must see that job 3 is not run before job 2.)

In addition to the task of controlling the stream of work that flows to the computer, the scheduler must arrange time for machine maintenance, training, demonstrations, rerunning, and internal computation, including

Name _____ REQUEST FOR KEYPUNCHING						Date _____
CHARGE NO.	JOB DESCRIPTION	CARD FORMAT	NO. OF SHEETS	TIME IN	TIME REQUESTED	PRIORITY
						AUTHORIZED SIGNATURE
NOTE: PLEASE INDICATE ANY SPECIAL INSTRUCTION						

computing center accounting and the maintenance of its programming systems.

In very large installations, computers may be set up to perform either more than one job at a time or more than one part of a single job at the same time. This is called *multiprogramming* and will be discussed in full in Chapter 21. There you will learn that the scheduling of a multiprogrammed computer is so complex that it is best performed automatically by a special computer program. (This program is also called "The Scheduler," although it is not human.)

KEYPUNCH OPERATOR

Once a program is developed and written out in detail on programming sheets, it is turned over to the keypunch staff to be prepared for machine operations. The keypunch operator reads from these sheets and punches the cards to convert the program to punched card form. These cards are later fed into a card reader by the computer operator. In this area of operation, the primary prerequisites of the employees are manual dexterity, dependability, accuracy, and speed.

TAPE LIBRARIAN

In a large computer center, the magnetic tape library may contain thousands of reels of tape. If you visit a center having several computers, each running 24 hours a day for six or seven days a week, you will find that several thousand reels of magnetic tape are required to contain files and programs for so many operations. There must be one and probably several persons to keep track of these tapes, as well as of the disc packs and decks of punched cards. The librarian must know the location and contents of all tapes and must follow a schedule to have them ready for the operator as soon as they are needed. Another function is to see that outdated obsolete tapes are made available for new use.

MACHINE OPERATOR

As his title implies, a machine operator operates the machines—which in this case are computers. Interestingly enough, the increasing complexity of the computers and peripheral machines has not caused a comparable increase in the complexity of operations because the complex parts of the operating job have been assigned to the computer programs referred to in Chapter 13.

It is the duty of the machine operator to follow the schedule prepared for his computer and to run the computer jobs according to that schedule. He may not change the schedule and must notify his supervisor if any difficulties arise that are not covered by his instructions.

In small computer centers, the programmers may actually come into the computer room while their program is being run. This is particularly true

SYSTEM/360 JOB INSTRUCTION FORM

CONTRACT #	JOB #		JOB TYPE:
TIME IN	TIME OUT		EST. RUN TIME:
SYSTEM: OS ☐ DOS ☐ TOS ☐ BOS ☐ OTHER ☐			NAME:

TAPES

UNIT #	REEL # OR LABEL	DEN.	I/P	O/P	DISPOSITION OF O/P's	SPECIAL INSTR. & CONSOLE ENTRIES:

DISK PACKS — OCCURRENCES & OPERATOR REMARKS:

UNIT #	PACK # OR LABEL	DISPOSITION OF O/P's

RDR. YES ☐ NO ☐   PRINTER FORM: PAPER: NO. OF PARTS:
PCH. YES ☐ NO ☐   SPC'L CHARGE: YES ☐ NO ☐

when new programs are being developed. Where there is this sort of direct contact between the programmers and the computer, the role of the operator becomes increasingly difficult. He must keep a constant eye on these wandering programmers to see that they don't tamper with the machine. He must also deal with temperamental personalities who don't appear on schedule with their programs.

As you may imagine, centers of this variety are less prevalent—but they do exist and continue to operate.

☐ TWO APPROACHES TO PROGRAMMING

There are two alternate types of operation in computer centers:

1 Closed shop
2 Open shop

We must define both of these operations before we can discuss the programming staff of the center.

At one time the terms referred only to the operation of the computer itself. In a closed shop, the programmers and other customers of the computer center were not allowed to touch the computer, this being exclusively reserved for the computer operators. In an open shop, each person who used the computer managed it totally, including pushing all the buttons, during his scheduled turn. As time went on, almost all computer centers became closed shops according to this definition; that is, only the operators touch the computer and push the buttons. Thus the names "closed shop" and "open shop" now refer only to the programming function.

CLOSED SHOP
In closed shop operations, all jobs are programmed by the professional programming staff of the computer center. These programmers and systems analysts are an actual part of the computer center. In a service center, their work is charged to a customer, just as machine time is charged.

As in all things, there are pros and cons regarding a closed shop. Having programs done within the center allows better control, both in the quality of the programs and in their scheduling. If mistakes are made, it can be more readily determined why and at what point in a job the difficulty exists. A closed shop also allows for better programs. Because a program belongs to the center in this type of operation, the center is able to improve and update the original package if performance is poor.

On the other hand, the closed shop may mean that there are too few systems analysts and programmers, who may be overworked far beyond their capacity at one period and have little to do at another. Because good programmers are in short supply, in a closed shop one may find these valuable men and women tied up for too long on one job.

OPEN SHOP

In an open shop operation, each customer must learn sufficient programming to do his own work. He generally uses programming languages (such as Fortran) to write his application. Because the user is aware of his own problems, he can produce his own programs simply and directly, bypassing the process of explaining it all to a programmer.

The major disadvantage is that all users must be trained in the use of the particular computer and language. Otherwise they will fail to get the major benefits from the center.

The open shop operates strictly as a data processing center and provides only machine time. In this type of center, the customer does his own programming and debugging. He sends it to the center to be processed.

COMBINATION SHOP

Practical computing centers operate as a combination of the open and closed shop. The computation center maintains a programming staff which is available to its customers just as the computer is available, on a priority schedule with some kind of charge-back system to account for the services rendered. Departments which make infrequent use of the computer will depend entirely on this staff for their work. Programs which for some reason must be very efficient will be constructed by the computer center staff. Departments which make frequent use of the computer will have their own staffs of analysts and programmers. They will have enough of them to cope with their average load, and will call on the computer center staff for programming help in overload situations. Even in cases where a definite corporate order has been issued stating that all programmers are to be in the computer center, outside managers will find ways to circumvent such an order if it impedes their work and will hide bootleg programmers in their own departments under innocuous job titles.

☐ THE PROGRAM STAFF

The programming staff includes the senior systems analyst and systems analysts. It is the primary work of the systems analysts to analyze the organization's needs and then design a system which best meets the requirements for the particular application.

As you may recall from Chapter 8, there are two types of analysts. The *applications analyst* is not a part of the programming staff. Although he may not have a deep knowledge of computers, he is well versed in the problems of his department. His major function is the development of systems for various applications. This involves a thorough understanding of his department's procedures so that he may successfully assist in developing required applications.

The *computer-oriented analyst,* unlike the applications analyst, must have a thorough knowledge of the computer. He must understand the computer's full capabilities for a given application. This involves a knowledge of its peripheral equipment, data storage methods, the available software for the machine; in other words, a knowledge of how the computer may be most efficiently used. Generally, the computer-oriented analyst is considered to be a part of the staff of the computer center.

It is the cooperation of these two analysts, the applications analyst and the computer-oriented analyst, that makes possible the highly technical applications that are becoming more and more successful. Not only are they scientifically interesting, but commercially successful beyond the wildest imagination of the first-generation computer users.

Frequently this classic differentiation between the two types of analysts is ignored. In certain centers, a systems analyst is expected and able to do both tasks successfully. This, of course, depends on the organization at the individual center and on the capabilities of the systems analyst in question.

As the systems analyst's staff plans new applications, it is the task of the programming staff to write the programs that will make these applications a working reality.

The breakdown of the entire programming staff is as follows:

1   Senior systems analyst
2   Systems analyst
3   Lead programmer
4   Senior programmer

5   Programmer
6   Systems programmer
7   Programmer trainee

Often the systems analysts are ex-senior programmers who have been promoted because of their experience and ability as programmers.

The systems programmer is a position generally filled only in larger computer centers. His responsibility is to maintain (and modify, if needed) the automatic programming systems distributed by the manufacturers to make the equipment function better. These systems, commonly called software and described in Chapter 13, are an essential element in modern computing.

☐ ORGANIZATIONAL PHILOSOPHY OF A COMPUTER CENTER

Traditionally there were two standard classifications for computer centers: business and scientific. Although both business and scientific applications are processed today, they now overlap. As a result, two new classifications have emerged. They are:

1   Unstructured operations (flexible, dynamic processing)
2   Structured operations (rigid, routine processing)

An *unstructured computer center* receiving a job from an organizational unit is expected to use ingenuity and flexibility in defining and solving the problem that is presented. It is in this work that the systems analyst is so important.

The *structured computer center* routinely processes sets of data in a highly defined and prescribed manner. Each job is done according to a standardized and rigid pattern. This rigidity is due frequently to the volume of data to be processed and because of the legal aspects dictated by the data requirements of the job. An example is the importance of tax laws when doing a payroll, or bylaws governing the processing of checks in a bank.

Because of the overlapping of the old classification, today's computer centers and equipment are expected to handle both structured and unstructured problems. It is rare to find a center devoted only to unstructured activities.

Internal computer centers will process both scientific and commercial problems originating from the same sources within the company. They will use the same computer for both kinds of work. But within the computer center, it is not unusual to find the programming staff divided into these two groups.

☐ USER'S VIEW OF THE COMPUTER CENTER

In this instance, the user refers to the one who has a program which must be run. The user expects, and should get, many services from the center. Obviously, there must be operators to run the machines. He also expects all the basic supplies such as tapes, card decks, printout paper, etc. He anticipates the support of a library of programs, short-term use of magnetic tape storage, and all other considerations that are essential if his job is to be successfully run.

☐ FLOW OF WORK IN A TYPICAL COMPUTER CENTER

In a smoothly functioning computer center, there is a regular flow of users' jobs through the center.

1   The user submits his request for machine time to the scheduler. This request is written on a special printed form on which the user gives the following information:

Who—He identifies himself and names his department and the date of his request.
What—He writes out the name of the program.
Where—He gives, according to the code of the particular center, the present location of the program so that the card decks and tapes can be gotten for the run.
When—The scheduler fills in the time for the run on the basis of priority.
How—Instructions to the operator—any special instructions are listed here:
How to set up the run
Special instructions, etc.

COMPANY – COMPUTATION CENTER   JOB REQUEST

NAME		PHONE	DATE	TIME SUBMITTED	SEQUENCE NUMBER

IDENT. NO.	INIT.	WORK ORDER NUMBER	PROGRAM NAME	TYPE	PRIORITY

CUSTOMER IDENT.	DAY IN	HOUR IN	DAY OUT	HOUR OUT	Check If Program To Be Supplied by Operations.

ITEMS SUBMITTED	NO.	ITEMS TO BE RETURNED	NO.	GEN.
ASSEMBLED DECK(S)		600 PRINTOUT(S)		
DATA DECK(S)		BINARY DECK(S)		
CODED SHEET(S)		KEYPUNCHED DECK(S)		

PROCESSED BY		
INIT.	TIME	DAY

LIB

KPCH

CTRL

MNTR

NAME/LOCATION

TAPE SERIAL NUMBERS	
INPUT	OUTPUT

NO. OF ACTIVITIES _____

IDENT. NO.	INIT.

MAX. CORE _____

MAX. TAPES _____

OPERATOR'S COMMENTS

BMC ☐ READER
☐ PRINTER
☐ PUNCH
☐ TAPE

PLEASE BRACKET MULTI-REEL FILES

SPECIAL INSTRUCTIONS TO OPERATOR

TERMINATED IN ACTIVITY

2   The scheduler then checks the request to make certain all is in order so that no machine time will be wasted. If the request is not as it should be, the program and request are returned to the user. If the scheduler finds no problems, he schedules the work and lists the time for the run on the request form and on a master schedule.

3   Once the job is scheduled, it is set up for processing. The proper magnetic tapes, punched cards, and disc pack are collected and set aside for the run. The program and data are transferred from cards to magnetic tape if necessary.

4   At the proper time, the material is brought to the computer prepared for processing.

5   The computer is run by the operator, who records the processing time in the computer log when the run is completed.

6 The output (cards and/or listings) is collected, identified, and returned to the scheduler. The identification is made according to the request form which accompanies the material, and the actual machine time is listed for billing.

7 The scheduler then sees that the completed material is returned to the user as soon as possible.

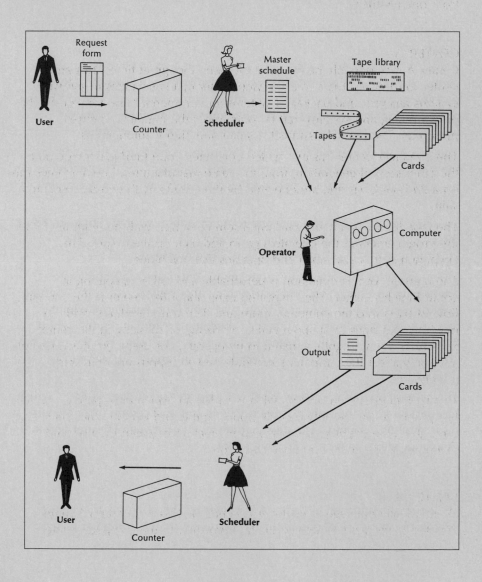

□ VARIATIONS ON A THEME

Because of requirements, available funds, and varying managerial viewpoints, each computer center is unique. To help prepare you for the variety of computer centers you will eventually be associated with, here are descriptions of two presently running operations that are quite different from one another.

CENTER A

Center A may possibly be the most pleasant, though at times frustrating, center to work in. It is a small service center that specializes in software, systems analysis, and packaged systems for commercial use. Obviously, the programming and systems staff far outnumber the machine-oriented personnel. The sales department is small and highly autonomous.

The computer center has two rented computers, one third-generation and the other second-generation, from the same manufacturer. The machines run on a 24-hour basis and are operated by three shifts, with two operators to a shift.

The tape library is a haphazard one-room operation with no librarian. Either the programmers or the operators go in and pick up their tapes. The keypunch staff is also small and operates five machines.

The manager of this operation is personable and rather easygoing in controlling his center. The interesting thing about the center is the constant flow of users into the computer room and their fond familiarity with the machine. No rules exist about eating, drinking, or smoking in the center. Schedules are not tightly adhered to by operators or users, but this does not adversely affect the customer's schedule and all reports are delivered punctually.

This type of operation runs on what is called an "open door policy," which has proved to be the only feasible policy in this and certain other centers throughout the country. The personal interaction between the user and the machines seems to be a motivating factor.

CENTER B

Diametrically opposed to center A is center B. This is an internal center devoted to the work of one particular company. In the computer center, there are six major machines plus six or eight much smaller computers for simple processing.

This organization buys, rather than rents, its equipment, which is centralized on one floor of the company's main building. In order to walk into the center, a pass must be secured from a guard who is one of a group on 24-hour duty. After the pass is secured a book must be signed, and signed again when one leaves the center.

This is a three-shift operation, but the number of people concerned run into the hundreds just for the machine operation, keypunch, and tape librarians. The three tape libraries contain thousands of reels of tapes.

The programming department is divided into three groups:

1   Procedure development programmers—A team of hundreds who perform programming, debugging, and development for work that is being done.
2   Program maintenance department—A smaller group that keeps programs updated, etc.
3   Software development group—A small group that designs new programming systems and works in an analytic and design capacity.

Altogether, there are about 500 persons working in this division. Quite obviously, just on the basis of numbers, no programmers can ever be allowed in the computer rooms. All jobs are submitted to the scheduler and are returned when completed. The personal contact of the programmer with the computer machine is practically nonexistent.

Aside from requiring a pass to enter the computing center, there are other rules for the center, such as:

No food in the computer room
Men operators should wear jackets during the day

Obviously, these two centers represent the two extremes in center management. Most computer centers fall somewhere in between them.

☐ QUESTIONS

1   Consider the aspects of closed and open shops in specific situations. Which would work best in a university atmosphere where most of the customers are students and professors? Which would work best in a

bank devoted entirely to dealing with files representing money amounts? Which would work best in a research laboratory having only scientists and engineers as customers for scientific computing?

2 Consider the organization diagram of the computer center and the duties of the three top managers. What aspects of the jobs of the manager of operations and the manager of programming and systems development would prepare them for the center manager's job? What qualifications for the lower job would work against their being promoted to the top job?

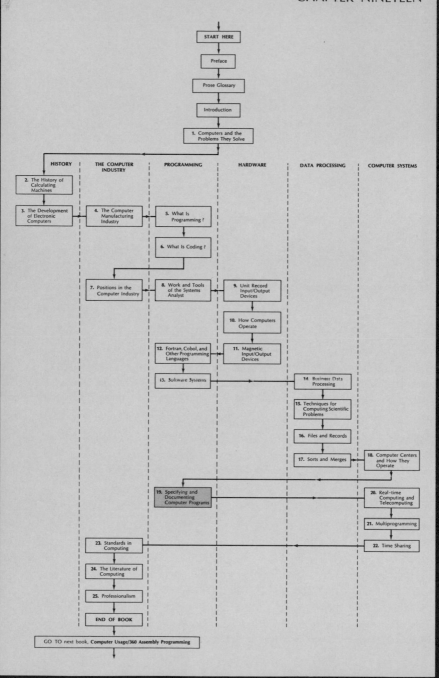

SPECIFYING AND DOCUMENTING COMPUTER PROGRAMS

A major part of every programmer's job is to explain his program. His explanation—which includes everything from printed listings and flowcharts to operating instructions and record formats—is called *documentation*. The programmer, when he explains in writing, is documenting.

In general, the documentation of a program consists of instructions for the people who will use the program, as well as information for the people who may later want to alter it or just be able to answer questions about it. Without some sort of documentation a program becomes a puzzle—possibly a mystery. It may confuse even the programmer who created it, for naturally he cannot recall every minute step in the logic of his program.

Thus, the programmer tells first how his program is to be used. He describes the input expected and the output produced. He explains the errors his program can handle, the limits it sets, the assumptions it makes. By giving this information, he improves the efficiency of his program. He allows the user to decide intelligently how to take full advantage of the program's features. Next, the programmer writes the instructions for the computer operator who actually runs the program. He tells the operator how to start the program and how to stop and restart it.

Also, the programmer supplies information for himself and for others like himself. He maps the logic of his program (with flowcharts and diagrams)

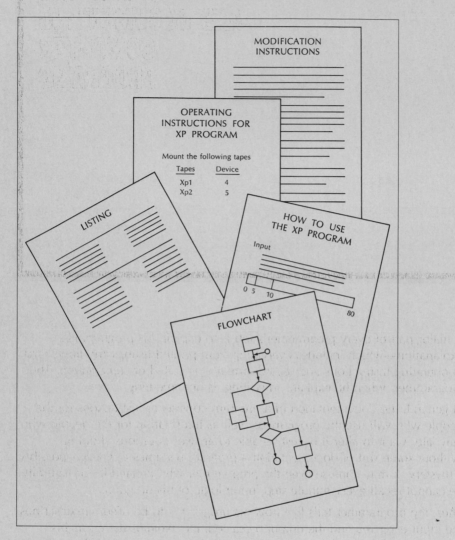

ELEMENTS OF PROGRAM DOCUMENTATION.

and explains his coding (by comments given in the program listing). To save himself trouble later, he shows how to alter data that are subject to frequent change.

A *specification* can be viewed as the documentation of a program that hasn't yet been coded. The specification is a guide for the programmer, establishing rules, limits, and boundaries. It defines the goals of the program and, perhaps, suggests ways to reach them. In brief, it states what the programmer must do.

Specifications vary from a few hints for an experienced programmer to a formal, detailed analysis of program organization, input, output, and operation. Usually, program size and complexity dictate the level of detail needed.

It should be clear that the *specification always precedes the documentation* for a program. Yet the experienced programmer knows that the specification is part of his documentation. For if he follows the rules set for him in the specification, then he can substitute those rules as a description of his completed program. Much of his documenting, therefore, is finished before he writes a line of code. In fact, one secret of good documentation—as well as of good programming—is to prepare a first-rate specification. To do so requires a solid grasp of the program's function, together with a knowledge of what is needed to explain that program. If this is done rightly, the program and its documentation proceed together and reach their final, unified, polished form at almost the same moment.

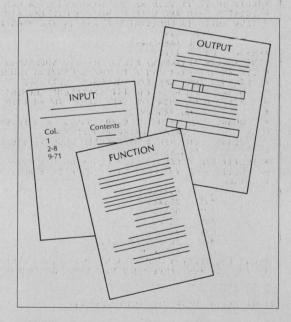

ELEMENTS OF A PROGRAM SPECIFICATION.

☐ DOCUMENTING A PROGRAM

Too often, programmers wait until they have finished their programs before turning to documentation. This is a serious mistake. The programmer can save effort and time, and make his documentation much better, simply by documenting his program as he prepares it. Programming and documenting should go hand in hand. To see this more clearly, consider what makes up program documentation.

FLOWCHARTS
First, there are the flowcharts that describe the general logic of the program. The programmer usually develops these while working out the design of his program, then uses them as a guide while coding. Since they are done in any case, all he need do is save them and incorporate them later in his completed documentation. To be sure, he may have to make changes in the

```
*REGISTER 11 IS USED AS THE BASE REGISTER FOR THE PROCEDURE
*REGISTER 1-10 ARE USED AS WORK REGISTERS AND HAVE NO  SPECIFIC FUNC-
* TION WHICH IS CONSTANT FOR THE ENTIRE PROCEDURE.
          CNOP  0,4
          USING YRESEL,11
YRESEL    LR    11,14
*INITIALIZE SWITCHES, REGISTERS AND ADDRESSES
* SET REGISTERS 1 AND 8 TO THE BEGINNING ADDRESS OF THE ELEMENT CODE
*   STRING. TURN OFF THE FOLLOWING SWITCHES -
*   BCSWA - ON WHEN THE 1ST STATEMENT ELEMENT IS BEING PROCESSED.
*   BCSWB - ON WHEN THE ITEM NAME  IN AN ITEM SWITCH DECLARATION IS BE-
*             ING RESOLVED.
*   BCSWC - ON WHEN THE DUMMY NAMES IN A PROCEDURE OR FUNCTION DECLARA-
*             TION ARE BEING PROCESSED.
*   BCSWD - ON WHEN A DIAGNOSTIC CODE IS STORED FOR THE STATEMENT BEING
*             PROCESSED.
*  INITIALIZE BCNADD, WHICH CONTAINS THE ADDRESS OF THE NEXT AVAILABLE
*  POSITION IN THE DATA TABLE ADDRESS STACK, TO THE 1ST ADDRESS OF THE
*  STACK.
          LA    8,YELEM
          MVI   BCSWC,0
          MVI   BCSWA,0
          MVI   BCSWB,0
          MVI   BCSWD,0
          MVC   BCNADD(4),BCADD7
          LA    1,YELEM
*SCAN THE ELEMENT CODE STRING FOR A CODE OTHER THAN 02 (LABEL). WHEN
*  THE 1ST NON LABEL CODE IS FOUND, DETERMINE IF IT IS SWITCH (CODE 37)
```

SAMPLE LISTING, WITH INSERTED COMMENTS.

```
            BNE     ERR5              WRONG DELIMITER
            CLC     JOB(TWO),TABA     TAPE REQUEST
            BE      SECSC             YES
            CLC     JOB(TWO),B        DIRECT ACCESS
            BE      SECSC             YES
            CLC     JOB(TWO),C        PAPER TAPE
            BNE     DLS
            B       SECSC             IT IS NOT
DLS         CLC     FL(ONE),LP        IS IT BATCH ENTRY
            BNE     ERR1              NO VALID REQUEST
BB          CLC     JOB(TWO),DD       PRINTER REQUEST
            BE      SECSC             YES
            CLC     JOB(TWO),EE       PUNCH REQUEST
            BE      SECSC             YES
            CLC     JOB(TWO),FF       READER REQUEST
            BNE     ERR1              NO VALID REQUEST
SECSC       L       R5,D              GET POINTER FOR SCAN
            LA      R5,ONE(R5)        CORRECT POINTER
            ST      R5,ST             STORE IN PARAMETER
```

SAMPLE LISTING, WITH END-OF-LINE COMMENTS.

flowcharts to reflect the refinements added during program development, but the basic information still remains.

THE LISTING

The programmer must prepare a final listing which represents his program as it was submitted for assembly. Here the programmer can easily provide an essential part of program documentation; all he has to do is include explanatory comments. Not only do they make the listing understandable to others, but they also help the programmer see his own creation more sharply. Commenting is the hallmark of a considerate, well-trained professional.

One word of suggestion: Comments can be handled more easily as insertions between instructions than as attachments to the instructions themselves. The first of the preceding sample listings of pieces of programs, for instance, shows a well-commented listing whose comments can be changed readily without having to repunch any instruction, because the comments are inserted between program steps. The second sample listing shows an equally well-commented listing; but the instructions must be repunched whenever a change in the comments is made, because each comment is directly attached to a program step. Repunching, of course, allows new errors to creep in, and thus may lead to further testing and correcting. The programmer can avoid trouble by inserting all comments.

THE RUN BOOK

The instructions for the program user are often contained in a volume called the *run book*, in which is collected all information needed to execute the program correctly. The exact information varies from program to program, but these general points are always covered:

1   *The function.* Briefly, this tells what the program is for and what the user can expect from it.
2   *The input.* This shows, precisely and exactly, every kind of input record accepted by the program. Included here are statements about the types of input mediums (magnetic tape, punched cards, disc, paper tape, etc.) and illustrations of file and record formats. Labels, when applicable, are described so that the user can supply them properly. Restrictions such as unacceptable characters, record sequence, length limits, padding, etc., are stated in detail.
3   *The output.* The output is described in the same way and in the same detail as the program input. In addition, all messages from the program are listed and explained. From this information the user should be able to tell what he would receive from the program under any conditions.

OPERATOR INSTRUCTIONS

These instructions tell how to run the program and what to do with its input and output. The specific information depends on the individual program, but below are the broad areas that must be considered:

1   *Setup instructions.* These tell the operator how to prepare for execution of the program. Typically, they describe the console switch settings involved; list the input and output devices needed; name the tapes, discs, cards, etc., that must be loaded or mounted; and note any special needs such as printer forms, card stock, carriage control tapes (for printers), etc.

When card input is involved, an illustration of the card deck format—showing position and order of control cards—is usually given. The operator is not responsible for the card input, but he can easily check for proper sequence when a control card is misplaced.

2   *Halts and messages.* Every program halt that can occur and every
    message that the program can send to the operator must be described.
    For both, the operator is told whether an error is involved or not, and
    what action (if any) is expected from him.

    These instructions are important and, if well done, can save much
    wasted computer time and programming effort.

3   *Takedown instructions.* These tell the operator how to end the run. They
    describe the order of removal (if that matters) and what must be removed,
    and explain what to do with it. The operator must be told what is to be
    saved and where to save it; what is to be labeled and how those labels
    are to be written; what may be discarded and where; and what is to be
    printed or punched in a separate run.

4   *Emergency procedures.* Unfortunately, programs often contain errors
    during their early runs. Operators therefore need directions on handling
    emergency situations. In most cases, instructions are given for dumping
    all or parts of core storage so that the programmer can examine the
    dump later and see what went wrong. In addition, the operator must be
    told what to do with the output generated up to the point where the run
    was ended. Instructions may also be provided so that the operator can
    restart the run after an emergency termination.

PROGRAM GUIDE

This part of documentation concerns programmers only, for it tells how to
alter the program itself. It is sometimes neglected by optimists, but not by
anyone who has ever had to update a single constant in some other person's
program. It is a sign of the truly professional programmer that in addition to
the commented listing and program flowcharts, he provides a guide to
modifying his program. This guide is helpful not just to others, but to the
programmer as well. Suppose he has to update the social security
calculations in a program written two years earlier. Suppose he wants to
change interest rate computation from 4 to 4¾ percent. If he did not
indicate how changes might be made, he might now have to rewrite the
entire program! Yet he could easily have told how to modify it when he
was writing the program, and thus saved himself from the long, sad chore
of rewriting. This documentation is essential for the program maintenance
mentioned in Chapter 8.

You have now been introduced to the major parts of program documentation.
Other information is sometimes included, depending on the particular

project. Written descriptions of program operation are generated; test cases and instructions for program testing are supplied along with the expected results and their meaning; and detailed flowcharts are drawn to guide new programmers through the listing—almost at the instruction level. But these are extras. If you produce fully commented listings, accurate flowcharts, clear instructions for the user and operator, and directions for modifying— then your program documentation is satisfactory indeed.

☐ DRAFTING A SPECIFICATION

A specification, as mentioned earlier, tells the programmer what his program is supposed to do. Although specifications vary considerably in detail, the general points are these:

1 *Function.* The specification defines what the program is intended to accomplish. This sets down the aim or goal of the program, usually in rather broad outline.
2 *Input.* The specification spells out the program input in as much detail as possible. The input—the exact file and record format and the device used—is the fixed, concrete base upon which the programmer builds his program. The more exhaustive the description is here, the better the resulting program will be.
3 *Output.* The specification describes the output expected from the program. Like the input, the output is presented in as much detail as possible, since it is truly the result expected from most programs. In fact, a clear, precise picture of input and output does much to define the program itself.

These three points are emphasized in almost every specification, even those for relatively simple programs. As the programs become more difficult and require interconnections with other programs, the specification grows more complex. Prepared by the most experienced and best programmers available, these complicated specifications supply much the same sort of information as the programmer's program documentation. The method of program operation may be depicted at length, and the basic logic of the program may be described both verbally and by flowcharts and diagrams. Input files and formats, along with output files and record formats, may be given in minute detail. These may be complete enough to serve as the final program documentation on those subjects. In addition, the specification may set a series of rules for the programmers it affects: it may set coding standards and conventions as to handling errors, checking on information passed between programs, allocating computer time and core storage, establishing schedules, describing test plans and techniques, etc.

Preparing a good specification requires a solid understanding of what will be needed to produce the desired program. It also demands an experienced, intelligent eye, able to see what is required and how it might best be done. A good specification demands a great deal of thought and work. Yet it is no surprise to learn that a good specification pays for itself many times over in the quality of the completed program, and in the speed and ease with which the actual programming can be done. A first-rate specification leads to first-rate programming.

☐ SUMMARY

To sum up, documentation is the exterior view of a program; it is the programmer's explanation of his effort, and reflects both strong and weak points of that effort. The documentation tells how to use the program most efficiently, thus aiding the user. It instructs the computer operator so that he can run the program with ease and confidence, thus aiding in execution. Finally, it supplies enough guidance—primarily through listings and flowcharts—to allow swift modification, correction, and understanding.

A specification looks at a program from the programmer's standpoint and directs him in his efforts. In a sense, it is a map: it tells the programmer which direction to take, and often suggests how he should travel. Many times, the carefully prepared specification provides much of what will ultimately become the documentation for the program. Thus, in a well-designed project, specification and documentation intentionally supplement one another so that no additional effort is needed to explain the program to users, the operator, or other programmers. The final result, in any case, is to explain; for only then can a program be truly useful and effective.

☐ QUESTIONS

1   The computer is able to use the program to do exactly what the programmer wanted it to do. Why is more documentation than the program itself needed?

2   It is often said that Cobol is self-documenting. What is meant by this? What parts of the documentation procedure are not provided for in a Cobol program, and what parts are provided for?

3   In the form of a block diagram, sketch the people associated with a computer and a computer program who are dependent on the programmer's documentation, and indicate the parts of the documentation that relate to each.

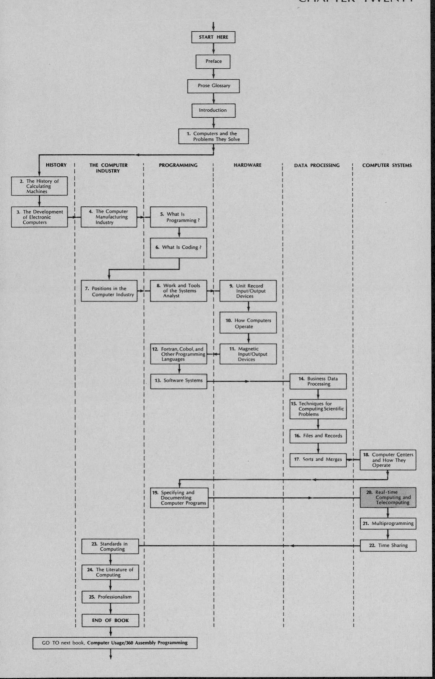

START HERE

Preface

Prose Glossary

Introduction

1. Computers and the Problems They Solve

| HISTORY | THE COMPUTER INDUSTRY | PROGRAMMING | HARDWARE | DATA PROCESSING | COMPUTER SYSTEMS |

2. The History of Calculating Machines

3. The Development of Electronic Computers

4. The Computer Manufacturing Industry

5. What Is Programming?

6. What Is Coding?

7. Positions in the Computer Industry

8. Work and Tools of the Systems Analyst

9. Unit Record Input/Output Devices

10. How Computers Operate

12. Fortran, Cobol, and Other Programming Languages

11. Magnetic Input/Output Devices

13. Software Systems

14. Business Data Processing

15. Techniques for Computing Scientific Problems

16. Files and Records

17. Sorts and Merges

18. Computer Centers and How They Operate

19. Specifying and Documenting Computer Programs

20. Real-time Computing and Telecomputing

21. Multiprogramming

23. Standards in Computing

22. Time Sharing

24. The Literature of Computing

25. Professionalism

END OF BOOK

GO TO next book, **Computer Usage/360 Assembly Programming**

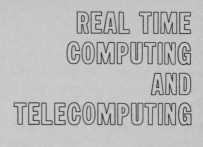

☐ THE MANY ASPECTS OF REAL TIME COMPUTING

Real time . . . on-line . . . fast time. You will hear these phrases quite often if you become a computer programmer. Most of the time they will be used correctly, but often they will not. For instance, there is some confusion about fast time, some programmers believing it to be the same as real time. Others think that on-line means real time. Now is the time to get these concepts straightened out, right at the beginning of this chapter.

ON-LINE

On-line refers to the use of input/output equipment that may be called upon at any time to transmit to or from a computer to which it is directly connected. An example is an on-line banking system, where tellers, using terminals, communicate directly with the computer, which responds within a second or two.

REAL TIME

In real time operation, a data processing system is synchronized with a physical process so that the results of the data processing are useful to the physical operation. Real time processing is usually identified with great speed, but speed is relative. Real time calculations of the movement of a glacier could well be very slow. The essence of real time is not speed but *concurrency*, or simultaneity.

Real time computing for high-speed situations has been possible only in the last few years. Before that, computers were too slow. Ten years ago, for example, if a telegraph company had wanted to use a computer to control the routing of all telegrams in a particular area, there was no computer available that could handle the job. The computers of that day simply couldn't have kept up with the flood of telegrams pouring in every second, each one requiring a different routing.

One characteristic of most on-line real time systems is that one or more human operators are often an integral part of the system. This means that problems of communication and human response time are among the significant factors in the design of the system. Another characteristic is the availability of a wide variety of input/output equipment. This includes not only keyboards and displays for communication with the operators, but also special purpose input equipment such as digitized radar, analog-to-digital converters, and outputs to many types of control devices and actuators for positioning valves, rotating shafts, or simply controlling off-on switches.

In order for a computer to operate in real time, it must be able to perform on the same time scale as the operation with which it is involved. That is, the computer must be able to keep up with the events that occur in the environment which the computer is controlling, simulating, or working in. Actually, the computer must be somewhat faster than that; it must respond to its environment faster than the environment is itself able to react, in order to be in control of the situation. But there are still many areas where the events occur too rapidly for a computer to be used in real time. One of these is nuclear research, where atomic particles react in much less than a billionth of a second—a speed that no computer of today can match.

There are at least six different types of real time computing: simulation, parallel operation with a process, hybrid operation with analog computer, performing an operational function, performing a remote communications function, and controlling the operation of one or more computers.

SIMULATION
In real time simulation, a computer executes a program with the time scale corresponding to that of the process being studied.

THIS HELICOPTER FLIGHT SIMULATOR OPERATES WITH A COMPUTER IN REAL TIME.

Flight trainers are one example of real time simulation. Using a real jet for all of a pilot's training is too expensive, so flight simulators are used. These large systems combine a precise mock-up of the pilot's cabin with all the instruments, audiovisual devices to produce the sights and sounds that a pilot would experience in flight, and a computer with a real time program to guide the trainer through all possible normal and emergency maneuvers. The computer must operate in real time so that the "aircraft" will respond in real time, and so that events are presented to the pilot just as they would occur under real conditions.

PARALLEL OPERATION WITH A PROCESS

In real time parallel operation with a process, a computer executes a program with a time scale that corresponds closely to a real process. In other words, the computer's time scale is just about 60 seconds to the minute.

The display of a missile's position is an important application of a real time parallel-operation program. The range safety officer at a missile launching must know exactly where the missile is, so that if it begins to veer off course, it can be destroyed in midair before doing any damage. Obviously, the computer that prepares the real time missile-position display must be

able to provide the latest up-to-the-split-second data on the missile's
position, to protect lives and property in case of missile failure.

HYBRID OPERATION WITH AN ANALOG COMPUTER

Just like a digital computer, an analog computer can in many cases be
programmed to operate in fast time or in slow time. If the analog computer
is operating in real time, and is connected to a digital computer for hybrid
operation so as to take advantage of the digital machine's large memory and
logical capabilities, then the digital computer must also operate in real time,
in order to be compatible.

At least two types of simulation may be used to study alternative systems
and evaluate their performance. Fast time simulation is used to examine the
approaches that have been shown by analysis to be possible, practical
solutions. In fast time simulation, the functions performed by a human
operator are simulated according to some set of rules. By eliminating the
human operator, fast time simulation can be used to examine many
alternatives in a relatively short time. In one hour, a computer in fast time
simulation may go through a whole day's cycle.

Real time simulation is then used to evaluate the alternatives that fast time
simulation has shown to be promising. Human operators are included in
the real time model. Thus the human factors that could not be considered
in fast time simulation, or that were considered only in a sketchy manner,
can be examined for their effect on the overall performance.

Slow time simulation, although not performed as often as fast time or real
time simulation, is often useful when real time occurrences take place too
rapidly for thorough observation of a particular event. This is especially
true in analog or hybrid computation, where simulation is almost always
used.

Take the example of a hybrid computer being used to study the effect of
supersonic speeds on wing designs for a jetliner. In fast time operation,
several hours of flight can be compressed into minutes for a quick,
comprehensive look at what will happen with each design. In slow time
operation, a detailed examination can be made of the events occurring
during a critical moment in a particular design. In real time operation, the
action of the wing can be observed as the pilot would experience it—to
see if, for instance, there is too much flutter of the wing for the pilot to be
able to control the craft properly. This could not be observed under
conditions of slow time or of fast time.

A HYBRID COMPUTER.

PERFORMING AN OPERATIONAL FUNCTION

When performing an operational function in real time, a computer is mainly an element in an external environment. That is, when a computer is involved in controlling an operation, the computer, although important, is usually a minor part of the overall picture.

In recent years, a breed of special purpose computers known as process control computers has grown up. These computers control an actual industrial or scientific process, using feedback mechanisms to sense the status of the operations being controlled. In a petroleum distillation process, for example, precise control of the "crude tower" is important in separating the various components that constitute the crude petroleum, in order to get maximum yield. A process control computer can supervise the entire operation, relying on various temperature and pressure sensors throughout the tower to provide indications as to just how the process is proceeding. These feedback devices monitor the operation and allow the computer to take corrective action if any part of the process begins to go wrong. This is

A PROCESS CONTROL CONSOLE.

especially important with unstable processes, as in the chemical industry, or with dangerous ones, such as nuclear reactions.

PERFORMING A REMOTE COMMUNICATIONS FUNCTION
A computer connected to and servicing a number of remote terminals must

perform this remote communications function in real time. The computer has to perform "on demand." The demands may come at any time, and they must be taken care of immediately.

In recent years, computers have become fast enough to be used for message switching, either for a telegraph company, as mentioned earlier, or to handle the vast number and variety of messages generated within a large corporation. In addition to the problem of the simultaneous arrival of two or more messages, the message-switching computer must also give priority to certain very important messages, must store some messages and retrieve them when required, and must convert from the code of one type of message to the code of another. In a few cases delays are tolerable, but during the peak hours, real time operation is vital.

One of the basic reasons that so many of today's giant far-flung corporations are able to function efficiently is that they use modern message-switching systems. Without such a system to speed orders, notices, confirmations, and

COMMUNICATIONS PROCESSING.

a host of other messages, many nationwide and worldwide companies would soon find themselves choked by a flood of their own paper work. Using a message-switching computer to get the right message to the right place in the least time, a company can fill orders overnight, make the most efficient management decisions, and keep up with, or stay ahead of, the competition.

CONTROLLING THE OPERATION OF ONE OR MORE COMPUTERS
Computers are rapidly approaching their maximum theoretical speed. They are already so fast that designers must take care to use the shortest possible lengths of wire to interconnect computer circuits. Many circuits operate in a few *nanoseconds*. A billionth of a second (nanosecond) is mighty short, but during that time a signal travels through 9 inches of wire. Every extra 9 inches of wire means another nanosecond of delay to account for.

Because computer speeds are reaching their maximum, manufacturers have to turn to other ways of increasing the computing power of their machines. One answer has been to design computer systems that can run more than one program at a time, which is called multiprogramming.

In order to perform multiprogramming, the computer must operate with a real time control program to handle the many simultaneous demands. Control programs, described in Chapter 13, are excellent examples of real time programs.

☐ TELECOMPUTING

In the early days, a computer was enthroned in the computer room and all work had to be brought to it. This was not much of a problem within a particular building. But as management gained confidence in their electronic computer, they wanted the branch offices to take advantage of the computer. This meant mailing punched cards or tapes to the main office, so that in some cases the branch offices actually lost time when the mails were slow.

Management asked for faster ways of communicating with the computer in the home office. The computer companies and the communications corporations went to work and came up with telecomputing devices that would allow data to be sent to—and received from—a central computer, from any branch office or from any location in the main office.

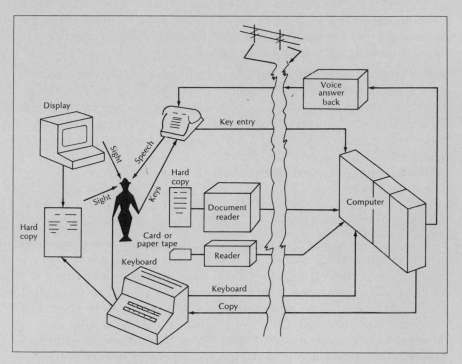

TELECOMPUTING: ALL INPUT/OUTPUT FUNCTIONS AVAILABLE AWAY FROM THE COMPUTER.

Note that this is not message switching. In message switching, a computer controls the switching of messages from line to line. Nor is it time sharing, in which more than one person can interact with the computer at the same time. Telecomputing means that the computer is connected to a device that will allow the machine to accept data over telephone lines or any other type of communication media (not excluding radio, satellite, etc.).

With telecomputing, branch offices at the end of the working day can transmit their data to the central computer at the main office. During the evening shift in the computer room, the orders from all the branch offices are sorted, merged, and sent to the factory for filling. The programs are run and output data sent back over the same wires, so that the branch office has the information the next morning. For more pressing needs, orders and problems can be transmitted during the day for immediate input to the computer.

Telecomputing has allowed companies to integrate their computer operations by having one computer room at a central location, instead of being forced to install a computer at each branch office.

More important, computers have allowed a lessening of the tide toward decentralization. As a typical company got bigger and its business spread across the country, there were too many details for management to handle. So branch offices were set up in various locations with branch managers to make local decisions. However, when a computer was installed at the head office, telecomputing permitted vital data to be received from each branch in time for central management to make meaningful judgments regarding branch operations. This meant that branch managers were less autonomous, as they now had the additional duty to collect data and transmit them to headquarters. Thus, management control was somewhat recentralized.

Even in a company that is contained within one building, telecomputing can offer many advantages. At a station down in the receiving department, information can be entered immediately about incoming shipments— information that otherwise might take considerable time to be transmitted to the right places. In a manufacturing operation, for instance, whether or not certain parts have arrived is vital information that the production department must know at once. Depending on the receiving department to telephone the information is hardly reliable, especially if several other departments are waiting for important shipments.

Most large companies are either using, installing, or considering telecomputing equipment. The cost is soon paid for by the savings in time and expense, smoother overall company operation, and increased and improved service to customers.

☐ QUESTIONS

1   Considering the methods of programming a computer that were described in Chapter 12, which are applicable to the types of real time computing described here? Why?

2   Discuss the implications of computer reliability as regards real time computing. What steps could be taken to cope with the inevitable computer failure? Which of the types of real time computing require high reliability, and which do not?

3   Discuss the implications to a branch manager if telecomputing gives
central management a look at the branch sales figures before he sees
them. Why could this be a problem? What could the branch manager do
about it? Why would central management prefer *not* to get this
information until the branch manager has screened it? What are the
relative responsibilities of the branch manager and central management?

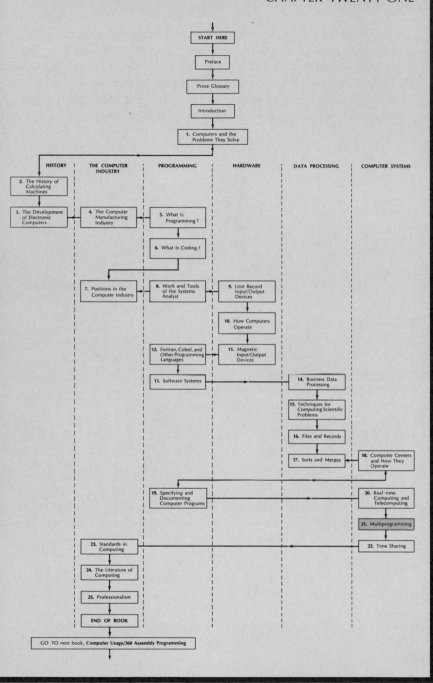

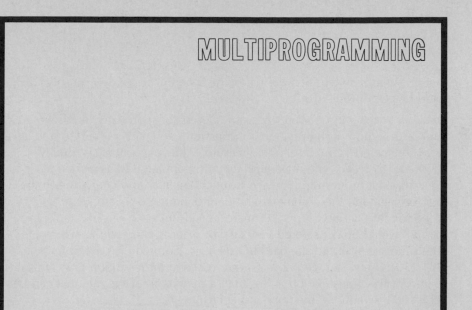

CHAPTER TWENTY-ONE

MULTIPROGRAMMING

Traditionally, problems to be solved by computers have been of two types—scientific computing and business data processing. In the past, scientific problems were generally regarded as requiring lengthy and involved computations on a relatively small amount of input data, and producing a relatively small amount of output data. On the other hand, business problems generally required only the most elementary computations, but the input and output data could be voluminous, with much of them in alphabetic form that merely accompanied the numerical data and did not enter into the computations at all.

In recent years, so many exceptions to the rule have been found, and so many new applications of computers have arisen, that a simple scientific-business categorizing of problems is no longer useful. Nevertheless, problems do vary greatly in the proportion of I/O and computing facilities required.

A problem is said to be *input/output limited*, or just *input limited*, or *output limited*, as the case may be, whenever the computations must be halted to wait for an input or output device to supply or accept data. A problem is said to be *computer limited* whenever the I/O devices must stand idle waiting for the processing to be completed. Because the matching of the speed of the I/O devices to the remainder of the system is mainly determined by the nature of the problem to be solved by the system, a good speed match is impossible to achieve when the system is to be used to solve a wide range of problems.

Because in general, no word-by-word address location is required with I/O data, a definition of information transmission rate is not as hard to find as it is for the memory unit. A simple measure of bits per second is usually adequate. However, the maximum rate of information transmission to or from an input or an output device is much less than the rate between the memory unit and the arithmetic and control units. For example, a bit repetition rate of one bit per 10 microseconds for each of nine tracks in parallel would be considered very fast for magnetic tape units, which are about the fastest of the standard I/O devices. (Some drums are faster: the IBM 2301 Drum Storage has a 3.3-microsecond bit repetition rate.) This rate of information transmission is less than a hundredth of the rate that can be achieved between the memory and control units.

For I/O limited problems, about the only help available is the use of several input or output devices operating simultaneously. Where it is not practical or desirable to distribute the input or output data among several devices, the procedure generally used is to work on several dissimilar problems at the same time. When the problems are as dissimilar as possible, the system has the best combination of I/O and computing. For instance, one job (such as file maintenance) may be mostly I/O (magnetic tapes) and involve very little computing; while another job (such as linear programming) may be mostly computing but have very little I/O. These two examples make a good mix, as they even out the I/O-compute usage.

The simultaneous solving of problems by one computer (*multiprogramming*) has received a great amount of study in recent years. It can be accomplished by suitable control programs for a computer that was basically designed for solving one problem at a time. The trend seems to be away from using hardware to handle the multiprogramming.

One way of looking at the situation is in terms of the *duty cycle*. This ratio indicates how much work is being performed in relation to the maximum that could be performed given the proper circumstances. An elevator used only half the time has a 50 percent duty cycle. In *unicomputing* (computing in which only one task at a time is performed), the expense is high because only one component is working at any one time. This means a very low duty cycle, much less than 1 percent, for many components.

How can the duty cycle of all the components be increased? By having the computer do *many* things at once.

The limitation on multiprogramming is basically due to a very human failing, in that the first computers were probably designed—unconsciously—like humans, able to do only one thing at a time. This "primitive" thinking resulted in primitive technology.

When a problem consists of a variety of parts that can be solved simultaneously, the best solution is often not to stack up the programs, like this:

0

0

0

0

0

but to do them simultaneously:

00000

Much of multiprogramming depends on hardware. When "compute-compute overlap" is available in hardware facilities, very powerful multiprogramming can be performed. Commonly, *read-write-compute overlap* is used.

☐ MULTIPROGRAMMING VERSUS MULTIPROCESSING VERSUS TIME SHARING

A good deal of confusion exists outside the computing world about the meanings of multiprogramming, multiprocessing, and time sharing. Fortunately, the definitions are fairly well understood among computer people.

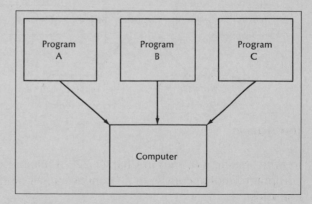

MULTIPROGRAMMING.

In *multiprogramming*, more than one program is run on a single computer. A few computers, such as the Honeywell 800 and the Control Data 6600 series, perform multiprogramming through the use of hardware. Most other computers that perform multiprogramming do so with software, making use of the interrupt system.

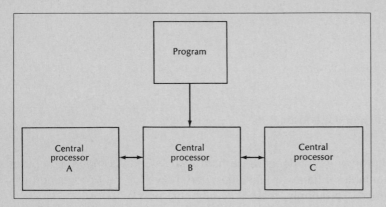

MULTIPROCESSING.

In *multiprocessing*, on the other hand, two or more interconnected central processors are used at the same time to solve problems.

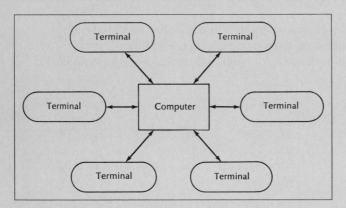

TIME SHARING.

In *time sharing* (covered in Chapter 22), a number of people use one computer simultaneously, in a "conversational mode" by means of remote consoles.

☐ MULTIPROGRAMMING

Multiprogramming is the execution of two or more programs on a single computer. The execution appears to be simultaneous.

WHEN IS MULTIPROGRAMMING DESIRABLE?

There are several different reasons for using multiprogramming. A simple one was discussed in the introduction: i.e., a computer is so much faster than the I/O devices that for some types of problems, the computer would be idle a large part of the time while waiting for the I/O devices to do their part. Problems that have complementary computational requirements may be solved together with the first problem. This greatly reduces the total amount of computer time required to solve all the problems.

Much of multiprogramming is concerned with performing a great deal of I/O all at one time. The computer's I/O channels have a much greater capacity, in bits per second, than any I/O device, so a primary concern is loading these I/O channels to capacity.

For example, one program is of such a nature that the computer is kept busy solving it, while another program to be run has large quantities of input data to be inspected with very little need for data processing. If enough I/O devices are available, this second program may be run simultaneously with the first, by making occasional brief interruptions to the first problem's program. In doing this, the first problem will not be solved at maximum computer efficiency, but when considering the two programs together, the efficiency may be nearly doubled by multiprogramming.

The programs will probably have different priorities, which introduces the question of just how to mix them. The "hot" job always has to be considered first. However, priorities can be changed automatically to take care of the possibility of a low-priority problem being neglected, if this is desirable. If a job is skipped over, it would then receive a higher priority number, thus giving it a better chance in the next go-around.

A third instance of the need for multiprogramming involves computers operating in real time, as in chemical process control or airline reservation recording. There may be periods of time when the input variables are changing rapidly, or when there is a large quantity of input information to be processed, requiring the full attention of the computer. At other times, only a small part of the computer's data processing capability may be used.

Rather than waste the unused data processing power, accounting problems, or other problems not related to the original purpose of the computer, can be solved simultaneously with the real time problem. Of course, the program for the real time problem has the highest priority, and the execution of the programs for other problems may be delayed when the computer is working at full capacity on the real time problem.

EARLY APPROACHES TO MULTIPROGRAMMING

An early approach to multiprogramming was to use one relatively simple stored program system which combined two or more problems that were to be executed simultaneously. This approach is called multiprogramming on a "pure programming" basis.

Another early multiprogramming approach was that offered by Honeywell. It involved using eight instruction counters that were operated one after the other. The different programs "took turns" at having one of their instructions executed. An exception was that, when a particular instruction was of a type which left useful information in registers that might be needed to execute other instructions, the next instruction was fetched under the control of the same instruction counter (same program), and the shift to the next instruction counter was postponed.

☐ MULTIPROGRAMMING WITH INTERRUPTS AND SUPERVISOR CONTROL

With the development of more advanced computer systems, the practice of multiprogramming has become increasingly practicable and popular, so that now it is a major aspect of computing.

Under modern multiprogramming supervisors, the execution of a single program proceeds in normal fashion until one of two conditions is met. One condition is that computation is interrupted (perhaps after it has started a particular I/O device), in which case an interrupt signal is generated. The system then comes under the control of the supervisor (also called the supervisory program). The other condition is that a signal is received from the internal clock indicating the end of a given time period—perhaps 10 milliseconds.

In either case, the supervisory program stops the work on the program currently being executed. The supervisor selects the program with the highest priority from the other programs currently in the system, then shifts the attention of the main data processing part of the computer system to this program.

THE ALLOCATION PROBLEM
The program on which work has been interrupted will ordinarily be reactivated as soon as a condition is reached where no work can be done on programs of higher priority. In some applications, two or more programs may be stored (with their associated data) in different portions of main memory, in which case the shift from one program to another is merely a matter of changing the contents of the instruction counter, or of changing to another instruction counter.

In other applications, the memory may not be large enough for this type of operation, in which case one or more programs may have to be "dumped" into a disc storage unit or other large-capacity storage device, to make room for the program of higher priority. In either case, the action is controlled by the supervisory program. Also in either case, the supervisor must provide for the storage of the contents of the instruction counter, the accumulators, the index registers, and all other special registers, so that a program can be resumed from the program step at which it was interrupted.

When a program is prepared (without multiprogramming) for a computer, the assembly program assigns relative addresses to each word of information. The core locations available to a given program will not be known at the time of program preparation. It is the function of normal software to see that the required relocation is made when the program is loaded. In multiprogramming, it is further required that programs be *movable* from one part of core to another.

As an example, assume that a computer is executing four programs, A, B, C, and D, on a multiprogramming basis, that the total memory capacity of the computer is used up by the four programs, and that each program uses a group of consecutively numbered addresses. The computer may complete programs B and D, at which time a fifth program, E, is to be executed by the computer. The memory capacity required by E may be greater than was required by either B or D, but not greater than the capacity required for B and D together. However, E may be the type of program that would be quite awkward to divide into parts, with one part stored in memory where B was, and the other part stored in the relatively remote area where D was. See the diagram on page 346.

In IBM System/360 only address constants require modification in order to

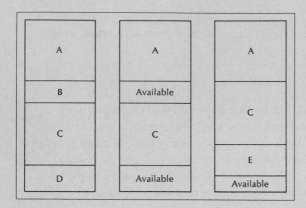

obtain relocation since System/360 memory, either for instructions or for data, uses a special addressing system called base-plus-displacement address. Whenever new programs are entered into the computer, the software must be able to shift programs already in the computer from their initial memory areas to other memory areas, and to assign new base addresses accordingly.

Occasionally in multiprogramming applications, especially where certain programs have a higher priority than others, situations can occur where sizable programs will never receive attention unless some special action is taken. One such special action is to include counts that enable the supervisor to gauge the size of the program or to determine the time that has passed since the execution of the last preceding instruction in each program. If this number or time is greater than a specified value for a given program, that program is automatically given a higher priority.

☐ THE PROBLEM OF PROTECTION

Unless there are means provided to prevent this situation, one program can disrupt the operation of another if the two are executed together on a multiprogramming basis. The disruption can be caused either by an error in a program, or by intention on the part of the programmer.

Disruption due to program error is a problem, because newly prepared programs are so likely to contain errors that they cannot be safely tested on a multiprogramming basis. Instead they must be tested individually, which not only takes up a great deal of computer time but also requires special monitoring techniques. These inform programmers that besides functioning correctly by itself, the new program does not at any point perform any function that would disrupt another program if operated on a multiprogramming basis. Even after a program has been extensively tested, unpredicted combinations of events and data sometimes arise which produce an undesired result.

Disrupt *by intention* is important in computer installation such as service bureaus, where the computer is to be used simultaneously by two or more customers who may be competitors. For the most part, there is no reason why the programs of competitors cannot be run together. However, there are certain instances where important information could be printed out or otherwise exposed undesirably, so that provisions must be provided for data protection to prevent revealing company-classified information to unauthorized persons.

MEMORY PROTECTION

Nearly all modern computers have some method of memory protection. The System/360 method, for example, uses a *protection key* (optional on certain models), which protects certain sections of code (control programs, code belonging to others in multiprogramming, etc.). The core storage is divided into blocks of 2,048 bytes. Each block is given a key numbered 0 to 15, using the insert storage key (ISK) instruction. A 32,768-byte protected memory might look like this (areas containing zeros are unprotected):

6	2	1	8
6	0	11	8
13	0	11	8
12	7	4	0

A program that is assigned key 11, in this example, can use only five particular memory areas for data storage.

Whenever information (data or instruction) is to be stored (written in core storage) in a protected area, the protection key in the PSW (program status word) is matched against the storage key corresponding to the addressed block. If the keys do not match, a program interrupt occurs. If the key in either is zero, protection is not checked, and storage will occur as requested.

Core is protected on all instructions that change contents, including arithmetic and data manipulation instructions that are storage-to-storage and register-to-storage such as the edit, move, and pack instructions.

☐ QUESTIONS

1   The definitions of multiprogramming, multiprocessing, and time sharing all use the words "simultaneously" or "at the same time." In which case is more than one program actually being executed at literally the same split instant, and in which case does it only appear that this is going on?

2   Consider two identical computers. One is operating in the multiprogramming mode and the other is operating as a uniprogrammed machine. The task is to execute two large programs, each of which is so large that it occupies almost all the available core. Which computer will complete the task first? Why?

3   Consider the same two computers, but now the task is to execute ten smaller programs which are ideally suited to multiprogramming in that several can be in core at once and the input/output time of several can be overlapped by the computer time of others. Now which computer will complete the total task first? Why?

4   In the situation described in question 3, consider only the first of the ten programs to go into each machine. Assuming that the first one is the same in each case, which computer will finish that first program first? Why?

START HERE

Preface

Prose Glossary

Introduction

1. Computers and the Problems They Solve

HISTORY	THE COMPUTER INDUSTRY	PROGRAMMING	HARDWARE	DATA PROCESSING	COMPUTER SYSTEMS

2. The History of Calculating Machines

3. The Development of Electronic Computers

4. The Computer Manufacturing Industry

5. What Is Programming?

6. What Is Coding?

7. Positions in the Computer Industry

8. Work and Tools of the Systems Analyst

9. Unit Record Input/Output Devices

10. How Computers Operate

12. Fortran, Cobol, and Other Programming Languages

11. Magnetic Input/Output Devices

13. Software Systems

14. Business Data Processing

15. Techniques for Computing Scientific Problems

16. Files and Records

17. Sorts and Merges

18. Computer Centers and How They Operate

19. Specifying and Documenting Computer Programs

20. Real-time Computing and Telecomputing

21. Multiprogramming

23. Standards in Computing

22. Time Sharing

24. The Literature of Computing

25. Professionalism

END OF BOOK

GO TO next book, **Computer Usage/360 Assembly Programming**

TIME
SHARING

A scientist enters a small room near his laboratory. He sits at a special typewriter and types a few characters. The machine types out a few more characters. Soon the scientist is solving a complicated problem using a computer many miles away. As far as the scientist is concerned, he is the only one using the computer.

A college student enters a large room where several other students are already at special typewriters. He finds one not in use, sits down, types in his name, number, and program desired. In a back-and-forth dialogue with the computer, located at the college computing center, the student proceeds to work his way toward the solution of a problem in advanced chemistry. Other students in the room are working on problems in mathematics, engineering, and physics. Each acts as if he were in sole communication with the computer.

A grammar school girl sits down at a console in a special classroom. The console contains a special typewriter and television screen. A map of a foreign country is projected on the screen, and the country's name is typed out for the girl. The screen gives the girl information on the country, then tests her to find if she has absorbed it. If not, the information is repeated in another form and tested again. The student proceeds at her own learning rate. She is one of a roomful of students, each of whom is learning at his or her own rate, all coordinated by a single computer.

These are among the more publicized uses of computer time sharing. In this lesson you will look into other time sharing applications which, although they do not make headlines, are just as important. One expert has said that time sharing may well become the most important computer application in the future.

Time sharing was created in response to a new approach to computer usage: "Bring the computer to the man, not the man to the computer." Using relatively new forms of hardware and software, each of many users may now have simultaneous access to one computer from a remote device, with no apparent interference from any other user. The resulting benefits to the user, in time saving and convenience, are apparent. Future application of these methods promises ever-widening use of computers.

How does time sharing work? Basically, it resembles—in principle—the distributor in an automobile ignition system. The distributor head rotates, connecting each spark plug in turn for a brief moment, to provide the electricity to make the spark that ignites the compressed mixture of gasoline and air in the cylinders. In computer time sharing, the system allots each user a tiny slice of time, and gives full attention for that brief moment to each user in turn. Thus, a number of users are able to use the computer in what *seems* a concurrent fashion, but which is actually consecutive.

☐ TIME SHARING FOR PROBLEM SOLUTION

Time sharing, oriented toward general problem solution, is particularly suitable for engineering and science. Based on conversational language processing and selective program execution, it is being used to perform a broad range of computational tasks.

In the field of education, time sharing is being used with great success to make computers available to many students. It allows a student to become familiar with the use of a computer and extends his capability of learning a specific subject. As the use of computers in business increases, the need for this training becomes more acute.

Information retrieval will no doubt become one of the biggest time sharing applications, allowing a user to conversationally refine his requests to the point where the system finally retrieves the exact information desired. Without time sharing, much time is wasted because the user is commonly unable to specify exactly what he wants right at the start.

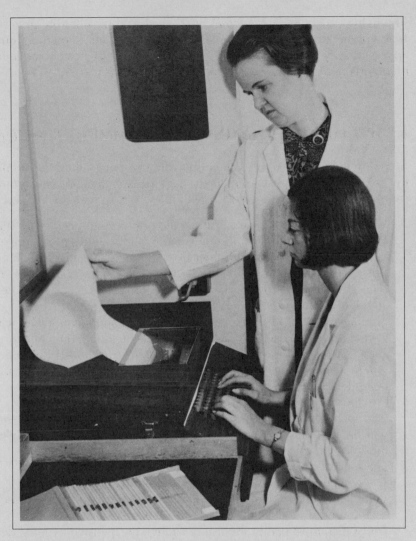

THESE TECHNICIANS ARE USING AN EXPERIMENTAL TIME SHARING COMPUTER SYSTEM AS PART OF A RESEARCH PROJECT CARRIED OUT BY THE MASSACHUSETTS GENERAL HOSPITAL AND BOLT BERANEK AND NEWMAN, INC., AND SPONSORED BY THE NATIONAL INSTITUTES OF HEALTH.

The field of accounting is another area which can benefit from time sharing. Many of the functions of a desk calculator can be performed more quickly and accurately by the computer. There are advantages here in reducing many laborious tasks.

☐ SPECIAL TIME SHARING PROGRAMMING LANGUAGES

Many time sharing users are unfamiliar with computers and programming. For this reason, several special languages have been created for use in time sharing. Each has been developed with a few simple features in mind:

1   Each must be easy to learn. (Although Fortran, Algol, and other standard languages are being used in time sharing applications, most noncomputer people are not familiar with their use.) The new languages, such as Joss, Basic, and Trac, are designed to be learned in a few hours rather than in days or weeks. Of course, they are more limited in scope than the standard languages.
2   The language must be easy to use. Programs can then be typed with few format restrictions and no complicated punctuation requirements.
3   Each statement in the program must compile quickly. Rapid response (one to five seconds) is a necessary feature of time sharing; therefore, compile-and-run time must be held to a minimum.
4   Previously written programs are held in storage. These must be susceptible to easy modification. Many of the programs in time sharing will be used only once; they will be modified if used again. Thus the modification operation must be simple.
5   The language must be usable in a conversational mode.
6   The computer must check statements upon input. Each program statement must be checked for validity to permit immediate correction by the user.
7   The system must permit the use of simple, inexpensive terminal devices.

☐ HARDWARE

There are several major hardware requirements in a time sharing system. The most important single hardware element, other than the computer itself, is a communications facility.

The communications can be handled by a separate smaller computer, or by

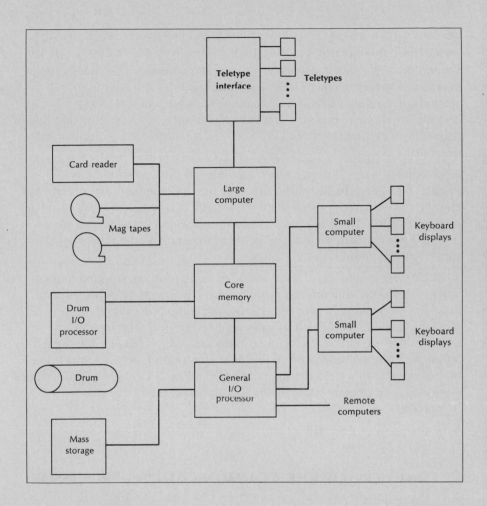

the use of a special communications module on the central general purpose computer. Each approach has its advantages, but the most important requirement is that the device used be able to handle the required number of lines and a variety of line speeds. Where a line controller is part of a general purpose machine, it must not dilute the system performance by taking up too much time or space.

In general, it is best to use a separate communications computer with a small-to-medium-scale system.

Another needed hardware component is a direct access storage device. All intermediate storage, and the collection of user programs, must be available to the system as rapidly as possible. Inadequate disc or drum storage will dilute performance to the point where system response is slow.

Several other hardware features are available that make time sharing more practical. Memory protect places hardware boundaries around specific sections of main memory. If the program "wanders" outside these boundaries, the user program is terminated at once. Thus, system destruction caused by user program bugs is avoided, as is interference with other users' programs.

Also required is an "interval timer" (an internal programmable clock) that permits the system to suspend a function after a certain amount of time has elapsed. When various users share the system, it is important that no single program retain control too long. When the allocated time for a given program has elapsed, a hardware interrupt occurs, and the time sharing supervisory program regains control.

Most existing systems have some capacity to perform background (normal batch) operations concurrently with the real time function. A background program is one whose completion is not dependent on time. Batch processing applications such as sales analysis, payroll, and tape file maintenance are typical background programs, which may be interrupted by a foreground program (the conversational time sharing activity) which has a higher priority. In a time sharing installation, all user-computer conversations are foreground operations, while the background system handles the behind-the-scenes work.

☐ FUNCTION OF THE COMMUNICATIONS PROCESSOR

The functions of the communications processor are many and varied. It must perform all the line service and control functions needed by the remote terminal. It is also best to perform all *code* conversion at this point in the system.

There are many types of terminals: communications terminals, Teletypes, IBM 1052 Printer-Keyboards, etc., all of which are used in different ways, have different outputs, and can be local or remote. The communications processor must make all these various terminal inputs look alike to the computer. It does this by changing the various input formats and codes to one format in one code for input to the machine.

☐ STORAGE ALLOCATION FOR USER PROGRAMS

One of the most difficult technical problems of time sharing involves allocation of core storage for each and every user. From the user's viewpoint, he writes his programs and executes them with little or no concern for their *actual* space requirements. After logging in, he may call for his program, which is stored in some direct address bulk storage device, to be brought into core storage for execution. He runs his program and, if he has changed it, he stores it away before logging out. In use, it appears to him that he has all the core storage he needs.

In actuality, his program is shuffled around a good deal while he thinks it is in core storage. Each of 10 to 100 active users may be using an average of 10,000 words of core storage (a total of 100,000 to 1,000,000 words), while the *real* storage has only 5,000 *real* words available for *all* the user programs. How can hundreds of thousands of words fit into this limited storage? The answer lies in the use of *virtual memory* and the *paging* concept.

VIRTUAL MEMORY AND PAGING

In most of the newest time-sharing computers, the concept of virtual memory is used, with these features:

1 Virtual memory is divided into *pages* of (typically) 1,000 to 4,000 words.
2 A large number of pages (often several hundred) is available to users.
3 Each time shared program may be contained on one or many pages.
4 The pages are stored on an external, fast, direct access device, such as a high-speed drum.
5 When needed, the pages are called into *real* (core) memory by a special page control program.
6 Addresses consist of two parts: *page number* and *word (or byte) within the page*. Fetching a command or a piece of data calls for page location followed by word (byte) location.
7 Several pages, typically three to ten, are in core storage at any one time. Hopefully:
   a References to pages not in core are few.
   b Most of the pages of a single program are in core at one time.
8 Assemblers and compilers see to it that proper page-oriented addresses are formed.

☐ TIME SHARING CONTROL SOFTWARE

One of the most basic elements of a time sharing system is the supervisor, which is generally a very large and complex program. Among its *major* functions are:

1 Scheduling each active user's time slice according to the priority schedule adopted.
2 Maintaining lists of all users, of current active users, of all programs, of current active programs, of their current locations, etc.
3 Interpreting all statements in the command language and executing them.
4 Allocating all storage resources, including pages, core, and bulk external storage.
5 Interfacing the communications controller on both input and output.
6 Performing accounting functions such as accumulating the actual time provided to each system user.
7 Transmitting and receiving system messages, special instructional text, etc.

☐ TIME SHARING AS SEEN BY THE USER

A good way to describe the operation of time sharing is to show what would happen if you were a typical user. You go to a console that looks like a typewriter. You turn it on, dial (or type) a number to connect the console to the computer, and wait a few seconds. The typewriter prints READY. You type LOGIN, your name and accounting number; such as LOGIN SMITH R1817. The typewriter prints PASSWORD. Every user has a secret number which identifies him to the computer, so that nobody else can impersonate him. You type your password. It isn't printed, so as to keep it secret, but it gets to the computer. Now you are logged in. The typewriter prints:

```
R1817 SMITH LOGGED IN AT 10.45 OCT 23, 67
THE NEW YARG COMPILER IS AVAILABLE. SEE MEMO 10.219.
```

This second line is the news item of the day. The typing continues:

```
DISC QUOTA 300 TRACKS. 152 USED.
TIME   ALLOW.   USED
  1      10      3.4
  2      10      7.1
  3      15      0.0
```

This means you are allotted 300 tracks for your programs and data stored on the disc, and you have already used 152 of the 300. Next follows the time accounting for the three shifts. The figures indicate the minutes of central processor time allowed for the week, and the time used so far.

You are using a command language, which is a simple language for primary conversations with a time sharing system. Once you get into your particular program, you will use the language in which that program was written, whether it be Fortran, Cobol, or another.

The machine types R, for READY. You might wish to check those 152 tracks, in which case you type LISTF, and the typewriter prints out the program names, number of tracks used for each, and date of filing of each program. You may wish to delete, modify, or give new names to some of these. Or you may be ready to run a program.

For simplicity's sake, let us say you have previously stored in disc memory a program to determine the location of addresses in Manhattan. You've called this program MANAD, which you have written in PLIC language. You type LOADGO MANAD PLIC. The supervisory program calls the PLIC compiler from the library of subroutines and stores it for quick access. The typewriter prints:

EXECUTION
TYPE THE ADDRESS

You type 51 MADISON. The computer may ask, DO YOU WANT THE ANSWER NOW? If so, you type YES. The computer performs a simple calculation, and prints:

26-27
EXIT CALLED
R 0.038

The computer has calculated that 51 Madison Avenue is between 26th and 27th Streets. That last figure, 0.038, is the time charged to your account, measured in seconds and thousandths of a second of central processor time.

In time sharing, the computer is programmed to inform the user exactly where he has made a mistake. Suppose you used your MANAD program to find out where 840 East 62nd Street is. After the preliminaries, you type 840 EAST 62. The typewriter will print:

NO SUCH ADDRESS
CHECK DATA

Again, if you requested the location of 219 81st Street, the typewriter would print:

EAST OR WEST

You type 219 WEST 81, and the typewriter prints BWAY-AMST, telling you the address is between Broadway and Amsterdam Avenue.

☐ TIME SHARING AS SEEN BY THE SUPERVISOR

The example just given describes external events: those seen by the user. Now consider the internal operations performed by the supervisory control program inside the computer.

Among its many activities, the supervisor (as it is called for short) keeps a variety of lists, such as:

Authorized users
Who is using the system at the moment
Active programs and their locations
Where each user's data is stored
Cumulative time for each user

The supervisor controls the scheduling of user processing. If there are ten users, all with fairly equal work loads, each will get one-tenth of the available time. But what if one user has a program that requires only half a minute, and another has a four-hour program? Or suppose one user is the director of the installation, and the only other user at the moment is a trainee? A scheduling algorithm makes the decisions. The algorithm must also take into account the system's availability. The situation at 2:35 A.M., with only two or three users, is quite different from a 2:35 P.M. jam-up of several dozen users, and different scheduling rules must be applied.

The supervisor handles the "broadcasting" of messages about the system and status to users and keeps records of who has received which messages, so that all users will be kept up to date. Another supervisory activity is to provide the type of protection required, for example, when two people are allowed access to a particular program, but not a third party. Or perhaps these two may both use some of the same programs, but each may be the only user allowed access to other programs that are to be used by him alone.

□ BENEFITS OF TIME SHARING

Time sharing can improve efficiency and productivity. When using it, there is no longer a need to struggle with the complex problem of computer scheduling. The turnaround time needed to get results from the computer no longer requires a period of two to ten hours, as in a conventional computer center (see Chapter 18). A problem can be programmed and submitted to the time sharing system through a remote console. The format is checked by the system automatically as it is entered. At this point, the program is compiled and checked. If errors are found, they are reported immediately to the remote user. If no errors are found, the program is executed and the results are returned to the user. If the results are incorrect, adjustments can be made in the program and new output obtained without the user leaving the terminal.

There are no major delays during which the engineer or scientist must find something else to occupy himself. He can stay with the problem until he has carried it to a conclusion. Much need for desk calculators and long manual operations also disappears. These operations can be done more accurately and in less time when using the computer. Many things that in the past were done by programmers may now be done by the problem originator at his console.

□ LIMITATIONS IN TIME SHARING

Time sharing is still young in many respects and far from its maturity. Cost is an important factor. The price of the computer, when divided by the number of time sharing users, may be cheap. However, the cost of the users' terminals, plus the cost of the communications equipment between these terminals and the computer, often adds up to an expensive system. The answer, of course, is to produce cheaper terminals and communications equipment, although this may mean some sacrifices in speed or flexibility.

Another important factor is the user himself, who still needs more education in the dos and don'ts of time sharing. Some people use a time sharing terminal for long program development, which can better be done by batch test methods. Also, there are users who play games at the terminals, such as impersonating other users by using their names or faking priority to get their problem solved sooner, or erasing their billing time for all or part of the week, or snooping into other users' files and programs. Although many users will grow up as time sharing matures, there will always be abuses. Additional safeguards will be added to prevent as many misuses as possible,

Computer breakdowns are bad enough in other applications; in time sharing they can be disastrous. There is seldom, if ever, a backup, such as a second computer that can be switched in for such emergencies, or another system that can be "borrowed" temporarily by cutting in on its I/O channels until repairs are made. And when the computer is restarted after the field service engineers have got it working, many of the users will find that they have to start all their programs over again, as too many data and interim results have been lost while the computer was down.

Slow response is another problem in time sharing. A time sharing system may originally be operated for 50 users, with a response time of 1 to 5 seconds for the computer to answer a query. But when the computer is loaded down with another 100 users, they no longer get their responses in a few seconds. With three times as many users as the system was designed for, response time may be 30 seconds, perhaps longer. This does not, to say the least, make users happy.

☐ THE FUTURE

Much can be done to improve the man-machine interface. Better, more flexible remote equipment, which is more natural and convenient to use, will be produced. Small computers will be developed for use in communicating the more complicated problems to a large time sharing system. The small system will have high-speed card and printing equipment to accommodate the jobs with high-volume I/O needs.

Software will certainly be improved. Languages will be developed to satisfy many different needs, from the most simple to the most complex. Extensions will be made to eliminate almost all the size and timing restrictions of some current systems.

Perhaps the most important improvements, however, will be in the area of systems integration. The various types of time sharing and batch oriented systems will tend to come closer together. There is, and will continue to be, a trend toward the creation of a single data base from which to work.

☐ QUESTIONS

1   Discuss the potential applications of time sharing in the areas of university use, scientific calculations, and business data processing. In which would it appear to have direct application, and in which would it appear to offer no advantage?

2   Compare the advantages of time shared access to a large computer, in company and competition with many other time sharing users, with the advantages of having one's own small computer. In what situations would one or the other be preferable? What difficulties of time sharing uses are avoided if one has one's own small, slow computer? What difficulties associated with the small computer are avoided by going to time sharing?

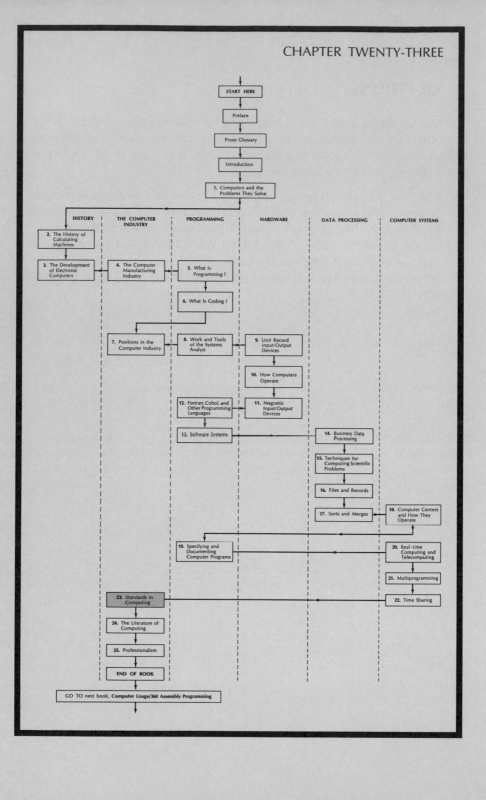

CHAPTER TWENTY-THREE

Transcontinental trains operate over tracks of the New York Central, Chicago and Northwestern, Union Pacific, and Southern Pacific Railways; color television programs are received by Admiral, RCA, Zenith, and Magnavox sets; Kodak, Ansco, and Dynachrome color film may be loaded into Yashica, Zeiss, or Hasselblad cameras. Did you ever stop to consider how remarkable—and how important—it is that there is interchangeability in these fields? Then stop to consider the fact that UNIVAC data cannot be read into Honeywell computers, Burroughs programs cannot be used with IBM computers, and Control Data Fortran programs cannot be compiled on RCA computers; or rather, these things *could not* be done in the early and mid-1960s. They probably will be increasingly possible in the 1970s.

Interchangeability results from *standardization*, the establishment and enforcement of identical technical characteristics. In railroads, it is the size and shape of tracks, the gauge (distance between rails), etc. In color television, it is the nature of the scanning signal, certain characteristics of the color transmitting and receiving tubes, etc. In film, it is the sizes and shapes of the film, perforations, and spools, and the characteristics of the emulsion that gives the film its speed, sensitivity, color fidelity, etc. In this lesson you will learn which characteristics of computers, programs, and data are susceptible to standardization, what the problems are, and what is being done to effect standardization.

☐ USA STANDARDS INSTITUTE

Within a single country, it is obvious that nationwide standards may be set and enforced by only *one* organization. In the United States that organization is the USA Standards Institute, a federation of about 150 trade associations, professional societies, and interested individuals. USASI, as it is generally called, is an old and highly respected organization which publishes all approved standards. To receive their catalog, write to them at 10 East 40th Street, New York, N.Y., 10017.

Maintaining published standards is not too difficult. Once they are accepted by the industry involved, violators simply place themselves out of the common market, since their equipment is nonstandard and thus noninterchangeable. When the users insist on interchangeability, the nonstandard equipment is soon bypassed.

Developing standards is another matter. This is generally a long and arduous task, and is assigned to a highly qualified group. Computer standards *development* has been assigned to the Business Equipment Manufacturers Association (BEMA), 235 East 42nd Street, New York, N.Y., 10017.

Development generally requires two to five years. Initial exploration is done by committees, subcommittees, and subsubcommittees. From the committee work a standard is proposed, submitted to the bodies empowered to approve it, modified, approved, established as tentative, published, and tried out. If no major flaw turns up or no violent opposition develops, the standard is adopted as final and published as such by USASI. All the work is done by professionals who volunteer great quantities of their precious time to serve on committees—often a tedious and frustrating, but critically important, activity.

☐ INTERNATIONAL STANDARDS ORGANIZATION

During World War I, a crisis of standardization arose. This was the first time that large quantities of American mechanical devices (tanks, planes, trucks) were taken overseas. When repairs were needed, it was found that neither British nor Continental bolts would work with American nuts, and vice versa. After the war, realization of the eventual *worldwide* need for interchangeability gave great impetus to strengthening the International Standards Organization (ISO). Originally, adopted national standards were submitted for international use. Conflicts led to monumental disputes as each nation refused to rescind *its* national standards in favor of any other.

Today the ISO is brought into the picture early. Generally, development of standards takes place simultaneously in a number of countries. Through ISO, the committees correspond and occasionally meet jointly. It is obvious that, as distances shrink and commerce becomes more and more international, merely establishing national standards without coordinating them internationally is insufficient.

☐ STANDARDS IN COMPUTING: THE X3 COMMITTEES

USASI has placed computers and information processing in the category X3 according to their classification scheme. Committees developing standards are called X3.1, X3.2, X3.3, etc. For example, Committee X3.3 is concerned with data transmission standards and X3.4 with programming language standards. Working groups get an additional number. For example, sub-working group X3.4.4.4 was concerned with one aspect of Cobol standardization (the area assigned to X3.4.4).

This book cannot give a list of adopted standards, since the list is constantly growing. Standards already adopted as final include:

Physical standards—For punched cards, perforated paper tape, and magnetic tape (all are interchange media)
Codes—On punched cards, paper tape
Character sets—And their representations
Programming languages—Basic Fortran, Fortran, and Cobol

Dozens of other aspects of computing are in various stages of development.

☐ WHEN TO STANDARDIZE

Many computer people *oppose* standardizing certain items at certain times— and with good reason. The great danger is in *premature* standardization. For instance, some standards that have been proposed *and rejected* would have resulted in very poor pictures on black and white television sets, and would have made it impossible for such sets to receive black and white versions of color telecasts. In a rapidly developing field, standards can act to throttle the whole field by freezing progress at a primitive level. You will notice that the computer areas standardized have been long-stabilized technologies— punched card dimensions, for example—or areas where progress was strangling the industry—data codes, for example. Cobol standardization was under way for years, but constant clarifications, improvements, and modifications fortunately slowed adoption of a Cobol standard of general acceptability, thus allowing improvements to be made. Finally, a standard Cobol was defined. *Good* standards make for interchangeability—at a level of development where change is *unlikely* to occur.

A question frequently raised about standardization is this: Should standards come before or after general acceptability? In the case of punched cards and paper tapes, the standards merely cover generally accepted practices. On the other hand, color television standards were required before the first set could be manufactured. In the one case, standards ensure adherence to general practice, while in the other, the standard was required first. This latter type of standard is difficult to develop, because considerable technical details are involved, yet those who promulgate the standards must be farsighted.

Standards are rarely rescinded, and even major modifications are rare. Standard setting is thus an activity not to be undertaken lightly or prematurely.

☐ THE DIFFICULTY OF STANDARDIZATION

Standardizing is not easy and not cheap. The major difficulties are those arising in the prestandardization and poststandardization periods.

Before final adoption, an enormous amount of work must be done by the development committees and work groups. Even the smallest decision can call for agonizing study. If you represent your company on a committee that is leaning toward a proposed standard which might simplify interchange but make your company's equipment obsolete, yours will not be an easy decision.

Although proposed standards may not become final for one or two years, the adoption of a standard might cause fantastic setbacks and expense to each of the companies involved. It *must* affect their planning for their next product, it *may* hurt the sale of the current product, and may require recall of existing equipment for modification. Standards are frequently such that they exempt existing equipment from conformity and depend on gradual replacement to make the new standard fully effective. However, many users of existing equipment may want immediate modification to the standard so that they can profit by interchange at the earliest possible date.

Lack of standards causes loss of the advantages of interchangeability, but the benefits of standardization must be weighed against the cost of disruption.

The most prevalent view is that standardization is a costly, difficult process that *must* be endured by each merging field—and computers cannot be exempted from the process.

☐ REQUIREMENTS FOR A STANDARD: AN EXAMPLE

To give you some insight into the difficulties faced in developing standards, here are the criteria used by Subcommittee X3.2.3 in developing a standard code for twelve-row punched cards:

The code, when punched in a card, shall not appreciably weaken the card, that is, the code shall cause a minimum number of holes to be punched. Another way of stating this is that the code shall be designed for:

1 Minimum hole density per unit area
2 Minimum hole density per column
3 Minimum hole density per row

The code shall be compatible with the common, de facto standard (Hollerith) code.

The code shall be compatible with international card standards.
The code shall be designed to be compatible with existing equipment.
The code shall provide for error detection (parity).
The code shall represent the full ASCII character set.
The code shall require minimum translation to and from ASCII.
The code shall provide for logical and orderly expansion to larger sets.
The code shall not decrease the present character storage capacity of the card.
The code shall preserve the logical arrangement of the ASCII columns.
The codes for the numerics shall be readily sight-readable.
No more than one column shall be used to represent one character.
Character representation shall be independent of column location.
All hole patterns in the set shall require the same number of punchable positions.
The code shall be such as to require the minimum number of passes in mechanical sorting.
The code shall be capable of being implemented in the standard card.

☐ STANDARDIZING PROGRAMMING LANGUAGES

Standardization is moving to firm up the physical interchange medias and the codes contained on them. The most pressing need, in this world of first-, second-, third-, and—soon—fourth-generation computers, is for *program interchangeability*. This would lead to enormous savings in effort and money by making *reprogramming* unnecessary.

Considerable effort has been spent on techniques for attacking the problem of running a program originally written for computer X on computer Y. The general approaches taken include:

1   Arranging for computer Y to accept and run programs written for computer X by means of:

   Simulating X on Y with a suitable simulating program
   Running X on Y with appropriate additional circuitry
   Emulating X on Y with a combination of hardware and software techniques.

2   Using a special computer program to *translate* programs for computer X into programs that will run on computer Y.

3   Writing in *standard* programming languages that are computer-independent.

Each approach has its proponents, but all methods sometimes produce imperfect and, very often, inefficient results on computer Y. Translation has not been demonstrably successful, simulation is inefficient, and additional circuitry is expensive.

The use of standard programming languages has a few drawbacks, but for most applications programming uses, it is becoming widely accepted. In fact, many organizations insist that all programming be done in standard languages. Fortran (and soon Cobol) are becoming mandatory languages in more and more computing shops.

PROBLEMS OF PROGRAMMING LANGUAGE STANDARDIZATION
Compared with standardizing the dimensions and physical characteristics of a punched card, the problems of programming language standardization are horrendous! Languages must be standardized, but that is not enough. Processors for each computer (and often more than one for the same computer) must be constructed that will accept programs written in these languages and *perform the same computations producing the same results from the same data!*

Among the many, many problems of language standardization are these:

1   The difficulty of precisely describing both the syntax (form) and semantics (meaning) of each element of the language

2   The necessity for machine-independent specification
3   Data interaction problems
4   Verifying conformity to the standard when adopted

MACHINE INDEPENDENCE

Complete machine independence cannot be obtained until all computers are alike—if that day should, or could, arrive. Originally, Fortran contained statements like:

```
IF (SENSE SWITCH 4)367,12
IF QUOTIENT OVERFLOW 13,90
```

which related to specific features of the IBM 704, the computer used to implement the first Fortran compiler.

It proved relatively easy to eliminate such *obvious* machine dependent features by relegating them to subroutine subprograms and replacing the above with CALL SSTEST (4,K), and CALL QOVFL(13).

Most of the difficulty stems from internal differences in computer characteristics. Some machines are word oriented, others character oriented, and still others, like the System/360, oriented to both. This makes defining the actual integers, real- and double-precision constants, and variables a problem. Furthermore, some machines have word lengths of 18 bits, while others range up to 40 bits. If you standardize to fit the smallest word, the user of the big machine must give up the much-needed precision produced by computing with long words. Double precision is another major area of incompatibility. Other areas involve the specifics of magnetic tape codes as well as how records and files are defined.

Naturally, problems of Cobol standardization were much more difficult—especially in specifying I/O behavior and data/procedure interaction.

The net effect of standardization of languages is that machine and data effects will be *minimized but not eliminated.*

☐ CERTIFICATION OF STANDARD LANGUAGE PROCESSORS

Suppose you are approached by representatives of two organizations both offering you compilers labeled USASI Standard Fortran. How would you go about satisfying yourself as to their conformity to the published standard? If you run two or three short Fortran programs and they produce the same results when fed the same input, you haven't *really* tested more than a tiny fraction of the possible combinations. In fact, testing for adherence to such a language standard is a very large and complex job.

In the United States, the National Bureau of Standards has developed techniques for checking processors and may act to issue a *Certificate of Conformity to Standard* to language processor/machine combinations that meet the standard. When certification is accepted, standard language will be easy to recognize.

☐ INSTALLATION STANDARDS

Most of this chapter has been devoted to the development of interchange standards that facilitate the free exchange of data and programs *between* installations or between present and successor equipment.

In a smaller way, there are standards often established *within* a single installation using only a single computer. Such standards are established to make programs, data, and documentation worked on—or likely to be worked on—by more than a single person conform to internal standards. Consider the graduation of standards needed by:

A single programmer
Three programmers working on parts of the same application
A team of forty programmers
All the programmers in one installation
All the programmers in a large multi-installation organization.

Very likely, standards would be established for some or all of the following:

Programming languages to be used
Program identification
Subroutine linkages
Supervisor services
I/O procedures
Tape and disc labeling
Flowcharting
Documentation

Many large organizations assign one or more persons to watch over conformity to both internal and industry-wide standards.

You may often chafe under what you regard as time-wasting conformity to standards, but such effort will assure that your work can be used for years and shared with many others.

☐ QUESTIONS

1 Discuss the advantages and disadvantages of industry-wide standardization. Among the specific things mentioned in the history of computers, which ones would have impeded progress if they had been adopted as standards? Why would computer vendors favor or oppose standardization? Why would computer users favor or oppose standardization?

2 Discuss the advantages and disadvantages of standards that are internal to a single company. What problems of industry-wide standards are the same? What problems are different? Are the benefits the same or different? How?

3 Can standardization arise without formal agreement? Under what conditions? Can you cite some examples of this from earlier chapters?

START HERE

Preface

Prose Glossary

Introduction

1. Computers and the Problems They Solve

HISTORY	THE COMPUTER INDUSTRY	PROGRAMMING	HARDWARE	DATA PROCESSING	COMPUTER SYSTEMS

2. The History of Calculating Machines

3. The Development of Electronic Computers

4. The Computer Manufacturing Industry

5. What Is Programming?

6. What Is Coding?

7. Positions in the Computer Industry

8. Work and Tools of the Systems Analyst

9. Unit Record Input/Output Devices

10. How Computers Operate

12. Fortran, Cobol, and Other Programming Languages

11. Magnetic Input/Output Devices

13. Software Systems

14. Business Data Processing

15. Techniques for Computing Scientific Problems

16. Files and Records

17. Sorts and Merges

18. Computer Centers and How They Operate

19. Specifying and Documenting Computer Programs

20. Real-time Computing and Telecomputing

21. Multiprogramming

23. Standards in Computing

22. Time Sharing

24. The Literature of Computing

25. Professionalism

END OF BOOK

GO TO next book, **Computer Usage/360 Assembly Programming**

THE
LITERATURE
OF COMPUTING

A good working knowledge of what is published and available in the field of computing must be part of the working tools of systems analysts, programmers, and all who would use computers. Naturally, no man will need to know everything, but he *must* know how to find anything he needs to know.

In this lesson, you will *not* be given a complete list of all available material and be told where to find it. But you will be given a description of the principal types of publications.

☐ LIFELONG LEARNING

To borrow the motto of the University of California Extension Division, lifelong learning is an essential part of every person's activity once he enters the computer world. The principal difference between a man who is standing still and a man who is growing is an awareness of what has been done and what is currently developing in the computing field. In a fast-growing, rapidly expanding field, you can't afford to be ignorant. Plan to read regularly and learn where to go for the information you need. As soon as you can, subscribe to one or more of the major computing magazines. Get into the habit of buying good computer books regularly.

☐ THE BREADTH OF COMPUTING LITERATURE

Compared with other technical fields, such as chemistry, electrical engineering, and astronomy, you might think that the publications on computers would be very limited. Actually, printed material parallels the growth of any field, and the amount of published material depends on the *age* of the field and the *number* of men in the field who actively publish the results of their work, or who write books and articles on the principal topics of interest. By 1950, there were less than a dozen books in print dealing with computers; by 1960 the list had not grown much beyond 50; by 1970 there will be over 500 books in print about computers. When computing is 100 years old, the literature may be as large as that for older technical fields. However, since computer information becomes "dated" quickly, the *active* literature may not be too large.

Printed material about computers tends to reflect the fact that computers:

1 Come in a great variety of makes, models, and configurations
2 Have been applied to nearly all *other* fields of knowledge
3 Involve complex logic and advanced components and concepts in their design and construction
4 Have been the subject matter of hundreds of research projects
5 Require the development of many automatic programming systems
6 Have had a profound effect on society and its economy, etc.

Consequently, to the newcomer a computer library looks like a terrible hodgepodge.

☐ CLASSIFYING COMPUTER SUBJECTS

To guide you in organizing material and in searching, indexing schemes to the whole of computing have been developed. The classification developed for *Computing Reviews*, the review journal of the Association for Computing Machinery, is recommended as a good starting point. It is quite general but is aimed more toward programming and applications than toward the design and construction of computers. In practice, every person—or every

1. GENERAL TOPICS AND EDUCATION
   1.0 General
   1.1 Texts; handbooks
   1.2 History; biographies
   1.3 Introductory and survey articles
   1.4 Glossaries
   1.5 Education
   1.9 Miscellaneous

2. COMPUTING MILIEU
   2.0 General
   2.1 Philosophical and social implications
   2.2 Professional aspects
   2.3 Legislation; regulations
   2.4 Administration of computing centers
   2.9 Miscellaneous

3. APPLICATIONS
   3.0 General
   3.1 Natural sciences
   3.2 Engineering
   3.3 Social and behavioral sciences
   3.4 Humanities
   3.5 Management data processing
   3.6 Artificial intelligence
   3.7 Information retrieval
   3.8 Real time systems
   3.9 Miscellaneous

4. PROGRAMMING
   4.0 General

4.1 Processors
4.2 Programming languages
4.3 Supervisory systems
4.4 Utility programs
4.9 Miscellaneous

5. MATHEMATICS OF COMPUTATION
   5.0 General
   5.1 Numerical analysis
   5.2 Metatheory
   5.3 Combinatorial and discrete mathematics
   5.4 Mathematical programming
   5.5 Mathematical statistics; probability
   5.6 Information theory
   5.9 Miscellaneous

6. DESIGN AND CONSTRUCTION
   6.0 General
   6.1 Logical design; switching theory
   6.2 Computer systems
   6.3 Components and circuits
   6.9 Miscellaneous

7. ANALOG COMPUTERS
   7.0 General
   7.1 Applications
   7.2 Design; construction
   7.3 Hybrid systems
   7.4 Programming techniques
   7.9 Miscellaneous

organization—that collects reference material is likely to evolve a plan based on a standard one but slanted toward its own needs. For example, if you work with an organization primarily concerned with space sciences, your index to the computing field will be greatly expanded to cover all types of computing applications and techniques involved in space problems (orbit computation, impact prediction, life support, guidance, etc.).

☐ PRINCIPAL TYPES OF COMPUTER PUBLICATIONS

Just as the subject matter of computer literature covers a wide range, so do the different forms of the publications. These will be considered under five categories:

1   *Trade publications*—which carry topical articles of current interest
2   *Technical journals*—and published "proceedings" of technical society meetings
3   *Books*
4   *Indexes, abstracts, and reviews*
5   *Compendiums of computer characteristics*
6   *Equipment manufacturers' manuals*—which describe the hardware, operating systems, programming languages, etc., for specific computers

TRADE PUBLICATIONS

The following are typical trade magazines in the computer field. *Computers and Automation* is the oldest, and *Datamation* the most widely circulated. *Computerworld* is a weekly newspaper.

Business Automation—288 Park Avenue West, Elmhurst, Ill., 60128
Computers and Automation—815 Washington Street, Newtonville, Mass., 02160
Data Processing Magazine—134 North 13th Street, Philadelphia, Pa., 19107
Datamation—94 South Los Robles Avenue, Pasadena, Calif., 91101
Data Systems News—200 Madison Avenue, New York, N.Y., 10016
Computerworld—60 Austin Street, Newton, Mass., 02160

To give you an idea of the type of material published, here are some titles of recent articles in these publications:

    On-line Business Data Processing
    Credit Checking by Computer
    The Language of Information Systems
    Advanced Shared-file Systems
    Univac Shows Multi-processor System
    Rent, Lease or Purchase?

Two additional trade publications related to computers are:

Electronic News—7 East 12th Street, New York, N.Y., 10003
Control Engineering—466 Lexington Avenue, New York, N.Y., 10017

The former is a weekly newspaper that deals with all aspects of electronics but provides a substantial section devoted to computers. It is oriented toward computer hardware. The latter is a monthly magazine of automatic control, a field in which computers are assuming a dominant role. The reader is assumed to be an engineer.

JOURNALS AND PROCEEDINGS

When a new aspect of any topic in computing is considered of interest, the originator submits it either to one of the publications devoted to new developments or to one of the four or five major computer meetings. In either case, the paper, as it is called, is submitted to referees who judge its originality and importance. If approved, it is published; or the originator is invited to present his paper at the meeting and to have it published in the proceedings of the meeting.

As a consequence, the complete sets of these journals and proceedings carry the basic pool of computer knowledge and form the heart of a reference library of computing. Such sets are often maintained by special technical libraries.

The following are among the most widely used journals:

Journal of the Association for Computing Machinery
Communications of the Association for Computing Machinery: Both published at 211 East 43rd Street, New York, N.Y., 10017

The Computer Journal
The Computer Bulletin: Both published by The British Computer Society, 23 Dorset Square, London, N.W. 1, England

Mathematics of Computation: Published by the American Mathematical Society, P.O. Box 6248, Providence, R.I., 02904

Except for *Communications of the ACM* and *The Computer Bulletin*, you will find the articles *very* technical and *very* advanced. However, as your knowledge of computing grows, you will find yourself more and more able to grasp the significance of these papers. Hopefully, some day *you* will be a contributor, too.

The above journals are devoted to programming or mathematics. Two journals dealing with the use of computers for commercial data processing are published by the Data Processing Management Association, 505 Busse Highway, Park Ridge, Ill., 60068:

Journal of Data Management
DPMA Quarterly

In the case of both publications, the reader is assumed to be a manager with an interest in the field of data processing. The content is more practical, down to earth, and immediately useful to a person involved in business data processing than any of the previously mentioned journals.

Journals dealing with the design and development of hardware are published by the Institute of Electrical and Electronic Engineers:

IEEE Transactions on Computers—Published monthly by IEEE, 345 East 47th Street, New York, N.Y., 10017
Computer Group News—Published bimonthly by the Computer Group of the IEEE, 3600 Wilshire Boulevard, Los Angeles, Calif., 90005

There are three major conference publications that you should be familiar with:

AFIPS Conference Proceedings—American Federation of Information Processing Societies, 210 Summit Avenue, Montvale, N.J., 07645
Proceedings of the ACM National Conferences—Association for Computing Machinery, 211 East 43rd Street, New York, N.Y., 10017
Proceedings of IFIP Congresses—International Federation for Information Processing, 23 Dorset Square, London, N.W. 1, England

You will undoubtedly find it easier to read papers in these proceedings than in the journals. Here are some sample titles from each class of publication:

JOURNALS

Fourier Analysis of Uniform Random Number Generators
Synthesis of Algorithmic Systems
Program for Algebraic Partial Differential Equations
Some Facilities for Speech Processing on a Computer
Compile-time Type-matching

PROCEEDINGS

Impact of Computers on Local and Regional Government
Real time Recognition of Handprinted Text
A System for Time sharing Graphic Consoles
Cost Performance Analysis of Integrated-circuit Core Memories
Satellite Lifetime Program

BOOKS ON COMPUTING

It is only natural that the publication of books on a subject lags three to five years behind the development of the subject. When a new idea is developed, it may first be presented as a talk at a conference. Later, it may be published in one of the important journals. Before long, a number of other aspects are brought to light; then the trade magazines present and discuss the techniques and their importance. Only after that point does a writer start to prepare a book on the subject—which may take about one to two years to appear in print.

This lag is called to your attention to give you some perspective on the value of books compared with other sources of computing information. Books are most useful in areas that have been well established and have shown little change in recent years—for example:

1   Books on first-generation computers
2   Books on punched card techniques
3   Books on basic numerical analysis, etc.
4   Books on programming in Fortran and Cobol, etc.

On the other hand, there are few, if any, books on the latest software production techniques, on fractional and conversational compiling, on large-scale integration devices, etc.

Someone who is actively working on the frontier of new developments will probably refer to primary publications much more than to books.

Nevertheless, books on computing that are of excellent quality are now appearing. Books are advertised and listed in the trade magazines, they are available in technical bookstores, and they may be found in the catalogs of technical trade book publishers who feature computer books. For example:

McGraw-Hill
John Wiley and Sons
Prentice-Hall
Addison-Wesley
Academic Press, etc.

Any publisher will send you one of his technical books for a ten-day free examination period. You will find the publisher's address on the back of the title pages of his books.

INDEXES, ABSTRACTS, AND REVIEWS
Fortunately there are a number of publications which ease your burden when you must look up some specific topic. Naturally, access to these is of central importance, since they will refer you to the exact articles or books containing the material. In this category are:

1   *Accumulative Permuted (KWIC) Indexes.* These computer-prepared listings are available for:

   Proceedings of AFIPS Conferences
   Computing Reviews
   Journal of the ACM
   Communications of the ACM
   Computer Literature Bibliography (National Bureau of Standards Miscellaneous Publication 266)

2   *Abstract and Review Publications.* These are regular publications containing several short abstracts or reviews in each issue. An *abstract* is a short summary of the article, while a *review* is a short critical comment about the article. *Computing Reviews*, the most important review publication, appears every month and covers books, articles, and college theses.

   Computing Reviews—published by the Association for Computing Machinery
   Computer Abstracts—published by the Technical Information Company, Ltd., London, W.C. 2, England
   Information Processing Journal—published by the Cambridge Communications Corp., Cambridge, Mass.

3   *Annual Reviews.* These represent a continuing yearly series of books containing long critical reviews of special topics by well known authorities. Such reviews, which generally give a long list of published references, are the best way to familiarize yourself with developments in a specific field. Among series now published are:

   Annual Review of Automatic Programming, Academic Press, New York, N.Y.
   Annual Review of Information Science and Technology, Interscience Publishers, New York, N.Y.
   Advances in Computers, Academic Press, New York, N.Y.

Other good sources of review material are the special computer issues published by the Institute of Electrical and Electronics Engineers every few years (October, 1953; January, 1961; December 1966). IEEE, 345 East 47th Street, New York, N.Y. 10017.

The use of these different sources depends very much on the breadth of your search. If you want to know about a whole subject, find a recent review. If you have a special topic or author in mind, use as many of the permuted indexes as possible. If you want an intermediate approach, look through the review/abstract publications under the appropriate classification.

COMPENDIUMS OF COMPUTER CHARACTERISTICS

The enormous variety of computer hardware makes it highly desirable to have at hand a comparative listing of the characteristics of all computers. Several such listings are available which go into considerable detail on each piece of equipment, but they are expensive. The lowest-priced such listing is that issued by Adams Associates. Its cost of $25 per year puts it out of the reach of most individuals, but it should be part of the library of any substantial computer-using group. It lists the salient features of all digital computers and related peripheral devices commercially available in the Free World and indicates comparative prices for several typical systems. It is updated quarterly. It attempts to cut through the hogwash of vendor puffs and make valid comparisons. Its listings, although compact, are comprehensive and dependable, being just what is needed for the first comparative view of any situation involving hardware.

> *Computer Characteristics Quarterly*—Adams Associates, 128 The Great Road, Bedford, Mass., 01730

Unfortunately, there is no compendium of this nature relating to software characteristics or performance.

MANUALS

In a somewhat different category from material published for general consumption are manuals generally published and distributed (either free or for a nominal charge) by computer manufacturers. These apply solely to the machines or programming systems produced by that manufacturer.

Most manufacturers have published so many manuals that they have been forced to publish indexes and listings of their many manuals.

One of the simplest ways to consider manuals is to divide them into three basic areas:

Hardware
Software
Applications

For hardware, there are basic manuals on the whole computer system, on programming the central processing unit, on every available piece of auxiliary or I/O equipment, on physical installation requirements, etc. Remember that manufacturers make constant small changes in their equipment, and it is important to have the revision of the manual that corresponds *exactly* to your equipment.

For software, there is often a bewildering collection of manuals needed, especially for large systems. Sometimes a *flowchart* of manual reading can be helpful! As a programmer, you may only need the *language* manuals in your everyday work, but access to manuals describing the operating system, details of the I/O system, and how jobs are set up is occasionally necessary. Be certain to avoid the pitfall of having manuals that do *not* correspond to the actual software.

Users of application packages supplied by the manufacturer must, of course, have access to the corresponding manuals. For large packages, like linear programming systems, general purpose simulators, etc., a number of manuals are needed for a full description of the whole.

☐ LIBRARIES OF PROGRAMS AND THEIR DOCUMENTATION

It is debatable whether programs (cards, tapes, listings, flowcharts, and documentation) should be considered here, since these generally come under the control of the computer center's librarian, who also keeps track of data tapes. However, as with all other forms of available material, these are precious to the people who need to use them. Be careful when you borrow material—preferably, leave the original with the librarian and borrow a copy for your own use.

Incidentally, everyone who originates and distributes material—articles, programs, manuals—is very generous. Please take good care of the material you receive. Pass it to others when you no longer need it. Avoid ordering materials you are unlikely to really need. The amount of printed materials distributed is prodigious, and you should cooperate to keep it under control.

☐ AVOID "REDISCOVERING THE WHEEL"

Some programmers and systems analysts studiously avoid looking at the published literature. They consider every job they undertake a challenge to their ingenuity. As a consequence, they painfully rediscover facts and techniques available in many publications.

Get into the habit of asking yourself questions like these:

Is this a totally new situation, or have others faced the same or similar ones?
Where would publications on this topic be found?
Have I satisfied myself that I am not duplicating someone else's effort?

□ ACQUIRE GOOD REFERENCE HABITS

In addition to avoiding duplication, there are many major reasons for getting into the reference habit. This chapter has dealt only with the literature of computing, but your problem assignments will cover application areas. If you are assigned to work with computers in banking, computers in medicine, or any other field, *you are not expected to be a banker or a doctor*! But you will be expected to track down pertinent references to your specific assignment—and they probably will not be found in the computer publications, but in the literature of the field in which you are working.

The fact that computer people are expected to work in a wide variety of fields makes it a real necessity for you to know how to find all the pertinent reference material to help you do your job perfectly.

START HERE

Preface

Prose Glossary

Introduction

1. Computers and the Problems They Solve

HISTORY	THE COMPUTER INDUSTRY	PROGRAMMING	HARDWARE	DATA PROCESSING	COMPUTER SYSTEMS

2. The History of Calculating Machines

3. The Development of Electronic Computers

4. The Computer Manufacturing Industry

5. What Is Programming ?

6. What Is Coding ?

7. Positions in the Computer Industry

8. Work and Tools of the Systems Analyst

9. Unit Record Input/Output Devices

10. How Computers Operate

12. Fortran, Cobol, and Other Programming Languages

11. Magnetic Input/Output Devices

13. Software Systems

14. Business Data Processing

15. Techniques for Computing Scientific Problems

16. Files and Records

17. Sorts and Merges

18. Computer Centers and How They Operate

19. Specifying and Documenting Computer Programs

20. Real-time Computing and Telecomputing

21. Multiprogramming

23. Standards in Computing

22. Time Sharing

24. The Literature of Computing

25. Professionalism

END OF BOOK

GO TO next book, **Computer Usage/360 Assembly Programming**

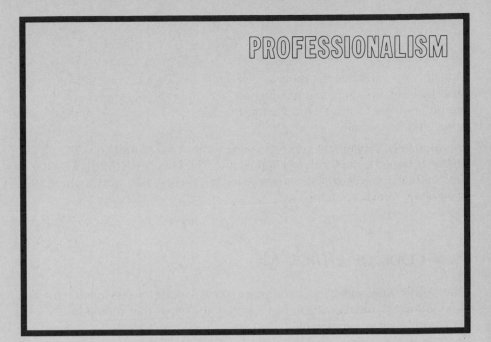

PROFESSIONALISM

Every profession is governed by standards of quality and ethics. A professional functions daily in a position of high responsibility. Everything he does, even actions seemingly unimportant, may later turn out to be crucial. Sometimes vast sums of money are involved; sometimes the integrity of an organization is at stake; sometimes even a matter of life or death is in the hands of a single person. Rockets have failed and bridges collapsed because of misplaced decimal points.

Doctors, lawyers, engineers, pharmacists, bankers—all have time-honored traditions to follow. Through the years, the public has learned to place its faith in these men. Without that faith, the professions would cease to exist and society would be impoverished.

A profession is distinguished from a craft by this element of responsibility Some years ago, it was assumed that programming was a craft. A good program was like a good ceramic pot—beautiful and functional. A programmer's main concern was to arrange his bits cleverly—even, one might say, artistically.

Nowadays, we live in a harsher world and the programmer has been burdened with vital responsibilities. Programming has become a profession. Computers have entered, often unseen, into every aspect of our life. The public accepts, *must* accept, the programs, often in blind faith.

Thus it is essential that the programmer attain the highest standards of honesty in his conduct, and technical quality in his work. It is essential to the programmer for his own sake, for the sake of his associates, and for the profession as a whole.

Unfortunately, programming is too young to have much tradition. The doctor is bound by his oath to Hippocrates. The lawyer is governed by the Bar. Architects and engineers are licensed to practice. But programmers are developing formal standards, too.

☐ A CODE OF ETHICS

One of the larger societies of computer professionals, the Association for Computing Machinery (ACM), has adopted guidelines that should be accepted by every programmer. They are quoted here in full:

The professional person, to uphold and advance the honor, dignity and effectiveness of the profession in the arts and sciences of information processing, and in keeping with high standards of competence and ethical conduct: will be honest, forthright and impartial; will serve with loyalty his employer, clients and the public; will strive to increase the competence and prestige of the profession; will use his special knowledge and skill for the advancement of human welfare.

1 Relations with the Public
1.1 He will have proper regard for the health, privacy, safety and general welfare of the public in the performance of his professional duties.
1.2 He will endeavor to extend public knowledge, understanding and appreciation of computing machines and information processing and achievements in their application, and will oppose any untrue, inaccurate or exaggerated statement or claims.
1.3 He will express an opinion on a subject within his competence only when it is founded on adequate knowledge and honest conviction, and will properly qualify himself when expressing an opinion outside of his professional field.
1.4 He will preface any partisan statement, criticisms or arguments that he may issue concerning information processing by clearly indicating on whose behalf they are made.

2 Relations with Employers or Clients
  2.1 He will act in professional matters as a faithful agent or trustee for each employer or client and will not disclose private information belonging to any present or former employer or client without his consent.
  2.2 He will indicate to his employer or client the consequences to be expected if his professional judgment is overruled.
  2.3 He will undertake only those professional assignments for which he is qualified and which the state of the art supports.
  2.4 He is responsible to his employer or client to meet specifications to which he is committed in tasks he performs and products he produces, and to design and develop systems that adequately perform their function and satisfy his employer's or client's operational needs.

3 Relations with Other Professionals
  3.1 He will take care that credit for work is given to those to whom credit is properly due.
  3.2 He will endeavor to provide opportunity and encouragement for the professional development and advancement of professionals or those aspiring to become professionals with whom he comes in contact.
  3.3 He will not injure maliciously the professional reputation or practice of another person and will conduct professional competition on a high plane. If he has proof that another person has been unethical, illegal or unfair in his professional practice concerning information processing, he should so advise the proper authority.
  3.4 He will cooperate in advancing information processing by interchanging information and experience with other professionals and students and by contributing to public communications media and to the efforts of professional and scientific societies and schools.

□ PROFESSIONAL ORGANIZATIONS

One of the important features that sets a profession apart from a craft is the professional emphasis upon communications between its members. Doctors, lawyers, and computer men all find that interaction with others in their professions is essential in keeping up with "the state of the art." Societies have been established to promote meetings, publish journals, and maintain standards.

Among the major societies for computer professionals are the Association for Computing Machinery (ACM), the Data Processing Management Association (DPMA), and the Institute of Electrical and Electronics Engineers (IEEE). Although there is much overlap in the membership, these societies have a general emphasis in three separate areas. The ACM consists primarily of systems analysts, applications programmers, and numerical analysts. They publish a monthly *Journal*, a scientific monthly *Communications*, and a monthly *Computing Reviews*. About fifteen "Special Interest Groups" are organized under the ACM, in areas such as business data processing, information retrieval, mathematical programming, design automation, and programming languages. Thousands of people participate in their local and annual meetings.

The DPMA consists primarily of members of business data processing organizations. This group arranges local and national meetings, maintains professional standards, and publishes periodicals, including the *Journal of Data Management* and the *DPMA Quarterly*. The DPMA sets standards for qualified data processors and awards certificates—on the basis of education, experience, and a stiff written examination—to members and nonmembers who apply for the certificate, meet the standards, and pass the examination. This series of books will help you to prepare for the examination. You should make it your goal to prepare yourself to qualify as a Certified Data Processor (CDP). Detailed information on the qualifications and the schedule of examinations, which are given every winter at about two hundred test centers, can be obtained from the Data Processing Management Association, 505 Busse Highway, Park Ridge, Ill., 60068.

Both the ACM and the DPMA represent computer professionals in public affairs. They testify at congressional hearings, advise other organizations and the press, and answer public questions in areas such as the possibility of automation creating mass unemployment and the intrusion of computing on the privacy of individuals.

Those with interests in the area of electronics and computer design should join the IEEE. Its publications include the *IEEE Spectrum* and the *Proceedings of the IEEE*. Occasionally, one of these journals contains an issue completely devoted to computing. A subgroup, the Computer Group, is particularly concerned with the development of data processing equipment and publishes the *IEEE Transactions on Computers* and *Computer Group News*.

The American Federation of Information Processing Societies (AFIPS) is a society of societies. Its members are such organizations as the ACM and IEEE. AFIPS holds spring and fall joint computer conferences each year, both of which include meetings and exhibits, and which are attended by more than 5,000 people. This organization represents all the American professionals in the International Federation for Information Processing (IFIP), which convenes a Congress every three years. Twenty-eight societies representing Japan, the USSR, Brazil, etc., are members of IFIP.

There are many other groups of particular interest to specialists, but most of these groups are sponsored by or directly affiliated with one of the organizations mentioned above. In addition to the publications from the professional societies, there are a number of excellent journals listed in Chapter 24.

Membership in these societies is open to all who have a professional interest. We recommend that you join one of the chapters in your area. Your affiliation will be both socially and technically rewarding, and it *may* lead you to a good job.

This book was set in Optima, printed on permanent paper by Halliday Lithograph Corporation, and bound by The Maple Press Company. The designer was J. Paul Kirouac; the drawings were done by John Cordes. The editors were John Maloney and Susan Davis. John F. Harte supervised the production.